"*Differentiation Strategy: Winning Customers by Being Different* should be required reading for every board and leadership team. Kevin's explanation of the principles and practice of differentiation is extraordinary."

G. Peter Bidstrup, *Founder and emeritus CEO of* Doubletree Hotels

"Kevin is our secret weapon. The process described in *Differentiation Strategy: Winning Customers by Being Different* has helped several of our clients differentiate their products and dominate their markets to the tune of hundreds of millions of dollars."

Sheila Kloefkorn, *CEO,* KEO Marketing, Inc.

"We retained Kevin to facilitate a workshop guided by the framework in *Differentiation Strategy: Winning Customers by Being Different.* Our new strategy played a major role in growing our company from 60 hotels under management to more than 100."

John Hamilton, *Executive Vice President,* Pyramid Hotel Group

"Read *Differentiation Strategy: Winning Customers by Being Different* and learn how to create a strategy that leaves your competitors in the dust. The chapter on creative thinking, alone, is worth the price of the book."

Woody Wade, *Author of* Scenario Planning: A Field Guide to the Future

T0331447

Differentiation Strategy

This comprehensive and richly illustrated book explains how to create a differentiation strategy—a strategy for being different in a way that causes customers to prefer your products and services to those of your competitors.

Filled with frameworks, tools, and templates, this book will enable you to create a compelling answer to your customers' most fundamental question: *Why should I buy from you instead of your competitors? What makes you different?* The first half of the book provides an in-depth analysis of the concepts and principles that underlie the practice of differentiation, including the meaning of *competitive advantage*, *competitive strategy*, and *customer-perceived value*. The second half of the book explains how to create a differentiation strategy by identifying the target of your strategy, using customer research and creative problem-solving to design a unique offering, devising a value proposition that emphasizes a key benefit and the reasons to believe you will deliver the benefit, and designing the activity system that will implement your differentiation strategy.

Business leaders in companies large and small, business students, and leaders in government, higher education, and the non-profit sector will gain a deep understanding of all that goes into creating a successful, difficult-to-copy differentiation strategy.

Kevin Holt uses a combination of facilitated workshops and customer research to help organizations devise differentiation strategies that work. His hands-on experience makes him uniquely qualified to write this book. He has worked as a development officer and consultant in the hotel industry, where he sat on the executive committee of a national hotel chain, owned a small business, and, since 2001, conducted consulting and workshop engagements in the USA and in London, Geneva, Singapore, and Delhi. Kevin received a BS degree from the University of Wisconsin-Madison and an MBA from Arizona State University. He has developed an e-learning course that complements this book. For more information, go to www.differentiationstrategy.com.

Contents

Acknowledgments

Up and along. This book is the result of a lifetime of being pulled up and along by others. Others who were smarter, wiser, and more disciplined than me. Others who deserve to be acknowledged and thanked.

I'll start with one of my oldest and dearest friends, Dick Binder. Dick was two years ahead of me in high school. He went off to college at the University of Wisconsin-Madison, where, when I visited him, I discovered he had transformed from my happy-go-lucky friend into a seriously serious student. It paid off. He went on to become a successful lawyer. I went home inspired to become a seriously serious student. Years later, I would tell my college-bound sons the "Dick Binder story" as part of explaining how important it was for them to get serious about their studies right from the start. They did, and they did well. And I imagine that years from now they'll tell their children the Dick Binder story. I thank you, my children thank you, and I expect my grandchildren will someday thank you, Dick. You were, and still are, an inspiration to me.

Next is Ray Monnat, M.D., who I roomed with at UW-Madison and who got me a part-time job as a research technician in Dr. Waclaw Szybalski's genetics laboratory. Ray's love of learning was extraordinary. He stirred the same passion in me. Ray went on to medical school and thereafter became a Professor of Genome Sciences and Pathology at the University of Washington. I went on to discover that I didn't have a future in science. So I moved on to "Plan B" and entered the MBA program at Arizona State University.

At ASU, I was fortunate enough to take a marketing course taught by Dr. Louis Grossman. Dr. Grossman was right up there with Ray on the love-for-learning scale, and he must have seen the same thing in me, for during and after my time at ASU, he encouraged me to get a Ph.D. and become an academic. During his 40's, Lou had left his job as a retail executive and earned a Ph.D. in marketing. He used to tell me, "I left the world of things for the world of ideas." I never did get the Ph.D., but I have Lou to thank for pulling me further into the world of ideas.

After I graduated from ASU, I worked on the real estate side of the hotel business, where I eventually came to work for Doubletree Hotels. The founder and CEO of the company was Peter Bidstrup, a West Point graduate and Harvard MBA. Pete was the sort of mentor who constantly moved the dial on your intellect. I can't count the number of times I walked out of his office mumbling to myself, "I can't believe I didn't think of that." And neither before nor after did I work for a company with a more inspiring culture, a culture that was the perfect blend of entrepreneurial enthusiasm, corporate professionalism, class, and caring. I would have gladly worked there for the rest of my life, but it finally came time for Pete to sell the company.

Woody Wade, also a product of Harvard Business School, is another person who has pulled me up and along. Woody occasionally calls on me to provide electronic brainstorming technology for his scenario planning workshops. And, periodically, we convene to "kick around ideas." Our conversations and his book, *Scenario Planning: A Field Guide to the Future*, helped motivate me to write this book. That his modesty matches his intellect makes him a pleasure to be around.

Marian Gerlich worked for the public relations company retained by Doubletree before she and her husband started their own PR firm, P&G Communications. We became friends and remain friends to this day. Never a more positive and encouraging person has God put on this earth. Nor a more knowledgeable grammarian. (I've always called her "Marian the Grammarian" behind her back. I guess this is as good a place as any to fess up.) Thank you, Marian, for your 30+ years of encouragement. (And the grammar advice.)

Another friend, and a business associate, is Sheila Kloefkorn, owner of KEO Marketing and digital marketer extraordinaire. We worked together to create and market the online course that complements this book. I have Sheila to thank for getting me to stop saying I'd like to write a book someday and start writing it. Thank you, Sheila. I'm sure the bruise on my butt will eventually fade.

While it may have been Sheila who kicked me over the edge, it was my son Matthew, a hedge fund trader, who got me there in the first place. The mental echo of, "Dad, you're never going to be happy until you're holding a book that you've written" was like two hands pushing me gently but relentlessly towards the edge. And as you will soon find out, once the book was started, it was my son David who helped to complete it. David, a graphic designer who has the unique ability to turn an idea into just-the-right visual, created many of the illustrations that are a part of this book. I am so thankful to have been blessed with you both. Your mother would have been so proud of you.

Then there is Elaine, who never once complained about being ignored when I disappeared into my study seven days a week while writing this book. Thank you, dear. Your encouragement and moral support were indispensable.

And finally, there is my sister Bonnie. Those of you who have had the pleasure of knowing her will know exactly what I mean when I say, "Thank you, Bonnie, for being Bonnie."

Introduction

This book explains how to create a differentiation strategy. Differentiation is about being different in a way that causes customers to prefer you. It's about having a compelling answer to the one-two question: *Why should I buy from you instead of your competitors? What makes you different?* Differentiation is crucial because it's the prime source of competitive advantage. The late Robert Guizetta, Chairman and CEO of The Coca-Cola Company, knew that. It's the reason he said, "In real estate it is all about location, location, location. In business, it is differentiate, differentiate, differentiate."[1] The advertising executive Jack Trout knew that too. It's why he coined the phrase *differentiate or die.*[2]

Differentiate or die. Faced with differentially advantaged competitors, a company is destined to die. It's only a matter of time until the competitors shrink its customer base below the threshold of survival. Fortunately, meaningful differentiation is rare. Not because it is difficult to do, but because managers in most industries tend to do what is safe and conventional, which is to say, what everyone else is doing. As Joan Magretta, a senior associate at Harvard's Institute for Strategy and Competitiveness, observes, "Nothing is more absurd—and yet more widespread—than the belief that somehow you can do exactly what everyone else is doing and yet end up with superior results."[3] The fact is that few companies have a convincing answer to the *What makes you different?* question. That spells opportunity. For you, if you choose to differentiate. For a competitor, if you don't.

The content of this book applies to businesses large and small. To businesses that offer products and services. And to businesses classified as B2C (business-to-consumer) and those classified as B2B (business-to-business). And while the content centers on competing for customers, it also applies to competing for others. The title of this book could just as well have been *Competing for Employees by Being Different.* For cities and states, it could have been about competing for *Employers,* or *Visitors,* or *Residents.* For universities, *Students.* Associations, *Members.* Nonprofits, *Beneficiaries.* And for everyone, *Funders.* The principles and practices in this book apply across the board.

Now that I've said what this book is about and why you should read it, let's turn to some miscellaneous matters. The first matter pertains to terminology. As it is used here, the term *customer* can mean either an existing customer or a prospective customer. The context will make clear which of the two meanings is intended. The second term is *offering.* Elsewhere, offering is often used as an umbrella term for a product or service. Here it is used as an umbrella term for a product or service, for a combination of products and services, or for some aspect of the customer's experience of a company. Again, the context will indicate which meaning is intended.

Second, this book is rife with references—three on the first page alone. The reason is that many of the topics we're[4] going to cover are themselves worthy of book-length treatments. So I've referenced books I think you'll find useful if you want to learn more about a topic.

DOI: 10.4324/9781003271703-1

Another reason for the references is that it's often impossible to improve on another person's words. So why try? Better to quote the person than tender a poorer-put paraphrase.

The third matter is that this book is full of figures—the graphical kind, not the numerical kind. That's because verbal and visual thinking together are better than either one alone. Graphical depictions convey what verbal descriptions cannot and vice-versa. Also, research shows that people are better at remembering material when they learn it using both images and words (a phenomenon known as *dual coding*).

Another matter worth mentioning pertains to the examples used to ground the principles and practices explained in this book. While I draw on a range of examples from a variety of industries, the hotel industry gets more than its fair share. That's partly because I spent much of my career in the industry, first as a development officer and later as a consultant. It's also because most people are familiar with hotels, especially business road warriors, who are the people most likely to read this book.

The final matter pertains to an idea arguably attributed to the philosopher Immanuel Kant. It runs along the following lines: *Theory without practice is empty; practice without theory is blind.* Above all else, this book is intended to be practical. That's why it includes the theory. When I say theory, I'm not talking about unproven, high-minded ideas that float free of reality.[5] I'm talking about the concepts and principles that enable you to understand why you're doing what you're doing.[6] And when I talk about practice, I'm not talking about guidelines that are so general as to be useless. I'm talking about detailed methods you can "put to work on Monday," as the saying goes. The first six chapters are mostly about the theory. The last eight are mostly about the practice. I say "mostly" because there's a sprinkling of practice in the first six chapters and a sprinkling of theory in the last eight.

Chapter 1 defines the terms *competition, competitive advantage,* and *competitive strategy*—seemingly simple terms that aren't so simple upon closer inspection. The chapter goes on to explain the two types of competitive strategy, cost leadership and differentiation, and then elaborates on the meaning of differentiation. It also explains how to tell when you have a competitive advantage.

Chapter 2 explores the concept of *value*, one of the most-used and least-understood terms in business. It explains that value is sometimes taken to mean the *monetary worth* of something. Other times it's equated with the sort of value with which we're concerned—*customer-perceived value*. Customers perceive that the value of an offering equals the benefits they obtain from it less the costs they must incur to obtain the benefits. In other words, customer-perceived value equals what customers get minus what they must give to get it.

Chapter 3 looks at the nature of benefits and introduces the *offering–function–benefit* trilogy. The trilogy summarizes the idea that an *offering* performs *functions* that generate *benefits*. The chapter next looks at various ways of classifying benefits, including a long look at a six-benefit typology that I've developed. The six kinds of benefits are physical, mental, emotional, social, economic, and cost/risk reduction. The long look will serve you well, considering that differentiation is fundamentally about providing more and better benefits than your competitors.

Chapter 4 examines the middle part of the offering–function–benefit trilogy. It starts by defining the *function* of an offering (to produce or help produce an outcome) and describing the proper way to state one (a verb-noun phrase). The chapter then explains how the same offering can perform different functions and how the same function can be performed by different offerings. It also explains the concept of *co-production* and the way that offerings *help* or *enable* customers to produce an outcome or *relieve* them of the task altogether. The chapter next explains how customers judge an offering by how well it *performs* a function. The final part of the chapter explains several ways to do *function analysis*.

Chapter 5 takes a deep dive into *offerings*, the first part of the offering-function-benefit trilogy. It first explains the adage, "Form [the offering] follows function." It goes on to examine offerings at the level of individual products and services, the level of bundles and complementary products and services, and the level at which the customer's experience is determined by other elements of the company. At the first level, the chapter explains the difference between a product and a service and then explains how both are more accurately described by employing the concepts *component*, *property*, *attribute*, *link*, and *configuration*. At the second level, the chapter explains bundling and complements (e.g., a core product and a complementary service). At the third level, the chapter explains the remaining things that determine the customer's experience of a company, chief among them being its sales and marketing activities, distribution channels, and customer relationship program.

Chapter 6 is the last chapter having to do with theory. It first defines the concept of *differentiation*. The chapter then describes different aspects of differentiation by asking and answering the questions: Different why? Different where? Different how? How different? Different for how long? Different at what level of abstraction?

The practice part of this book starts with Chapter 7. It's impossible for a company to be all things to all people. For this reason, differentiation strategies are segment specific. The chapter first explains how to identify and target a supply chain segment. It then explains how to use top-down and bottom-up methods to identify and target one or more of the market segments that comprise a supply chain segment. It also explains how to use segmentation to identify differentiation opportunities.

Chapter 8 explains three ways of using attributes to identify differentiation opportunities. Surprisingly few management teams can accurately list the attributes that the customers in their industry consider when deciding from whom to buy. Fewer still can identify the unique attributes that distinguish their offering. The three attribute methods are intended to overcome these problems. The first method utilizes a *strategy canvas*. The second method employs an *attribute map*. And the third uses the concept of *attribute lines*.

Customers engage in certain *actions* (behaviors, jobs, tasks, steps) before, during, and after they use an offering. Chapter 9 explains four ways of using the actions to identify differentiation opportunities. The first method centers on what customers are trying to do at each step of the *consumption chain*. The second method, known as the *jobs-to-be-done method*, considers the jobs customers are trying to do at each step of a job map. The third method builds a *mental model* of the tasks customers are trying to perform as they work through a process. And the fourth method focuses on what customers want at each step of a *journey map*.

Superior strategies stem from superior insights into segments, attributes, and actions. Superior insights stem, in turn, from superior research. Chapter 10 explains how to do the two traditional types of qualitative research—interview research and observation research. It also touches on survey research, a form of quantitative research, as well as two non-traditional forms of research—employee idea systems and living labs.

Superior insight into your customers' problems—obtaining the attributes they want but don't have and performing the actions they want to do but can't—gets you only part of the way to a differentiation strategy. The next part is finding creative solutions to their problems, solutions that will cause them to prefer you to your competitors. Chapter 11 explains three ways of creating superior solutions—expertise, logic, and analogy. It also explains the significant role your subconscious plays in problem-solving and how to use it to generate creative ideas. Finally, it explains the role that experimentation plays in growing the seed of an idea.

The next part of devising a differentiation strategy is to translate your superior solutions into a value proposition. The value proposition answers the two-part question: *Why should I buy from you instead of your competitors? What makes you different?* Chapter 12 explains that the value proposition is essentially a benefit proposition. It also explains why the value proposition should emphasize a single key benefit and how to decide which benefit to emphasize.

And it explains why the value proposition should include one or more of the seven kinds of reasons to believe that you will deliver the promised benefit. Finally, the chapter explains how to distill the value proposition down to a short micro-script that customers will remember and repeat to others.

The last part of devising a differentiation strategy is designing the *activity system* that will implement the strategy. This is where the rubber meets the road. Every company consists of a system of activities that produces the benefits that customers desire. Some of the activities are "onstage" activities that customers are able to see, and other activities are "backstage" activities that produce the onstage activities. In both cases, differentiation requires that you, as compared to your competitors, do the activities differently or do different activities. Chapter 13 explains three frameworks for designing the activity system—the *value chain*, the *strategy wheel*, and the *dependency diagram*.

Chapter 14 summarizes the process for devising a differentiation strategy, which, up to the point of this chapter, was spread across the previous chapters. The process is to develop a coherent set of answers to the following five questions: (1) Who are we targeting? (2) What benefits do they desire? (3) What offering will provide the benefits? (4) What compelling answer can we give to the "What makes you different?" question? and (5) What system of activities can we create to profitably produce and deliver the benefits? I debated whether to make this the first or last chapter of the book. I settled on making it the last chapter so that readers would understand the concepts that are incorporated in it—*targeting*, *benefits*, *offering*, *value proposition*, and *activity system*. But you may want to read the last chapter first to understand why you're learning the concepts in the first place.

Now, on with the show.

Notes

1 Robert Guizetta, https://quotepark.com/quotes/19285-robert-goizueta-in-real-estate-it-is-all-about-location-location/.
2 Jack Trout with Steve Rivkin, *Differentiate or Die: Survival in Our Era of Killer Competition* 2nd Ed. (Hoboken, NJ: John Wiley & Sons, 2008).
3 Joan Magretta, "Stop Competing to Be the Best," *Harvard Business Review*, November 30, 2011, https://hbr.org/2011/11/stop-competing-to-be-the-best.
4 When I say "we," "we're," and other like terms, I'm referring to you the reader and me the author.
5 Which reminds me of the old line in economics, "Sure it works in practice, but will it work in theory?"
6 In my workshops, I first present the theory that is relevant to the step of the differentiation strategy process upon which we are about to embark. Unfortunately, there is a limited amount of time for me to present the material and for my clients to absorb it. Much of the impetus for this book was the observation that managers would do a better job of devising their differentiation strategies if they first read a book that thoroughly grounds them in the theory and practice of differentiation.

1   Competition

The concepts of *competition*, *competitive advantage*, and *competitive strategy* seem simple enough. That is until you try to define them. Give it a try. What's the meaning of competition? Is there a difference between competing in a race and competing for a customer? In business, what does it mean to have a competitive advantage? And how do you know when you have one? What is a strategy? What is a competitive strategy? Are there different kinds of competitive strategies? In this chapter, we take a closer look at each of these terms and the questions that surround them.

Competition Defined

If you had a tough time defining competition, don't feel bad. You're in good company. James Case starts his book *Competition: The Birth of a New Science* by noting that competition is a surprisingly difficult term to define. Despite repeated attempts, he explains, modern lexicographers have failed to improve on the definition given by Samuel Johnson in the 1755 edition of the *Dictionary of English Language*, where Johnson defined "competition" as a noun meaning "the act of endeavoring to gain what another endeavors to gain at the same time; rivalry; contest."[1]

Johnson's definition evokes the image of two children tugging on a teddy bear, each endeavoring to gain what the other is endeavoring to gain at the same time. From there, it's a short leap to imagining the two children as adult business rivals, each endeavoring to gain a customer the other is endeavoring to gain at the same time. Case, an expert in game theory, goes on to explain that in a two-party competition the contest amounts to a zero-sum game—the winner wins what the loser loses, be it a teddy bear, a customer, or something else. But, he says, the definition of competition gets a lot more complicated, and inescapably mathematical, when the contest is a non-zero-sum game among three or more competitors. Fortunately, for those of us who didn't get the math gene, we can get by with Case's amended version of Johnson's definition, which says that competition is the act of endeavoring to gain what *others* endeavor to gain at the same time.

Competitive Advantage

Most people think of a *competitive advantage* as something that gives one party a better chance of beating another in a contest or competition. With wrestlers, for example, that "something" is strength. Stronger wrestlers have a competitive advantage relative to weaker ones. In basketball, it's height. Taller basketball players have a competitive advantage compared to shorter ones. And in most sports, the team playing at home is considered to have a "home-court" or "home-field" advantage.

But the concept of competitive advantage is a bit more complicated in business. As

DOI: 10.4324/9781003271703-2

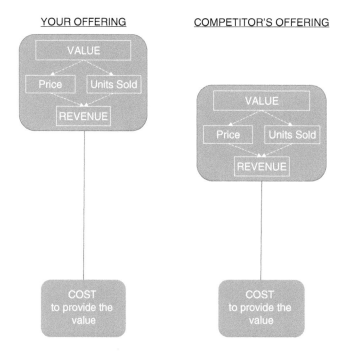

Figure 1.1 You have a competitive advantage when your offering has a bigger gap than your competitor's.

Source: Adapted from *Strategic Learning: How to be smarter than your competition and turn key insights into a competitive advantage*, Fig. 2.1. Reproduced with permission.

explained in the book *Strategic Learning: How to be Smarter Than the Competition and Turn Key Insights Into Competitive Advantage*, authored by Willie Pietersen, formerly the CEO of several multi-billion dollar companies and now a professor at Columbia University Business School, a company's offering has a competitive advantage when, relative to a competing offering, there is a bigger gap between the amount of value customers perceive that they derive from the offering and the cost the company incurs to provide that value.[2] The idea is illustrated in Figure 1.1, where you can see that the gap between your offering's customer-perceived value and the cost of providing that value is bigger than the gap between your competitor's customer-perceived value and its cost of providing that value.

Pietersen goes on to explain that the amount of customer-perceived value is something you can objectively assess because price and volume (units sold) are derivatives of value. You know you're providing more customer-perceived value than your competitors when you can charge a premium price without sacrificing volume or you can improve volume at comparable prices. But when customers perceive that you offer comparatively less value, you can expect to see a decline in price, volume, or both.

It's tempting to think that, like superior strength in wrestling, superior value is the "something" that gives you a competitive advantage in business. But there's more to it than that. If your costs were so high that you lost money on each transaction (i.e., the cost box in Figure 1.1 moved above the value box), you wouldn't be able to say you have a competitive advantage. Nor would you be able to say you have a competitive advantage if, as shown in Figure 1.2, your costs were so high that your competitor was making more money than you on each transaction—in other words, if there were a smaller gap between the amount of

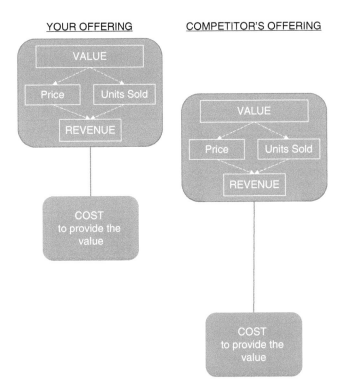

Figure 1.2 Competitive advantage is all about the gap between value and cost.

Source: Adapted from Strategic *Learning: How to be smarter than your competition and turn key insights into a competitive advantage*, Fig. 2.1. Reproduced with permission.

customer-perceived value of your offering and the cost to provide that value as compared to your competitor's offering.

In both cases, the question is *why*. Why are you unable to say you have a competitive advantage? In the first case, where you're losing money on each transaction, the answer is obvious. It's hard to argue you have a competitive advantage when you're gradually headed out of business. In the second case, where you're making comparatively less on each transaction, the answer is basically the same. The only difference, as next explained and illustrated in Table 1.1, is that it will take you longer to go out of business.[3]

Table 1.1 contains five-year profit and loss statements for your company and a competitor company. The two of you compete in a market that totals 10,000 units in size. In year 1, you and your competitor each capture 50% of the market, which means you each sell 5,000 units. Both of you charge $100 for your product. In years 1–5, you both incur costs equal to 80% of revenue. And in year 1, you both achieve a gross profit of $100,000. Where you and your competitor differ is in the amount of gross profit you reinvest in your offerings. You reinvest 10% of your gross profit every year in, say, advertising, training, product improvement, or something else that increases the value of your offering, while your competitor reinvests nothing. The result is that your sales volume increases in years 2–5, while your competitor's sales volume decreases. The further result is that in years 2–5, your revenue, reinvested funds, and net profit become progressively greater than your competitor's.

Putting the foregoing in terms of Pietersen's gap, we can say that your company's offering has a competitive advantage relative to your competitor's because your offering has a larger

Table 1.1 Competitive advantage and comparable performance

Market	Yr. 1	Yr. 2	Yr. 3	Yr. 4	Yr. 5
Total Units	10,000	10,000	10,000	10,000	10,000
Your Company					
% Market share (% Unit Share)	50%	55%	60%	65%	70%
Sales volume	5,000	5,500	6,000	6,500	7,000
Price	$100	$100	$100	$100	$100
Revenue	$500,000	$550,000	$600,000	$650,000	$700,000
Cost (% of revenue)	80%	80%	80%	80%	80%
Cost	$400,000	$440,000	$480,000	$520,000	$560,000
Revenue	$500,000	$550,000	$600,000	$650,000	$700,000
Less: cost	$400,000	$440,000	$480,000	$520,000	$560,000
Gross profit	$100,000	$110,000	$120,000	$130,000	$140,000
Profit reinvestment rate	10%	10%	10%	10%	10%
Reinvested profit	$10,000	$11,000	$12,000	$13,000	$14,000
Net profit (Gap)	**$90,000**	**$99,000**	**$108,000**	**$117,000**	**$126,000**
Profit margin	**18%**	**18%**	**18%**	**18%**	**18%**
Competitor					
% Market share (% unit share)	50%	45%	40%	35%	30%
Sales volume	5,000	4,500	4,000	3,500	3,000
Price	$100	$100	$100	$100	$100
Revenue	$500,000	$450,000	$400,000	$350,000	$300,000
Cost (% of revenue)	80%	80%	80%	80%	80%
Cost	$400,000	$360,000	$320,000	$280,000	$240,000
Revenue	$500,000	$450,000	$400,000	$350,000	$300,000
Less: cost	$400,000	$360,000	$320,000	$280,000	$240,000
Gross profit	$100,000	$90,000	$80,000	$70,000	$60,000
Profit reinvestment rate	0%	0%	0%	0%	0%
Reinvested profit	$0	$0	$0	$0	$0
Net profit (gap)	**$100,000**	**$90,000**	**$80,000**	**$70,000**	**$60,000**
Profit margin	**20%**	**20%**	**20%**	**20%**	**20%**

gap between the amount of customer-perceived value it provides and the cost required to provide that value. Because price and volume are derivatives of value and the product of price and volume is revenue, an equivalent way of putting this is to say that your company's offering has a competitive advantage because there is a larger gap between the revenue generated by your offering and the cost of producing and delivering it. In other words, your offering has a competitive advantage because it generates more profit than your competitor's offering, some of which you reinvest in the business.

So how do you know when you have a competitive advantage? How do you know when the gap between your customer-perceived value and costs is larger than that of your competitors? Pietersen has already provided half of the answer. You know you're providing more customer-perceived value when you can charge a premium price without sacrificing volume, or you can improve volume at comparable prices. But what about costs? How do you compare your costs with those of your competitors? Sometimes you can use what you know to estimate a competitor's costs. But if you have no way of knowing your competitor's costs, a solution is to look to industry benchmark data and assume your competitor's cost or profit margin approximates the industry average.

There are several lessons to learn from the foregoing. The first is that value enhancement and cost control are equal partners in the quest for competitive advantage. Focusing on one at the expense of the other gets you nowhere. To have a competitive advantage, you must

Size of Gap (Profitability)

Figure 1.3 The rich get richer while the poor get poorer.

make sure the gap between your value and cost is larger than that of your competitors. The second lesson is to reinvest enough money to increase customer-perceived value by a meaningful amount, whether on advertising, training, product improvement, or something else. But keep in mind that spending money on value enhancement may require cutting costs elsewhere in order to maintain a larger gap. The third lesson concerns what economists call *increasing returns*. This is the concept that underlies the aphorism, "The rich get richer, while the poor get poorer," or as author Mitchell Waldrop puts it, "Them that has gets."[4] You saw increasing returns at work in Table 1.1, where reinvesting 10% of your gross profit resulted in more revenue and profit the following year, which resulted in more money to reinvest, which resulted in still more revenue and profit the year after that, which resulted in even more money to reinvest, and so on. The net result, as shown in Figure 1.3, is that while you grew progressively richer, your competitor grew progressively poorer. *Them that has gets!*

One glance at Figure 1.3 should tell you why the late Jack Welch, GE's legendary emeritus CEO, said, "If you don't have a competitive advantage, don't compete."[5] As you'll next learn, there are three generic strategies for achieving a competitive advantage.

Competitive Strategy

Let's start the discussion of *competitive strategy* by defining the two halves of the term. You already know that *competition* is the act of endeavoring to gain what others are endeavoring to gain at the same time. In our case, we'll say that competition is the act of endeavoring to gain the *customers* that competitors are endeavoring to gain at the same time.

The second half of the term is *strategy*. A strategy is a way of achieving an objective. A simple example, illustrated in Figure 1.4, is a person who has the objective of getting to the other side of a wall and employs the strategy of climbing over it. Another person with the same objective might use the strategy of digging under the wall. A third person might utilize the strategy of busting through the wall. All have the same objective, but each adopts a different way of achieving it. In other words, they each have different strategies for achieving the objective.

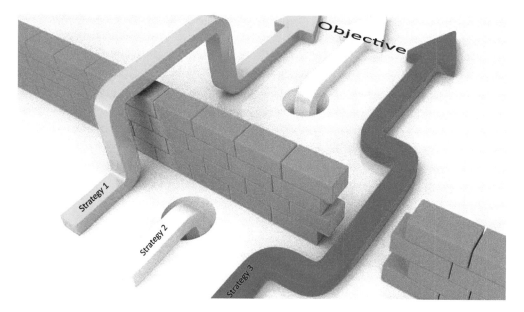

Figure 1.4 A strategy is a way of achieving an objective.

Source: Shutterstock, as modified.

So our definition of competition is *the act of endeavoring to gain the customers competitors are endeavoring to gain at the same time*, and our definition of strategy *is a way of achieving an objective*. Combining the two gives us this definition of competitive strategy: *A competitive strategy is a way of gaining the customers competitors are endeavoring to gain at the same time*. Context and comparison are good ways to flesh out a definition, so let's next consider the question, "Of what more general strategies is competitive strategy a part?" The answer, as illustrated in Figure 1.5, is that a competitive strategy is a kind of growth strategy, and a growth strategy is a kind of problem-solving strategy, which means that a competitive strategy is a kind of problem-solving strategy.

In the broadest sense, all strategies are problem-solving strategies. Developing a problem-solving strategy entails establishing an objective, identifying the factors that are preventing the achievement of the objective, and devising a strategy to eliminate, avoid, or otherwise overcome the factors. This is what you saw in Figure 1.4, where the objective was to be on the other side of the wall, the factor preventing the achievement of the objective was the wall, and three ways to overcome the factor were to go over, under, or through the wall. The traditional strategic planning process is essentially about problem-solving. As shown in Figure 1.6, the first step is to establish the company's objective, the second step is to perform a strengths, weaknesses, opportunities, and threats[6] analysis (SWOT analysis) to identify the external and internal factors that stand in the way of achieving the objective, and the third step is to devise alternate strategies for overcoming the factors and then select the best alternative.

One kind of problem-solving strategy involves finding a way to grow a business. The idea that a growth strategy is a kind of problem-solving strategy is illustrated by placing it inside the problem-solving ring in Figure 1.5. There are various ways to grow a company. For example, you can grow by entering an altogether different industry, by adding to your existing stable of offerings, or by selling more of an existing offering. In turn, you can sell more of an existing offering by acquiring a competitor, by expanding into new geographic

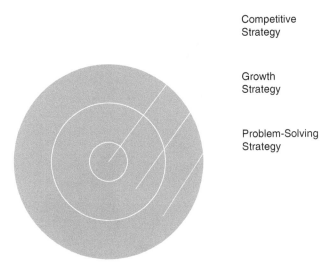

Competitive
Strategy

Growth
Strategy

Problem-Solving
Strategy

Figure 1.5 A competitive strategy is a kind of growth strategy, which is a kind of problem-solving strategy.

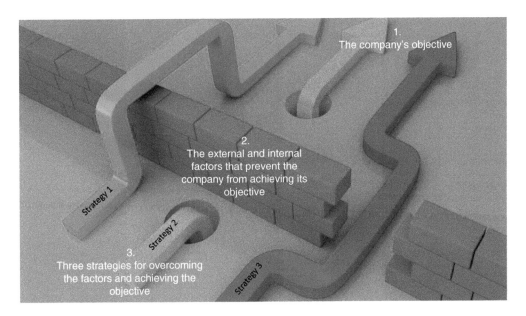

Figure 1.6 Traditional strategy making is about problem-solving.

Source: *Image Source:* Shutterstock, as modified.

areas, or by taking business away from your competitors. To take business away from your competitors you must find a way to gain the customers your competitors are endeavoring to gain at the same time, i.e., you must create a competitive strategy, which means that a competitive strategy is a kind of growth strategy. So, to summarize, a competitive strategy is a kind of growth strategy, and a growth strategy is a kind of problem–solving strategy.

Kinds of Competitive Strategy

Michael Porter, a professor at Harvard Business School, identifies three generic competitive strategies in his seminal book *Competitive Advantage: Creating and Sustaining Superior Performance*[7] and in his earlier book *Competitive Strategy: Techniques for Analyzing Industries and*

Figure 1.7 Differentiation is about being different in a way that causes customers to prefer you.

Source: David Holt Design, Adobe.

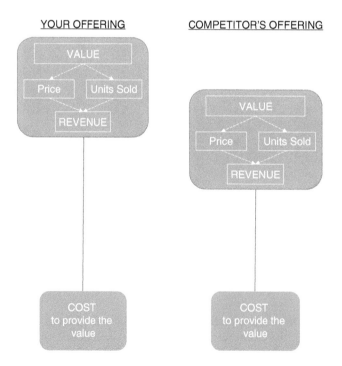

Figure 1.8 Customers prefer you when you provide more customer-perceived value than your competitor.

Source: Adapted from *Strategic Learning: How to be smarter than your competition and turn key insights into a competitive advantage*, Fig. 2.1. Reproduced with permission.

Competitors.[8] The three strategies are differentiation, cost leadership, and focus. The third type of strategy is simply a more focused version of the first two, which is to say, a differentiation or cost leadership strategy that focuses on a niche market segment. Each of the three kinds of strategies is a fundamentally different way of achieving a competitive advantage. In other words, each of the strategies is a different way of managing the gap between the amount of customer-perceived value and the cost to provide the value.

As earlier explained, to differentiate is to be different in a way that causes customers to prefer your offering to competing offerings. Consider Figure 1.7, where the (not very bright) chickens are competing to be selected for the farmer's chopping block. The two chickens in the left panel are the same size, which is to say, they are undifferentiated, so the farmer has no preference for one or the other. In other words, the offerings in this barnyard are *commoditized*. Compare this to the right panel, where the plumper chicken is different in a way that causes the farmer to prefer him to his competitor. In this barnyard, the plump chicken is *differentiated*.

Figure 1.7 illustrates that customers prefer an offering when they perceive that it provides more value than alternative offerings. This brings us back to Pietersen's gap. One way to achieve a competitive advantage, as illustrated in Figure 1.8, is to increase the amount of customer-perceived value by differentiating your offering while keeping the cost to provide the differentiated offering on par with your competitor's cost.

The *cost leadership* strategy takes a different route to competitive advantage, which is to say, it employs a different way of achieving a bigger gap. Here, as shown in Figure 1.9, the

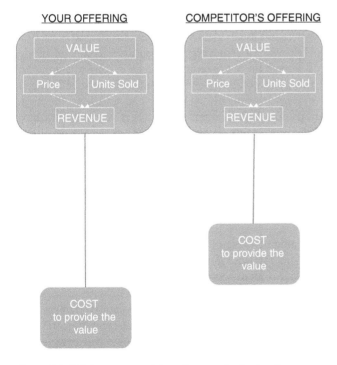

Figure 1.9 Gaining a competitive advantage by having lower costs.

Souce: Adapted from *Strategic Learning: How to be smarter than your competition and turn key insights into a competitive advantage*, Fig. 2.1. Reproduced with permission.

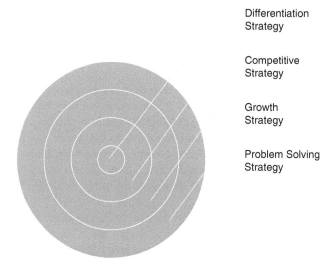

Differentiation
Strategy

Competitive
Strategy

Growth
Strategy

Problem Solving
Strategy

Figure 1.10 A differentiation strategy is a kind of competitive strategy, which is a kind of growth strategy, which is a kind of problem-solving strategy.

strategy is to be the lowest-cost producer in the industry—not *a* low-cost producer, but *the* lowest-cost producer. Were you to use this strategy, you would achieve a bigger gap by keeping the amount of your customer-perceived value on par with that of your competitor and the cost to provide the value significantly lower than your competitor's cost.

The third generic strategy is *focus*. This way of achieving a competitive advantage applies one of the first two strategies to a smaller segment of the entire market, i.e., to a niche market segment. With a *differentiation focus* strategy, a company seeks to differentiate its offering in the niche segment. With a *cost focus* strategy, a company seeks a cost advantage in the niche segment. For a focus strategy to be successful, the customers in the target segment must have atypical needs, or the production and delivery system that best serves the target segment must differ from the system used to serve the other segments. A focus strategy is a viable option when you want to enter a market in which there are competitors who possess an over-whelming competitive advantage. In this circumstance, it is usually the case that the only way to compete is to identify a niche market segment with unique needs or that requires a different system to serve it and then build a competitive advantage in the niche with a differentiation or cost leadership strategy.

Now that you know what a differentiation strategy is, we can expand Figure 1.5. As shown in Figure 1.10, a differentiation strategy is a kind of competitive strategy, which is a kind of growth strategy, which is a kind of problem-solving strategy. Or, reversing the order, one kind of problem-solving strategy is a growth strategy; one kind of growth strategy is a competitive strategy; and one kind of competitive strategy is a differentiation strategy.

This book is about achieving a competitive advantage by using a differentiation strategy. As the gap diagrams illustrate, competitive advantage is a function of value and cost. So far, I've relied on your intuitive understanding of value. But we'll need to dig deeper into its meaning to move this discussion down the road, which is what we're going to do in the next chapter.

Notes

1 Samuel Johnson, as quoted in James Case, *Competition: The Birth of a New Science* (New York, NY: Hill and Wang, 2007), *vii*.

2 Willie Pietersen. *Strategic Learning: How to be Smarter Than Your Competition and Turn Key Insights Into Competitive Advantage* (New York, NY: John Wiley & Sons, 2010), 16–24.

3 Note that both competitors start out equal in size. In the case of a much smaller competitor with a competitive advantage entering an industry in which there are much larger competitors, it's likely that the larger competitors will put the smaller one out of business before it can use its competitive advantage to grow to a competitive size. In this circumstance, the smaller competitor would be better off focusing on a market niche in which it can rapidly build a defensible competitive advantage.

4 M. Mitchell Waldrop. *Complexity: The Emerging Science at the Edge of Order and Chaos* (New York, NY: Simon & Schuster, 1992), 17.

5 Jack Welch, as quoted by Eric Sherman, "Think You Know Your Competitive Advantage? Maybe Not. Competitive advantage is a simple idea. Identifying yours can be harder than you think." Inc.com: https://www.inc.com/erik-sherman/think-you-know-your-competitive-advantage-maybe-not.html.

6 The opportunities and threats are things that exist in the external environment of a company, whereas the strengths and weaknesses are things that exist in its internal environment.

7 Michael Porter. *Competitive Advantage: Creating and Sustaining Superior Performance* (New York, NY: The Free Press, 1985), 11–15. In addition to this summary, the book dedicates whole chapters to cost advantage and differentiation.

8 Michael Porter. *Competitive Strategy: Techniques for Analyzing Industries and Competitors* (New York, NY: The Free Press, 1980), 34–40.

2 Value

Value has to be one of the most-used and least-understood terms in business. Books and articles are peppered with phrases like *value added, value proposition, value chain, value innovation, economic value, shared value, superior value, company value, stock value, lifetime customer value,* and *competing on value*. Yet most managers have little more than a superficial notion of what the word means. In this chapter, we're going to give value a thorough going over. You'll get more out of it if you first take a moment to say what the term means to you.

Customer-Perceived Value

In business, value is used to mean two different things. In the first case, it's taken to mean *monetary worth*, as when someone says the value of their house is $400,000 or that a stock is valued at $25 per share. In the second case, the meaning of value combines the concepts of *worth* and *appeal*, as when a customer considers something "worth buying" because it's a "good value." Business professors call this sort of value *customer-perceived value* or simply *customer value* or *perceived value*. Unfortunately, when it comes time to define these terms, the professors are hard-pressed to agree. In their book titled *Value Merchants: Demonstrating and Documenting Superior Value in Business Markets*, James Anderson, Nirmalya Kumar, and James Narus explain a number of the definitions that have been proposed, as detailed at this endnote.[1] Doriana Dumitrela Morar provides more definitions in her overview of the consumer value literature.[2]

The most widely accepted definition of customer-perceived value is based on a study in which customers were themselves asked to define value. The author of the study summarized their definitions in this way, "[P]erceived value is the consumer's overall assessment of the utility of a product based on perceptions of what is received and what is given."[3] The definition can be boiled down to the equation *Value = Received − Given* or, more pithily put, the equation *Value = Get − Give*. Another version of this definition is, "From a customer's perspective, customer value is what they 'get' (benefits) relative to what they have to 'give up' (costs or sacrifices),"[4] which distills down to the equation *Value = Benefits − Costs*. In both cases, the terms used in the definitions and equations warrant a closer look at their meaning.

First is the term *benefits*. As the first two equations make clear, one way of defining benefits is to say they are what customers "receive" or "get" from a company's offering. To "get" something is to "gain" something. The terms "get" and "gain" are consistent with the dictionary definition of a benefit, which says a benefit is "a gain or advantage."[5] Combining the terms "gain" and "advantage" adds the idea that the thing which is gotten is something good or positive. In the next chapter, you're going to learn there are six kinds of good things to be gotten, which is to say, there are six kinds of benefits—physical, mental, emotional, economic, social, and cost/risk reduction benefits.

DOI: 10.4324/9781003271703-3

The second term in need of definition is *costs*. Most people equate the cost of an offering with its purchase price. But there are more kinds of costs than the initial purchase price. The cost of an offering also includes the monetary costs incurred during the offering's lifecycle (e.g., downtime costs, repair and maintenance costs, and disposal costs) as well as non-monetary costs like the time and effort required to find, purchase, and learn how to use the offering.

The third term requiring more definition is *relative to*. As used in the sentence "Customer-perceived value is the perceived worth of benefits relative to costs," the phrase *relative to* is equivalent to *compared with*. So, an equivalent way of defining customer-perceived value is to say, "Customer-perceived value is the perceived worth of the benefits compared with costs." If benefits are what you "get" and costs are what you "give" to get the benefits, you want to compare them to make sure you are getting more than you are giving. In other words, you want to make sure that the worth of the benefits is more than the worth of the costs. Which leads to the question: *How do you know when the worth of the benefits is more than the worth of the costs?*

Answering the question requires us to deal with the fourth thing in need of more definition—the concept of *worth*. We will take worth to mean "the amount or quantity of something that may be had...."[6] With this definition in mind, one way to answer the foregoing question is to quantify the monetary worth of the benefits and the monetary worth of the costs and calculate the difference between the two. Imagine, for example, a business that is considering buying a manufacturing machine that costs $10,000, all in (where "all in" means the purchase price and other monetary costs, such as maintenance costs). If, during its useful life, the machine will benefit the company by generating more than $10,000 of profit—say $12,000—then the company will consider the monetary worth of the benefits to be more than the monetary worth of the costs and conclude that the machine has value.[7]

But the worth of benefits and costs can't always be reduced to dollars and cents. For example, how do you monetize the emotional benefit of a thrill ride or a painting or a museum exhibit? How do you attach a dollar value to the physical benefit provided by a shaver that shaves closer or a weed killer that kills faster? How do you translate the social esteem derived from a luxury car into monetary terms? And how do you calculate the economic cost of the extra ten minutes spent driving to your barber's new location? In circumstances like these, the only way for you to answer the question "How do you know when the worth of the benefits is more than the worth of the costs?" is to simply say that you *think* or *feel* or *believe* that it is. In circumstances where people are unable to calculate the *monetary worth* of benefits and costs, they are somehow able to compute their *cognitive worth*.

The mental machinations are even more mysterious when people must add two or more incommensurable benefits—say, the monetary worth of one benefit and the cognitive worth of another.[8] Just like you can't add apples and oranges in algebra, you can't add dollars and pleasurable emotions to calculate the total worth of the two. The same holds true for two or more incommensurable costs—say, the price of a product and the physical effort required to use it. Money and physical effort do not have a common measure and are therefore things that cannot be summed algebraically. So, if you can't add the worth of incommensurable benefits and you can't add the worth of incommensurable costs, how do you know if the sum of the benefits is more than the sum of the costs? Again, the most you can say is you just *think* or *feel* or *believe* that it is.

The last thing requiring more definition in the sentence "Customer-perceived value is the perceived worth of benefits relative to costs" is the word *perceived*.[9] The term is included (twice) to emphasize that value judgments are subjective. People are free to assign whatever monetary or cognitive worth they please to benefits and costs. And that's exactly what they do. Different people perceive the worth of things differently. One man's trash is another man's treasure, as the saying goes. For example, where a boy racer might perceive that a manual transmission is worth more than an automatic transmission, an elderly person might perceive the opposite.

Conditional Value

The fact that customer-perceived value is subjective has several important consequences.[10] One consequence is that value is *conditional* or *contextual.* The value people assign to something depends on their circumstances. Put our boy racer in the circumstance of having to commute in Los Angeles's stop-and-go traffic and he might decide that an automatic transmission isn't such a bad thing after all. Put our old man in the circumstance of climbing a long, steep hill in an underpowered car and he may prefer to do the shifting himself rather than put up with an automatic transmission that can't decide what gear it wants to be in. Ask the two of them to tell you the worth of the two types of transmission and they will tell you, "It depends on the circumstance."

Not only do circumstances influence *what* people want, but they also influence *how much* monetary worth they are willing to attribute to it. Consider, for example, that on a hot day in the park most people are willing to feed a vending machine $2 for the same can of soda they can buy at the supermarket for $0.25.[11] The same logic applies to buying a bag of popcorn at a movie theater, a hot dog at a baseball game, and a coffee at Starbucks, as compared to buying the items at a supermarket. What a person is willing to pay for something is set subjectively and depends on the circumstances.

The second consequence of the subjective nature of customer-perceived value is that it is *dynamic.* People change their minds about what things they value and the monetary or cognitive worth of those things. Various things cause them to change their minds.[12] For example, a decrease in the personal income of a car owner may cause her to value higher gas mileage. An increase in the size of her family may cause her to value a larger vehicle. And a move to a snowy climate may cause her to see more value in a four-wheel-drive vehicle.

Relative Value

The third consequence of the subjective nature of customer-perceived value is that people perceive it *relative to* other alternatives. Anderson et al. explain that there are four kinds of alternatives to buying a company's offering:[13]

- Competitor Offering: In most cases, the customer evaluates a company's offering relative to the alternatives offered by one or more of the company's competitors.
- Do-It-Yourself: In some cases, the customer considers the alternative of providing the offering itself, as would be the case if a business customer decided to implement its own call center rather than outsource the service or if a consumer decided to clean his own house rather than hire a cleaning service.
- Status Quo: Sometimes the customer chooses the alternative of doing nothing. The customer doesn't buy from anyone, and he doesn't do it himself. This would be the case where a consumer decides not to have a contractor build an addition on his house, nor does he build the addition himself.
- Past Offering: This is the alternative of continuing to use a past offering rather than upgrading to the most up-to-date version, such as when a customer is satisfied with a past version of a software product.

To gain more insight into how people perceive value relative to alternatives, let's revisit the earlier example of the business that is considering buying a manufacturing machine (Machine

Table 2.1 Customer-perceived value equals perceived benefits minus perceived costs

	Value	=	*Benefits* − *Costs*
Machine A	$2,000	=	$12,000 − $10,000
Machine B	$3,000	=	$15,000 − $12,000

A) that costs $10,000 and delivers $12,000 of profit during its useful life. Now let's assume there is an alternative manufacturing machine (Machine B) that delivers $15,000 of profit during the machine's useful life and costs $12,000. If, as shown in Table 2.1, we transform the sentence "Customer-perceived value is the perceived worth of benefits relative to costs" into the equation *Customer-Perceived Value = Perceived Worth of Benefits − Perceived Worth of Costs* or, more simply, *Value = Benefits − Costs*, we see that the value of Machine B is more than the value of Machine A.

The Value Equation

The equation *Value = Benefits − Costs* is easy enough to understand. The difficulty is putting it into practice. As previously explained, not everything can be monetized. Also, incommensurability—the idea that you can't add things that don't have a common standard of judgment or measurement—makes it impossible to sum the worth of dissimilar benefits and dissimilar costs. Fortunately, there are ways to work around the problem.

The first workaround is to forget about calculating the precise amount of value and simply use the value equation to understand how you can increase customer-perceived value. Or, to employ some common business terms, use the value equation to understand how you can *add value* or provide a *value-added* solution. You don't have to be a mathematician to use the equation *Value = Benefits − Costs* to see that there are three ways to increase value. The first way is to hold the customer's costs steady and increase benefits, either by providing more benefits, increasing performance on existing benefits, or both. The second way is to hold benefits steady and lower the customer's costs, either by lowering the price, decreasing other monetary and non-monetary costs, or both. The third way is to simultaneously increase the customer's benefits and decrease the customer's costs. In all three cases, the objective is to provide the customer with more value, i.e., to *add value* or provide a *value-added solution*.

The second way to work around the difficulty of putting the value equation into practice is to, again, forget about calculating a precise amount of value and simplify the equation even further. The equation is simplified by transforming all costs, other than price, to their opposite and treating them as benefits. For example, rather than treat *maintenance costs* as a cost, treat *maintenance cost savings* as a benefit. Similarly, instead of treating the *time required to learn how to use the product* as a cost, treat the *time saved learning how to use the product* as a benefit. We'll see how to put this into practice in a later chapter. For now, the important thing to understand is the idea of treating cost savings as benefits in order to separate costs from price. Doing this enables us to transform the equation *Value = Benefits − Costs* into *Value = Benefits − Price*. In other words, *value equals the benefits received for the price paid*. From here, it's a short step to seeing how the equation can be used to compare the value of your offering (the benefits minus the price of your offering) with the value of a competing offering (the benefits minus the price of the competing offering).

Anderson et al. offer a different version of the value equation and a more precise way of putting it into practice.[14] They do so by limiting its application to business customers, whose chief concern is monetary benefits. Their approach to separating out *Price* is to treat the

Benefits part of the equation as *Net Benefits*, i.e., as the monetary benefits net of the monetary costs the customer incurs to obtain the benefits. Then they treat *Value* and *Net Benefits* as meaning the same thing. This, they explain, enables you to do two things. First, it enables you to think of *Value* (net benefits) as something that is exchanged for *Price*. Second, it enables you to compare your offering with your competitor's offering by using the following equation (where the subscript "y" stands for your offering and the subscript "c" stands for your competitor's offering): $(Value_y - Price_y) > (Value_c - Price_c)$. As indicated by this formulation, the goal is for the difference between the value and price of your offering to be greater than the difference between the value and price of your competitor's offering.

Now that the concept of value has been thoroughly defined, some qualifications are required to avoid confusing the concept of customer-perceived value as it's been used in this chapter with the concept of value as it was used in the last chapter in Pietersen's gap diagram (Figure 1.1). The fundamental difference is that the costs referred to in this chapter are the costs the *customer incurs to obtain* the desired benefits, whereas the costs referred to in Pietersen's gap diagram are the costs the *company incurs to provide* the desired benefits. The value in the gap diagram is best conceived of as the customer's net benefits, as defined by Anderson et al., which means that the customer is willing to pay a certain price for the net benefits. This definition squares with Pietersen's explanation that price and volume are derivatives of value or, said differently, that net benefits drive price and volume. As you think about volume, remember that the price and volume referenced in Pietersen's gap diagram pertain to a population of customers rather than a single customer.

We started this chapter by defining customer-perceived value as what customers "get" (benefits) relative to what they have to "give up" (costs or sacrifices) in order to get the benefits. Putting the definition in the form of an equation yields *Value = Get − Give*. Another way of defining customer-perceived value is to say that it is the perceived worth of benefits relative to the perceived worth of the costs required to obtain the benefits. We boiled this definition down to the equation: *Value = Benefits − Costs*. Then we transformed all the costs, except price, into benefits by treating them as cost savings, which yielded the equation: *Value = Benefits − Price*. Spoiler alert. When we get to the chapter on the value proposition, we're going to go even further by putting price in the back of our minds so that we can treat value and benefits as meaning the same thing. This yields the equation: *Value = Benefits* and enables you to think of the *value proposition* as the *benefits proposition*, which is easier to think about than the (more correct) *benefits-price proposition*. Clearly, benefits are the key concept to consider when thinking about customer-perceived value. The logical next step is to take a closer look at the concept of benefits, which is what we're going to do in the next chapter.

Notes

1 James C. Anderson, Nirmalya Kumar, and James A. Narus, *Value Merchants: Demonstrating and Documenting Superior Value in Business Markets* (Boston, MA: Harvard Business School Press, 2007), 22. The authors note that different business scholars have proposed different definitions of "customer value" including the idea that it is perceived quality adjusted for the relative price of the product, the maximum price the customer will pay, the benefits received relative to the price paid, and the total savings or satisfaction that the customer receives from a product.
2 Doriana Dumitrela Morar, "An overview of the consumer value literature—perceived value, desired value," *Conference: Marketing from Information to Decision—At: Cluj-Napoca Volume 6*, 2013, https://www.researchgate.net/publication/271585009_An_overview_of_the_consumer_value_literature_-_perceived_value_desired_value, 169–186.
3 Valeri Zeithaml, "Consumer Perceptions of Price, Quality, and Value: A Means-End Model and Synthesis of Evidence," *Journal of Marketing*, 52, Jul. 1988, 14.

4 J. Brock Smith and Mark Colgate, "Customer Value Creation: A Practical Framework," *Journal of Marketing Theory and Practice* 15 (Winter 2007), 7.

5 *Webster's New World College Dictionary,* 4th Ed., (Cleveland, OH: Wiley Publishing, Inc., 2004), 135.

6 *Ibid*, 1651.

7 For those familiar with the concept of *present value*, both figures are assumed to be in present value dollars.

8 Anderson et al., *op. cit.*, 23. The authors introduce the idea of commensurability and the difficulty it presents with regard to calculating value.

9 It would be more correct to use the term *conceived* rather than *perceived*. Technically speaking, the term perceive refers to perception, which is not how we determine worth—we do not see, hear, smell, touch, or taste worth. Conceive comes closer to the intended idea of judging the worth of something or believing or holding the opinion that something has some level of worth. However, the term perceive is so widely used that I decided to stay with it to avoid confusion.

10 Smith and Colgate, *op. cit.*, 8. The authors note that some of the key characteristics of value are that it is perceived uniquely by individual customers; it is conditional or contextual; it is relative to known or imagined alternatives; and it is dynamic.

11 Niraj Dawar, *Tilt: Shifting Your Strategy from Products to Customers* (Boston, MA: Harvard Business Review Press, 2013), 29–30. This example is taken from Dawar.

12 Cinzia Parolini, *The Value Net: A Tool for Competitive Strategy* (New York, NY: John Wiley & Sons, 1999), 117. Parolini cites the following types of factors that influence the value perceived by customers: individual factors, environmental factors, cost of complementary goods and competitiveness of substitute goods, the configuration of the received offer system, and the configuration of alternative offer systems.

13 Anderson et al., *op. cit.*, 25.

14 *Ibid*, 24–27.

3   Benefits

Chapter 1 explained that the two ways to gain a competitive advantage are differentiation and cost leadership, that differentiation is about being different in a way that causes customers to prefer you, and that customers prefer you when you provide more customer-perceived value than your competition. Chapter 2 explained that the customer-perceived value of your offering equals the benefits customers receive from it less the price they pay for it. In other words, *Value = Benefits − Price*. Together, the two chapters highlight the fact that differentiation is fundamentally about providing more and better benefits than your competition, which is why it is vital that you dig deep to understand them.

The Meaning of Benefits

The first shovel-full of understanding is the recognition that when customers talk about wanting or needing something and sellers talk about providing something, they're both talking about the same thing—a benefit. A benefit is that which is wanted or needed by the customer and provided by the offering. In Figure 3.1, for example, the lady says she needs pain relief, and the company says its aspirin provides pain relief. The needed benefit is pain relief, and the provided benefit is pain relief. What all this means is that the old advice to "find a need and fill it" is more accurately, though less pithily, put as "find a benefit that's wanted or needed and provide it."

The next thing to understand is what it is, exactly, that is providing the benefit. In the foregoing example, most people would say that it is the aspirin that is providing the benefit and most people would be wrong. As shown in Figure 3.2, it's more accurate to say that it's the *function* of the aspirin—what it does—that provides the benefit. The function of aspirin is to block pain signals to the brain. By performing the function, aspirin provides the benefit of pain relief. Figure 3.2 illustrates a handy way to talk about an offering, function, and benefit from the customer's perspective. The offering is *what it is* (aspirin), the function is *what it does* (blocks pain signals), and the benefit is the *desired consequence*, or *what it does for me* (provides pain relief).

The last thing to understand about the meaning of a benefit is that desires, wants, and needs are mental entities, which is to say, they are things that exist in the customer's mind. But that doesn't square with the idea that a benefit is an end or consequence that the customer "gets" or "receives"—like the pain relief a person gets from an aspirin or the fixed car a person receives from a car repair service. To square the corner, we need to make the distinction between a *desired benefit* and a *satisfied benefit*. That might strike you as hairsplitting but failing to make the distinction is sometimes a source of confusion.

Types of Benefits

As just explained, a desired benefit is something that is wanted or needed. The classic classification of wants/needs is the psychologist Abraham Maslow's hierarchy of needs (Figure 3.3).

DOI: 10.4324/9781003271703-4

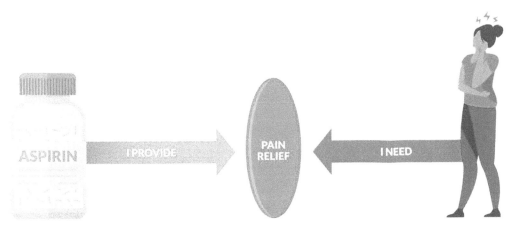

Figure 3.1 A benefit is that which is wanted or needed by the customer and provided by the seller.
Source: David Holt Design, Adobe.

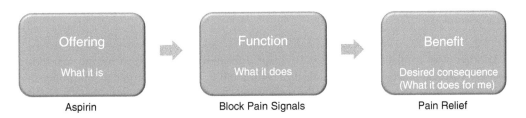

Figure 3.2 Offering-function-benefit trilogy.

The hierarchy is usually depicted as a pyramid in which the most basic and most frequently sought needs serve as the base of the pyramid, and the progressively less basic, less frequently sought needs are stacked on top of it. Maslow proposed that people must satisfy a lower-level need before they will be strongly motivated to satisfy a need at the next higher level. At the bottom of Maslow's hierarchy are physiological needs like air, water, food, shelter, sleep, clothing, and sex. Above that are safety needs, such as personal security, employment, resources, health, and property. Still higher are love and belonging needs, which include friendship, intimacy, family, and a sense of connection. Next to the top of the hierarchy are esteem needs like respect, self-esteem, status, recognition, strength, and freedom. And at the top of the hierarchy is self-actualization—the need to be the most you can be.

The Bain & Company consultants Eric Almquist, John Senior, and Nicholas Block offer an alternate version of Maslow's hierarchy.[1] Their hierarchy is filled with thirty "elements of value" that address four kinds of needs. Adapting this to the language used here, we can say that there are 30 kinds of benefits classified into a hierarchy of 4 progressively more general types of benefits. At the bottom of their hierarchy are *functional benefits,* such as saves time, makes money, and reduces risk. On the next step of the hierarchy are *emotional benefits*, such as reduces anxiety, rewards me, and provides access. Above that are *life-changing benefits*, including self-actualization, motivation, and hope. And at the top of the hierarchy is the *social impact benefit* of self-transcendence.

Figure 3.3 Maslow's hierarchy of needs.

Source: Shutterstock.

Another way to classify benefits is to adapt a framework developed by the marketing professors Brock Smith and Mark Colgate.[2] Smith and Colgate performed a comprehensive review of journal articles having to do with value, from which they developed a classification scheme consisting of four fundamental types of value—functional/instrumental value, experiential/hedonic value, symbolic/expressive value, and cost/sacrifice value. Substituting "benefit" for "value" and using their definitions of the four types of value produces four fundamental kinds of benefits. An offering provides a *functional/instrumental benefit* when it has desired characteristics, is useful, or performs a desired function. *Experiential/hedonic benefits* are provided by offerings that create appropriate experiences, feelings, and emotions. *Symbolic/expressive benefits* are about the extent to which customers attach or associate psychological meaning to an offering, such as an enhanced sense of self-worth or self-expression. *Cost/sacrifice benefits* are provided when an offering minimizes the economic, physical, and psychological costs associated with purchasing, owning, and using an offering.

The anthropologist Lionel Tiger classifies pleasures in a way that can be used to create a taxonomy of benefits.[3] Tiger's taxonomy consists of physiopleasure, ideopleasure, psychopleasure, and sociopleasure. *Physiopleasure* is the physical pleasure we derive from our sensory system. *Ideopleasure* is the intellectual pleasure associated with ideas and using the mind. *Psychopleasure* relates to pleasant emotions. And *sociopleasure* is the pleasure we obtain from being and bonding with other people. Replacing "pleasure" with "benefits" yields the four-benefit taxonomy: *physiobenefits, ideobenefits, psychobenefits,* and *sociobenefits*.

I've borrowed from the foregoing four classification schemes to create a six-benefit taxonomy that I find is easier to put into practice. The six kinds of benefits are labeled *physical, mental, emotional, social, economic,* and *cost/risk reduction*.[4] The rest of this chapter describes each of the benefits. But before we get into that, note the following five things:

- Smith and Colgate and the Bain & Company consultants distinguish functional benefits. To my way of thinking, considering that all benefits are the product of a function (remember the offering–function–benefit trilogy), it seems appropriate to say that all benefits are functional benefits.
- In some instances, it's hard to say whether the function of an offering produces one type of benefit or another, or both and maybe more. This is usually because the function delivers a laddered set of benefits in which higher-level benefits are stacked on top of lower-level benefits.
- One can fairly argue that many, if not all, benefits end in an emotional benefit, which would mean that of the six types of benefits, five are simply a means to the end of some emotional benefit. Here, again, consider that an emotional benefit can be a higher-level benefit laddered on top of a lower-level benefit.
- We'll discuss the concepts of *enablement* and *relief* in the next chapter. For now, as you consider the six kinds of benefits, keep in mind that the function of an offering provides a benefit when it *helps* or *enables* a customer to perform a physical, mental, emotional, social, economic, or cost/risk reduction action. Or the function of an offering provides a benefit when it *relieves* a person of having to perform the action.
- The final and most important thing to keep in mind is that differentiation is ultimately about benefits. You can be different by providing significantly more of a desired benefit than is provided by your rivals, by providing desired benefits that your rivals do not provide, or both. The more you know about benefits, the more differentiation opportunities you will be able to identify, so it's well worth taking the time to gain a thorough understanding of them. You'll get much more out of the following if you routinely stop and ask yourself how your company could differentiate itself by providing, or providing significantly more of, the kind of benefit that is being discussed, especially the benefits that initially strike you as being unrelated to what you offer.

Physical Benefits

Physical benefits pertain to the material world. Some pertain to the world outside the body, some to the interface between the body and the world, and some to the world on or inside the body.

The first type of physical benefit exists when customers perceive that an offering's function will help or enable them to perform a physical task in the world outside their body. For example:

- The *support weight* function of a cane helps or enables the user perform the physical task of walking—or *help walk*, for short.
- The *cut substance* function of a kitchen knife enables the user to perform the physical task of slicing food—or *slice food*.
- The *extend hands* and *transmit force* functions of a shovel enable the user to perform the task of digging a hole—or *dig a hole*.
- The *infrared emitter* function of a television remote control reduces the physical effort required to change channels—or *change channels*.
- The *transmit signals* function of a telephone enables the user to communicate at a distance across physical space—or *communicate at a distance*.
- A digital recorder's *store signals* function enables the user to transmit information across space and time—or *communicate across space-time*.
- The *transport things* function of car enables the user to perform the task of traveling through physical space from point A to point B—or *travel across space*.

The second place that an offering's function delivers a physical benefit is at the interface between the body and the world. Here, the function serves to augment the human sensory system. The traditional view of the sensory system recognizes the five senses of sight, sound, smell, touch, and taste. Scientists now know that people also sense temperature, pain, vibration, balance, the relative position of the parts of the body (referred to as the kinesthetic sense), and chemicals in the blood, such as salt and carbon dioxide concentrations.[5] (Strictly speaking, the last three senses detect things inside the body, but to keep things simple, let's ignore that so as not to complicate the classification scheme.) Since the senses detect things that exist in the physical world—e.g., wave-particles of light, sound waves, and molecules—we can say that anything that functions to help or enable a person to sense something provides the person with a physical benefit. Consider the following examples (where I dispense with the verb-noun descriptions of functions and benefits):

- Eyeglasses, microscopes, and telescopes help or enable people to see small things and distant things.
- Hearing aids and megaphones help or enable people to hear things they would otherwise be unable to hear.
- Dogs enable people to detect odors that they are unable to smell on their own, and there are now "smell machines" that do the same thing, including those that can detect the odor of specific types of cancer and of bacterial odors that indicate that an operating room has not been adequately sterilized.
- Artificial hands are now equipped with sensors that enable people to regain their sense of touch.
- Wine tasters often use crackers to enhance their sense of taste. And the wine itself enhances the taste of food.

Sensory benefits also include Tiger's *physiopleasures*. This is about helping or enabling people to derive pleasure from what they sense. Imagine, for example, a spa where every aspect of the customer's sensory experience is attended to. The décor and beautiful views are designed to be visually pleasing. Soft, serene music relaxes the spa's patrons and pleasant aromas improve their mood and sense of well-being. The temperature is perfect and the massages, mud baths, and other spa treatments make masterful use of the sense of touch to sooth and stimulate. Yoga and other exercise classes enable people to explore the outer reaches[6] of their body's kinesthetic sense, after which they are given sports drinks to quench their thirst and replenish their blood electrolytes. To finish things off, customers are treated to a healthy, good-tasting meal. All in all, a day at the spa is a sensory feast.

The third place that an offering's function delivers a physical benefit is on or inside the body. Following are some examples of offerings that have a positive impact on the body:

- Soaps and shampoos that clean the body.
- Oils and lotions that prevent skin from drying out and wrinkling.
- Topical medicines that cure rashes.
- Products that protect the body from the elements, such as sunscreens that block ultraviolet radiation, clothing that keeps the body warm or cool and prevents scratches and bug bites, and shoes that cushion and prevent damage to feet.

Other offerings benefit the world inside the body, usually by maintaining or recovering a person's physical health or relieving pain and discomfort. For example:

- Physicians, psychologists, nurses, dentists, physical therapists, and other health-care professionals do various things to help people stay well or recover from an illness.
- Hospitals, pharmaceutical firms, diagnostic laboratories, and other health-care companies provide medicines, vitamins, stents, artificial hips, and all manner of other things that have a positive impact on the inside of the body.
- Antacids relieve the discomfort of an upset stomach.
- Aspirin, morphine, and other drugs provide pain relief.

Mental Benefits

The second of the five types of benefit is a *mental benefit*. Users perceive that an offering's function delivers a *mental benefit* when it helps or enables them to perform a mental action. Where a physical action occurs "out there," in the physical world outside our heads, a mental action occurs "in here," in the mental world inside our minds. Another term for mental actions is cognition. A formal definition of *cognition* is, "The collection of mental processes and activities used in perceiving, learning, remembering, thinking, and understanding, and the act of using these processes."[7] Cognitive scientists have yet to develop a comprehensive inventory of the mental processes and activities, although, as next explained, various ways of classifying them have been attempted.

A way of classifying the content of the mind is to divide it into *mental acts* and *mental states*.[8] A mental act is a mental performance. When we perform a mental act we are *doing,* or trying to do, some mental thing like calculate a number or remember a name. In contrast, a mental state is a temporarily static state of mind. We refer to mental states using words like *being* and *having*, such as when we talk about being satisfied, having the knowledge we need, and possessing peace of mind.

One way of classifying mental acts is "Bloom's Taxonomy," named after Benjamin Bloom, who chaired the committee of educators that developed and published the taxonomy. As illustrated in Figure 3.4, the taxonomy identifies three lower-order and three higher-order mental acts. The lowest-order act is to *remember* relevant knowledge by retrieving it from long-term memory. After having remembered the knowledge, the next act is to *understand* its meaning. Once the meaning of the knowledge is understood, the person *applies* it by, for example, using it to solve problems in new situations. The three lower-order mental acts support or enable the implementation of the three higher-order mental acts. The first is *analyzing* the knowledge by breaking it into its constituent parts and determining how the parts relate to one another. The second is *evaluating* the knowledge by judging or critiquing it. The third is *creating* something by using the existing knowledge to hypothesize, plan, or produce new knowledge.

An offering provides a mental benefit when it helps or enables a customer to perform a mental act, such as when a calculator helps a person multiply two large numbers. Or an offering provides a mental benefit when it relieves a person of having to perform a mental act, such as when a smartphone relieves a person of the task of remembering a phone number or a "To Do" item. People also benefit when an offering helps or enables them to eliminate an undesirable state of mind, like the state of being conflicted or confused about what to do. Finally, people benefit when an offering helps or enables them to have a desired state of mind, such as the state of mind that exists when their sense of curiosity is satisfied or when their sense of wonder is induced.

Curiosity and wonder are what Smith and Colgate call *epistemic* benefits, so called because they pertain to knowledge and the act of knowing. Tiger refers to them as *ideopleasures*. An offering provides epistemic benefits, or ideopleasures, by satisfying a person's curiosity, providing a novel experience, stimulating the imagination, or taking the person on a flight of

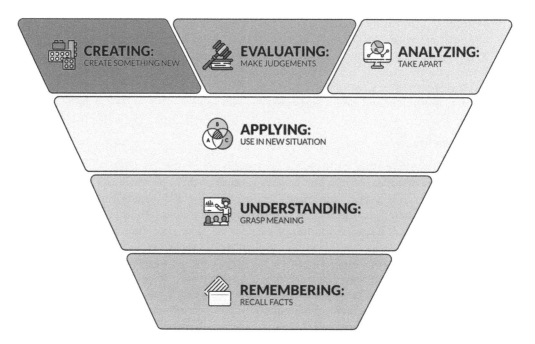

Figure 3.4 Bloom's taxonomy.

Source: Shutterstock.

fantasy. Tiger identifies two kinds of ideopleasure. The first kind is "what people receive from experiencing or creating theoretical entities such as movies, buildings, plays, music, art objects, [and] books. Or, when they do crossword puzzles, or create scientific problems and excitedly try to solve them."[9] The second kind of ideopleasure, he says, is "the pleasure found in nature—in landscape, the look and smell of animals, the general impact of natural circumstances."[10] Tiger's examples only begin to describe the many types of offerings that provide epistemic benefits. Travel tours, theme parks, space camps, games, museums, newspapers, magazines, television shows, documentary films, hobbies, parks, botanical gardens, zoos, pets, and plants are just some of the many things that provide people with ideopleasure.

One omnipresent and important state of mind is *self-esteem*. Self-esteem consists of two interrelated components.[11] The first is *self-efficacy* (aka *self-trust* and *self-reliance*). People who have a high degree of self-efficacy are highly confident in their ability to face life's challenges. The second part of self-esteem is *self-respect* (aka *self-worth*). People possessing a high degree of self-respect are assured of their worth or value, their right to be happy, and their right to assert their thoughts, wants, and needs. Customers benefit from offerings that increase their sense of self-efficacy and self-respect. Examples of the former are educational, training, and information products that increase a person's or company's ability to overcome challenges. An example of the latter is a customer relationship program that assures customers of their value and provides them the opportunity to assert their thoughts, wants, and needs.

A related sort of mental benefit has to do with *self-expression*. The word "express" is derived from the Latin root meaning "to press out." Self-expression is about revealing or exposing—i.e., pressing out—an aspect of the self to show to others. Some definitions of self-expression focus on the expression of a person's thoughts and feelings. Other definitions emphasize the expression of the person's individual traits or individuality. In both cases, a person's *self-concept* is the set of beliefs that he or she has about him- or herself.[12] The nineteenth-century psychologist William James was among the first to classify the things people believe about themselves.[13] James divided the beliefs into three fundamental categories—beliefs we have about the material self, the social self, and the spiritual self. He also identified an "I" self, which he called the pure ego, that perceives the three kinds of beliefs.

The *material self* (or *empirical self*) consists of things that belong to us or that we belong to. Our body is the most intimate part of our material self, with clothing being a close second, followed by our family, our home, and other material possessions, including money. Among the offerings that enable people to express the individuality of their body are tattoos, hairstyles, fragrances, bodybuilding, and plastic surgery. Ways of individuating clothing include different fashion styles—e.g., classic, western, preppy, bohemian, arty, chic, and punk—and unique combinations of clothing and accessories. Material possessions like homes are individualized by adopting different architectural styles—e.g., contemporary, cape cod, gothic revival, and mission home—and unique combinations of furniture and art. There are all manner of ways for people to display their wealth, ranging from owning a luxury car to belonging to an exclusive country club.

The *social self* consists of the recognition we get from others. James explained that we have an innate desire to get ourselves favorably noticed by others, that we have as many different social selves as there are distinct groups of persons about whose opinion we care, and that we show a different side of ourselves to each of these different groups. James' social self is similar to the self that exists in the *social identity theory* of consumer behavior.[14] There are two parts to the theory. The first part proposes that people are motivated to take actions and consume products, at least in part, by the desire to enact identities that are consistent with their ideal self-images. The second part says that a person does not enact just one global identity, but multiple identities (e.g., mother, professor, employee, friend, etc.), each of which is triggered by a particular social context. An offering that helps or enables a person to do a better job of expressing a social role is one that provides that person with a desired mental benefit. Consider, for example, how diapers that do a superior job of keeping a baby dry help a mother do a better job of expressing her ideal mother self to other mothers and the way gifts and greeting cards help people express their ideal friend selves to their friends. In B2B settings, a polished report format or slick slide deck helps a manager express his competent employee self to his superiors and his competent seller self to buyers.

The *spiritual self* consists of a person's core values and conscience. One way for people to express their values is by purchasing offerings that are consistent with them. If a person values the environment, for example, he or she is more likely to buy an environmentally friendly offering, such as an electric car, a non-aerosol deodorant, a magazine that focuses on green issues, and so forth. The person is also more likely to engage in environmentally friendly practices, such as volunteering for clean-up efforts, using a recycling bin, and joining the Sierra Club. Whatever the means, people seek to express the values that distinguish their spiritual selves, and they obtain mental benefits from offerings that help or enable them to do so.

Another sort of mental benefit has to do with *personal meaning*. Personal meaning is something other than the *lexical meaning* found in dictionaries and the is-a, has-a, is-a-kind-of, and other factual associations that comprise *conceptual meaning* (which is explained later in this chapter). Personal meaning consists of the entire constellation of thoughts, images, and emotions that something evokes in a person.[15] This is particularly, though not exclusively, the case with things that are salient and significant for a person because of past experience. One sort of past experience is growing up in a certain culture or society, where a person learns what offerings symbolize or stand for. Sometimes it is the brand of an offering that does the symbolizing, such as the way the Mercedes-Benz and Rolex brands signify wealth and a degree from an Ivy League school signifies intelligence. Other times it is the nature of the offering that does the symbolizing, such as the way a red "power tie" signifies power and the cut of a person's clothes signifies whether the wearer is conservative, classy, or trashy. Things other than personal possessions also communicate socially shared meanings. The size and class of an office building, for instance, signifies things about the occupant's prestige and economic well-being, which is why banks, law firms, and stockbrokers prefer to occupy prominent Class A office buildings. Consider how none of these things—the Mercedes brand, the red tie, the office building, etc.—would have the same personal meaning, or any personal meaning at all, for a person who grew up in a remote Amazon Indian tribe.

Clotaire Rapaille, a French psychiatrist turned marketing consultant, explains that many meanings run deep in the sense that they are imprinted on a person early in life and are largely subconscious.[16] For example, in American culture the deeper meaning of cars is *identity*, whereas in German culture cars are most strongly associated with *engineering*. A fascinating example of a subconscious, culturally driven meaning is the fact that Americans subconsciously associate Jeep with a *horse* because of the way it is used to drive on the open land, free of the restraints of the road. In contrast, the deeper meaning of Jeep in France is *liberator*, owing to their memories of the Jeeps American troops drove when liberating the country during World War II.

As any psychiatrist will tell you, subconscious meanings and memories hold great sway over our thoughts and behaviors, including our purchasing behavior, which means that knowing the deeper meaning of an offering has practical benefits for those who design and market it. Rapaille gives the example of how the deeper American meaning of Jeep explains the positive impact on US sales that resulted from replacing Jeep's square headlights with round ones. Just as real horses have round eyes instead of square ones, so should Jeeps have the same. After the change, Jeep fan clubs went so far as to distribute T-shirts imprinted with "Real Jeeps have round headlights." The moral of the story is that the more people perceive that an offering is consistent with its cultural meaning, the more mental benefit they derive from it.

Another example, also provided by Rapaille, is the deeper meaning of food.[17] The social meaning of food in America is *fuel*, whereas the deeper meaning of food in France is *pleasure*, and its deeper meaning in Japan is *perfection*. As a result, those who create and market food items in America, France, and Japan would do well to ask, "What are the implications of food's deeper meaning in these cultures?" In America, Rapaille explains, some key implications are that food should contain things that power the body, such as protein for energy, healthy fats for brain function, and magnesium for relaxation. Another implication is that more food (fuel) is better than less, which explains why serving sizes in America are larger than serving sizes in France and Japan. Yet another implication is speed. Just like Americans hurry to fill their car with gas, they hurry to fill their bodies with food—thus the American preference for fast-food restaurants and fast service in full-service restaurants.

Where cultural meanings are shared by all the people who grow up in a culture, other meanings appear to be shared by many cultures. The customer experience consultant Steve Diller and his colleagues list the fifteen meanings that were mentioned most frequently in the thousands of interviews they've conducted in countries and cultures around the world.[18] Among the fifteen meanings are *accomplishment*, *beauty*, *creation*, and *community*. Offerings provide a mental benefit when they evoke these meanings or a stronger sense of them. As examples, they note how Nike's "Just Do It" campaign evokes a sense of accomplishment, Apple's computer designs evoke a sense of beauty, salad bars evoke creativity, and Harley-Davidson and their Harley Owners Group (HOG) evoke a sense of community.

Rather than being widely shared within or across cultures, some personal meanings are limited to the members of certain groups. An example is the constellation of thoughts and emotions shared by the group of people who attended a particular university, such as the memories of football games, fight songs, mascots, academic departments, and prominent landmarks that the university uses when trying to get graduates to donate to their alma mater. Another example is the personal meanings shared by those who have visited a particular vacation destination (e.g., Hawaii), such as the landmarks, food, weather, and pleasant emotions that the destination uses to induce visitors to return.

A final form of personal meaning is the meaning that people attach to a brand because of its advertising, their personal experience of it, or both. For example, people are more likely to associate the Apple brand with "entrepreneurial" and the Microsoft brand with "corporate." There is also the personal meaning that an offering has for a person because of his role or circumstance. For a boy racer, a car with superior acceleration means he can win races. For a police officer, it means she can catch bad guys.

Emotional Benefits

The third type of benefit is an *emotional benefit*, or what Tiger calls a *psychopleasure*. I will use the terms *emotion* and *feeling* interchangeably even though some scientists consider them to be two different things.[19] Fussing over the distinction between emotions and feelings is just the start of the scientific arguments having to do with emotion. There is also widespread disagreement about how to define an emotion, what causes emotions, and the most accurate way to classify them. Following are what appear to be the commonly held views on these issues.[20]

Emotions combine mental and physical states. A good way to imagine the combination is to recall a time you had to speak in public. Chances are you had the bodily symptoms of a dry mouth, tense muscles, accelerated heartbeat, and butterflies in your stomach. On top of the bodily symptoms, you probably had some mental symptoms. If you're like most people, the most prevalent symptom was the mental urge to be "anywhere but here," which is the latter half of the "fight or flight" response that kicks in when we experience fear.

There are hundreds of emotions and blends of emotions, probably more than we have names for. There are numerous proposals for classifying them. One of the most prevalent classification schemes employs three levels of structure.[21] The first level classifies emotions as positive (pleasant) and negative (unpleasant). The second level contains the six *primary emotions*—love, joy, surprise, anger, sadness, and fear. Love and joy are considered positive emotions. Anger, sadness, and fear are classified as negative emotions. Surprise can go either way depending on whether a person is pleasantly or unpleasantly surprised. The third level divides five of the six primary emotions into finer grades—135 of them, in all. Some of the finer grades of *love*, for example, are adoration, arousal, attraction, caring, and longing. *Joy* includes the emotions of amusement, enthusiasm, contentment, pride, eagerness, and relief. Among the finer grades of *anger* are aggravation, exasperation, rage, disgust, envy, and torment. *Sadness* includes the emotions of anguish, grief, displeasure, guilt, alienation, and pity. And *fear* subdivides into emotions such as alarm, shock, anxiety, and distress. There are no finer grades of *surprise*.

Other classification schemes extract some of the finer grades of the primary emotions to form a class of emotions called *secondary* or *social emotions*,[22] or what others call *self-conscious emotions*[23] because they rely on having a sense of self and they involve injury to, or enhancement of, the self. Self-conscious emotions divide into social comparison emotions and self-evaluation emotions. The two *social comparison emotions* are envy and jealousy, and the five *self-evaluation emotions* are guilt, shame, embarrassment, pride, and hubris.

Most of the time we do not experience any of the six primary emotions or the self-conscious emotions. Instead, we experience *background emotions*, so called because they are in the background rather than the foreground of our mind and body.[24] Examples are fatigue, energy, excitement, wellness, sickness, tension, relaxation, surging, dragging, stability, instability, balance, imbalance, harmony, and discord. We sense the background emotions in others when we describe them as being tense, edgy, down, discouraged, enthusiastic, or cheerful.

An offering provides an emotional benefit when it helps or enables the customer experience a pleasant emotion or avoid or eliminate an unpleasant one. In his book titled *The DNA of Customer Experience: How Emotions Drive Value*, the customer experience consultant Colin Shaw describes four clusters of emotions.[25] The *destroying cluster* consists of unpleasant emotions that diminish or destroy value. It includes stress, frustration, and irritation. The *attention cluster* contains emotions that have a proven link to increased customer spend. It includes the feelings of being stimulated, energized, and interested. In the *recommendation cluster* are emotions that cause customers to recommend an offering when they are asked about it. This cluster includes emotions like feeling safe and valued. The *advocacy cluster* consists of the two emotions that cause customers to proactively promote an offering—feeling happy and feeling pleased.

Psychologists explain that thought and emotion are indivisibly linked. Thoughts are always accompanied by emotions and emotions are always accompanied by thoughts.[26] The cognitive scientist and consultant Donald Norman elaborates on the connection between the two in his book titled *Emotional Design: Why We Love (or Hate) Everyday Things*. He explains, "Emotions are inseparable from and a necessary part of cognition. Everything we do, everything we think is tinged with emotion, much of it subconscious. In turn, our emotions change the way we think, and serve as constant guides to appropriate behavior, steering us away from the bad, guiding us toward the good."[27] He goes on to explain how offerings that are designed to evoke pleasant emotions enable us to think and behave more intelligently. In the opposite direction are offerings that trigger unpleasant emotions, like fear and anger, which narrow our focus of attention, thereby reducing our ability to attend to relevant information.[28]

The Japanese practice of *Kansei engineering*, originally called *emotion engineering*, utilizes the fact that people respond to things with a mixture of thought and emotion. As explained in Mitsuo Nagamachi and Anitawati Mohd Lokman's book *Innovations of Kansei Engineering*, there is no English word that exactly translates the meaning of *Kansei*.[29] An approximate translation is to say that "a Kansei" is the combination of thoughts and emotions that is evoked by an offering (or any other stimulus). Together, the combination of thoughts and emotions could be called our overall impression of a thing. Kansei engineering is the practice of designing the desired combination of thoughts and emotions into an offering. It has been used to design offerings as varied as cars, brassieres, and housing. In broad brush, Kansei engineering entails breaking down the overall product concept into a hierarchy of progressively more specific meanings until reaching the point where the meanings can be translated into physical aspects of the product.

Nagamachi and Lokman give the example of the overall product concept used for the Mazda MX-5 (originally called the Mazda Miata)—*the rider and horse are one*. This concept was subdivided into a hierarchy in which the branch headings were *tight feeling*, *direct feeling*, *running feeling*, and *communication*. *Direct feeling* was subdivided into *driver wish* and *maneuvering feeling*. One place where the concept *maneuvering feeling* was physically realized was the shift lever, where Mazda experimented with different lengths until they discovered one that did the best job of conveying the feeling of maneuvering the shift lever into a new gear. If you read car magazines, as I do, you know that car reviewers consistently laud the Mazda MX-5 for doing precisely what the driver wants it to do (*driver wish*) and for the feedback it gives the driver when shifting, steering, and braking (*maneuvering feeling*).

Again, a Kansei is a combination of thought and emotion. A thought (roughly, a sentence) is comprised of concepts (roughly, words). The idea of concepts brings us back to the notion of conceptual meaning, which was briefly mentioned in connection with mental benefits. *Conceptual meaning*, also called *semantic meaning*, consists of the facts associated with a concept. James Spradley (1933–1982), a professor of anthropology and practitioner of ethnography, proposed that the following are *universal semantic relationships* because they are found in every culture: *strict inclusion* (X is a kind of Y), *spatial* (X is a place in Y, X is a part of Y), *cause-effect* (X is a result of Y, X is a cause of Y), *rationale* (X is a reason for doing Y), *location for action* (X is a place for doing Y), *function* (X is used for Y), *means-end* (X is a way to do Y), *sequence* (X is a step or stage in Y), and *attribution* (X is an attribute or characteristic of Y).[30] As just explained, a part of Kansei engineering is to explicate the concepts that are to be designed into an offering. Spradley's universal semantic relationships are a useful tool for doing so. The more the semantic meaning of a concept is understood and physically embedded in the offering, the greater the mental-emotional benefits customers will derive from it.

Another way of explicating concepts when doing Kansei engineering is to use a thesaurus. *Roget's International Thesaurus*, now in its eighth edition, is a unique form of thesaurus that is particularly helpful.[31] Rather than the usual collection of synonyms and antonyms, Peter Mark Roget (1779–1869), an English physician, used zoological principles of classification to organize his thesaurus into collections of ideas.[32] His thesaurus is essentially a reverse dictionary. Where a dictionary is organized in a way that enables you to look up a word to find its meaning, in Roget's Thesaurus you start with an idea (meaning) and then use the organization of the thesaurus to search until you find the word that best expresses the idea.

Social Benefits

The fourth type of benefit is a *social benefit*, or what Tiger calls a *sociopleasure*. This type of benefit includes personal interaction benefits, bonding and connectedness benefits, network benefits, and trust and commitment benefits. Examples of offerings that provide social benefits are bars, brokers, business networking organizations, customer relationship management (CRM) software tools, social media platforms, and personal matchmaking services. Sometimes social benefits are best thought of as an end in themselves (e.g., a marriage commitment), and other times they are better thought of as a means of obtaining other types of benefits (e.g., emotional and economic benefits). Consider, for example, that one of the emotional benefits of personal interaction is to combat feelings of isolation and loneliness and another is to obtain joy and happiness. People and companies derive economic benefits by developing good relations and being part of a network.

Two people are considered to be in an *interpersonal relationship* "if a change in the state of one produces a change in the state of another" or, said differently, "if the behavior of each is dependent on the behavior of the other."[33] If two persons do not influence each other's behavior, they are not in a relationship, which is why growing indifference to the behavior of another person is a symptom of a dying relationship. An exception to the "interdependent behavior" criterion of interpersonal relationships is the case where two people are simply acting out social roles, such as the roles of being a customer and a retail clerk or a doctor and a patient. In role-based interactions, each person's behavior is governed by social norms rather than the other person's behavior.

People have interpersonal relationships with family, friends, acquaintances, co-workers, romantic partners, customers, clients, and others. Identifying the types of persons with whom people have relationships is one way of classifying them, e.g., family relationships, romantic relationships, customer relationships, and so on. Another way of classifying interpersonal relationships pertains to the primary concern of the relationship partners.[34] The types of primary concerns are: (1) *communal sharing*, where both people treat each other as equals, share a common identity and are primarily concerned with each other's happiness and welfare, (2) *authority ranking*, where people are primarily concerned with and attend to each other's status in a hierarchy, (3) *equality matching*, where people's principal concern is with quid pro quo social exchange rules, whereby each attempts to reciprocate what is given to the other, and (4) *market pricing*, where the primary concern of each person has to do with judging the utility of his or her behavior in achieving desired outcomes when interacting with the other.

Romantic relationships and friendships progress through a series of stages on the path towards closeness.[35] While theories differ regarding the number and sequence of the stages, they all suggest that increased interaction, disclosure, communication, behavioral and goal synchrony, investment, and positive emotions (e.g., love, liking, trust) are associated with the progression. The development and maintenance of a relationship are also influenced by various types of environmental factors. Social factors include the approval or disapproval of the relationship by society at large or by others in the partner's social network. Another social factor is the presence or absence of attractive alternatives. Physical factors include proximity and comfort. Being physically close to one another and interacting in a comfortable environment promote the development and maintenance of a relationship, whereas being physically distant and interacting in a physically uncomfortable environment inhibit the progression of a relationship. Economic factors, such as the degree to which the partners are economically dependent on each other, also influence the development and maintenance of a relationship.

In addition to the emotional and economic benefits described above, interpersonal relationships (good ones, at least) also have physical and mental health benefits.[36] Research indicates that people live significantly longer and healthier lives when they are more *socially integrated*. Indicators of social integration include marital status, the degree of contact with friends and relatives, and participation in formal and informal organizations. But the social integration itself isn't what accounts for the health and wellness effect. The effect is caused by the *social support* a person receives in his or her social network, where social support consists of *emotional support* (e.g., expressions of love, sympathy, and empathy), *appraisal support* (e.g., advice and guidance), and *instrumental support* (e.g., physical and economic assistance).

The theory of *social capital,* which pertains to the importance of social relations in achieving goals, explains other ways that individuals and organizations benefit from being embedded in a social network.[37] The first is the fact that networks facilitate the flow of useful *information*, such as the presence and nature of threats and opportunities. The second is that social ties exert *influence* on those who are making decisions that will affect a person, as would be the case, say, where a college admits an unqualified applicant because his father is a prominent politician. The third way that social ties benefit people is by certifying their *social credentials*, such as the case where admission to a country club certifies the person's wealth and the esteem in which he is held. Finally, social relations provide *reinforcement* in the twin senses that they reinforce a person's identity (self-image and self-worth) and others' recognition that the person is a part of a group and therefore entitled to possess or use certain resources. The sum of the foregoing, and the basic premise behind the idea of social capital, is that people *invest in social relations with the expectation of receiving a return in the marketplace*, that is, with the expectation of obtaining a resource or some other sort of return in the economic, political, labor, or community market.

There is growing recognition of another kind of return on the time and energy invested in building a social network, which is the intellectual return provided by the group's *collective intelligence*. The idea of collective intelligence is expressed by the old adage that asserts, "Two heads are better than one" and the newer one that proclaims, "No one is as smart as everyone." As the author and MIT Media Lab researcher Michael Schrage explains, groups of people with complementary skills are often able to "create a shared understanding that none [of the people in the group] had previously possessed or could have come to on their own."[38] It's as if each member of the group is holding a piece of a jigsaw puzzle and the only way to solve the puzzle is for each member to insert his or her piece.

MIT computer science professor Alex Pentland, who helped create the MIT Media Lab, uses the "social physics" framework to explain how a social network—be it a small group, company, city, or entire society—makes us smarter. He coined the term *social physics* because, "Just as the goal of traditional physics is to understand how the flow of energy translates into changes in motion, social physics seeks to understand how the flow of ideas and information translates into changes of behavior."[39] The two most important concepts in social physics are *idea flow* and *social learning*. The flow of ideas within social networks involves *exploration*—going outside of one's network to other networks in order to find new ideas. And it involves *engagement*—the network members engage with each other to exercise collective judgment to select the best ideas and collective intelligence to think of ways to exploit the ideas they have selected. Social learning relates to how learning can be shaped and accelerated by social pressure and how new ideas become habits. Together, the concepts of idea flow and social learning are used to understand "how human behavior is driven by the exchange of ideas—how people cooperate to discover, select, and learn strategies and coordinate their actions[.]"[40]

The social physics framework applies to every offering in the world that is made manifest by a network of individuals or companies, each of which possesses a distinctive set of skills and resources and many of which must be coordinated. Consider, for example, the myriad skills and resources of the companies that contribute to manifesting the idea of a car—the mining companies that mine the metals, the foundries that mold the metal into parts, the suppliers of the many other components of a car, the car manufacturers that assemble the components, the advertising agencies that help to market the car, and the car dealerships that sell the car to customers. Each member of the network benefits, directly or indirectly, from the skills and resources of the other members of the network. And all benefit when the network is made more effective and efficient by improving idea flow and social learning.

Whether the relationships exist in a network of suppliers or a network of friends, all relationships are glued together by an epoxy-like combination of trust and assurance.[41] *Trust*, which is defined as the belief in the responsiveness and beneficence of another in a time of need, is important in relationship development because entering into a relationship means becoming more dependent on a partner (emotionally or economically), which puts the partners in a position of risk. One person increases another's trust in him or her by always doing what they say they will do and doing it in a responsive way, i.e., without "dragging their feet." The other half of the epoxy that cements relationships is termed *assurance*. Assurances, which are more often the case in commercial relationships, are penalties that incentivize the partners to be trustworthy. They include things like contract terms that impose penalties on a partner that violates the contract and the social condemnation that will result from being known to be untrustworthy.

The long and short of this section is that any offering that helps or enables a person or company to form or enhance a social relationship is an offering that provides a social benefit, which is to say, a benefit that is derived from the social relationship.

Economic Benefits

People and companies enjoy an *economic benefit* when an offering helps or enables them to gain an economic resource. Economic resources include money, things that can be exchanged for money, and things that can be used to generate money. Ways for an individual to obtain money include a gift or grant, a loan, earnings from an investment, and the salary and wages derived from a job. Examples of things that can be exchanged for money are land, stock, jewelry, and fine art. The resources a person can use to generate money include information and the education, experience, and instruments (e.g., references or a car) that enable a person to gain and hold a job.

Commercial enterprises enjoy an economic benefit when they obtain money from sales and when they have the resources required to generate money. Economists define resources as *the factors used in producing goods or providing services*.[42] The six kinds of resources cited by economists are *land* (natural resources), *labor* (physical and mental talents of individuals, including management skills), *capital* (cash and manufactured items, such as tools and equipment), *information and innovation* (assembling information about buying and selling opportunities and creating production technologies), *business reputation* (industry network, member of industry's supply chain, business ethics), and *accepting or bearing the risk of business ownership* (a willingness and ability to bear the risk of owning and controlling a business that may incur a net operating loss).[43] Examples of resources that help or enable a company to generate money include a loan or equity contribution for expanding capacity, a sales training course that makes salespersons more productive, machinery that is more productive, more effective advertisements and advertising media, a franchise brand that attracts customers (e.g., McDonald's), and an internet platform where companies can sell their goods (e.g., Amazon).

TRIZ is an acronym that stands for the Russian way of saying the Theory of Inventive Problem Solving. One part of the TRIZ method lists several hundred resources that can be used to solve problems. Many of the resources are more specific members of the economist's six broad categories of economic resources. In one treatment, the TRIZ resources are divided into internal resources, external resources, complementor resources, human resources, cultural resources, low-cost resources, and unexpected resources.[44] A separate taxonomy identifies tool and object resources, environmental resources, macro-level resources, micro-level resources, time resources, space resources, energy resources, and other resources.[45] A major objective of the TRIZ method is putting underutilized resources to work. An example is using high school classrooms for adult training during the evening, when they would otherwise sit empty. Similarly, a company might provide its customers with an economic benefit by allowing them to use its underutilized meeting rooms, warehouse space, or equipment.

Cost and Risk Reduction Benefits

The last type of benefit pertains to *cost and risk reduction*. Recall that in Chapter 2 we "cheated" our way from the equation *Value = Benefits − Costs* to the equation *Value = Benefits − Price* by treating cost reductions, other than price, as benefits. When people think about the cost of an offering, they usually think about its price. But, as next explained, price isn't the only kind of monetary cost, and monetary costs aren't the only kind of cost.

Monetary costs have to do with (what else) money. One of the monetary costs of an offering is its price. Other monetary costs include the cost of traveling to buy or use the offering, the cost of paying someone to deliver and install the offering, the cost of learning how to use the offering, the cost of operating the offering, the cost to maintain and repair the offering, the cost of complementary goods and accessories, the cost to update the offering, the cost of switching from one offering provider to another (switching cost), and the cost of selling or otherwise disposing of the offering.[46] In short, there are monetary costs associated with purchasing, using, and disposing of an offering. Consider, for example, how you've incurred each type of cost when purchasing, operating, and selling a car, a house, a computer, or a mobile phone

Also, think about how these kinds of costs relate to the purchase, operation, and disposal of a piece of factory machinery. Finally, think about how you personally, or as the factory manager, would consider any reduction of these monetary costs as a benefit.

Another type of cost is time. As the saying goes, "Time is money." Time *literally* is money for a commercial enterprise that incurs labor costs, downtime costs, and other monetary costs related to time. The same goes for an hourly worker (e.g., a waitress) who loses money when she must go to the doctor, wait at home for a repair person, take care of a sick child, or do something else that pulls her away from her job. Time is *metaphorically* money when we think about *spending* time and *saving* time. Whether literally or metaphorically, we perceive that we benefit from an offering that saves us time while finding it, purchasing it, using it, and/or selling or otherwise disposing of it.

Monetary costs are *economic costs*.[47] Economic costs aren't the only kind of cost. The other benefit categories—physical, mental, emotional, and social—also involve costs. There are two kinds of *physical costs*. The first is the energy cost of motor movement. We lose bodily energy when we walk, talk, or otherwise use our body, and we regain it when we eat, rest, and sleep. Thus, an offering will be perceived as providing a physical benefit when it decreases the amount of energy (effort) required to perform a physical activity and when it replenishes that energy or enables us to start with even more of it.

The second kind of physical cost pertains to our senses. Something imposes a sensory cost when it makes it more difficult or impossible for us to see, hear, smell, taste, feel, or use one of our other senses or when it makes the experience unpleasurable. A dirty windshield makes it more difficult to see, a loud background noise makes it difficult or impossible to hear, a cold makes it hard to taste and smell, and gloves reduce our ability to touch and feel. Offerings provide a benefit when they eliminate or mitigate these sensory costs. There are also sensations that are downright unpleasant. A bright light hurts our eyes, and a loud noise hurts our ears. The smell and taste of rotting food are revolting. And it's hard to sleep in a hot room on a hard bed. We benefit from offerings that eliminate or reduce sensory costs like these.

Mental costs are a third type of cost. Just as we lose energy when we perform a motor action, we lose it when we perform a mental action. We've all had the experience of being mentally exhausted after concentrating on something for a long time. Offerings that conserve and replenish mental energy will be perceived as offerings that provide a benefit. And just like a dirty windshield makes it difficult for us to see clearly, distractions make it difficult for us to think clearly. Examples of mentally costly distractions are annoying background noises, people that pop into our office to ask a question, phone calls, emails and text messages that pull our attention away from whatever we are working on, and newly assigned projects that sidetrack our thinking for a week. Whatever the case, offerings that remove or diminish mental distractions will be perceived as offerings that provide a benefit.

Another type of cost is *emotional costs*. One way of defining emotional costs is to say that we incur them when we experience one of the negative emotions—anger, sadness, fear, and sometimes surprise. Another way to define emotional costs is to say they are, "The emotional value a subject pays, in terms of suffering and discomfort, when faced with extreme or traumatic situations. It leads to a weakening of emotional health."[48] This includes things like the emotional burnout experienced by nurses and others who are routinely exposed to emotionally traumatic events and the lasting emotional trauma of combat veterans, first responders, and victims of bullying and abuse. However we define it, the elimination or diminution of an emotional cost will be viewed as a benefit by the people who experience it and, possibly, by those who surround them.

The last kind of cost is *social costs*. Just as social bonds are made stronger by increases in trust and assurances, they weaken or break when trust and assurances decrease or drop to zero. The social costs of a weakened or broken social bond include the loss of the information, influence, credentials, and reinforcement we gain from others as well as the ability to think and act collectively. Thus, people and companies benefit from offerings that strengthen trust and assurances or that replace the information, influence, credentials, reinforcement, and collectivity that is lost when a social bond is broken.

Sometimes it might not be enough to reduce or eliminate a cost. You might also need to reduce or eliminate a customer's *perception* that he is at *risk* of incurring the cost. The dictionary defines risk as "the chance of injury, damage, or loss."[49] This definition captures the two fundamental facets of risk, which are "a 'chance' aspect where the focus is on probability and a 'danger' aspect where the emphasis is on the severity of negative consequences."[50] Behavioral scientists cite five forms of what they call *consumer-perceived risk*—physical risk, psychological risk, social risk, monetary risk, and functional risk.[51] Other than functional risk, the five types of risk identified by behavioral scientists are similar to the five kinds of cost we just reviewed. Functional risk, sometimes referred to as performance risk, is the risk that an offering won't work or do what it's supposed to do. Considering that a cost is a loss or negative consequence, we can say that a prospective customer perceives that she is at risk when there is a chance of incurring one or more of the five kinds of cost discussed in the previous paragraphs—physical, mental, emotional, social, and economic—or the sixth kind of risk, alternately known as functional risk or performance risk.

But this six-headed taxonomy of risks seems incomplete when considering some of the examples given by Naraj Dawar in his book *Tilt: Shifting Your Strategy from Products to Customers*. Dawar lists eighteen questions customers might ask themselves about the risks of doing business with a company, including: "Can I trust the seller's promises? Will I be able to use [the product] successfully? What are the side effects? Is the product compatible with other products I use? Will the product become obsolete? Will the seller be around for repair and maintenance?"[52] His questions indicate that there are also *side effect risks, useability risks, compatibility risks, obsolescence risks, stock-out risks, seller trustworthiness risks,* and *seller viability risks* to consider. Another source goes so far as to identify 53 types of risk.[53] Whichever taxonomy you use, the important thing to remember is that you provide a benefit when you eliminate or reduce a consumer-perceived risk.

In this chapter, we took a deep dive into benefits, the central element of the *Value = Benefits − Price* equation and the third element of the offering-function-benefit trilogy. As I emphasized at the beginning, a deep reading (or re-reading) of this chapter will provide you with numerous ideas for providing your customers with benefits that set your offering apart. In the next chapter, we're going to take a closer look at the second part of the trilogy—functions—and the way they can be used to differentiate your offering.

Notes

1 Eric Almquist, John Senior, and Nicholas Bloch, "The Elements of Value," *Harvard Business Review* (September 2016), https://hbr.org/2016/09/the-elements-of-value

2 J. Brock Smith and Mark Colgate, "Customer Value Creation: A Practical Framework," *Journal of Marketing Theory and Practice* 15 (Winter 2007), 7–23.

3 Lionel Tiger, *The Pursuit of Pleasure* (Boston, MA: Little, Brown and Company, 1992), 53–60.

4 If this was an academic paper, I would say there are "at least" six kinds of benefits to provide for the possibility that there are additional kinds of benefits, which there well may be.

5 Wikipedia contributors, "Sense," *Wikipedia, The Free Encyclopedia,*https://en.wikipedia.org/w/index.php?title=Sense&oldid=672867376 (accessed July 25, 2015).

6 If you've ever taken a yoga class, you know exactly what I mean by "outer reaches."

7 Mark H. Ashcraft, *Fundamentals of Cognition* (New York, NY: Addison-Wesley Educational Publishers, 1998), 5.

8 Matthew Lipman, *Thinking in Education* 2nd Ed. (Cambridge, UK: Cambridge University Press, 2003), 139–161.

9 Tiger, *op. cit.*, 59.

10 *Ibid*.

11 Nathaniel Branden, *Six Pillars of Self Esteem* (New York, NY: Bantam Books, 1994), 26–27.

12 Wikipedia Contributors, "Self-Concept," *Wikipedia, The Free Encyclopedia*, https://en.wikipedia.org/w/index.php?title=Self-concept&oldid=672318230.

13 William James, *The Principles of Psychology*, Chapter 10, downloaded from the Classics in the History of Psychology website by Christopher d. Green, http://psychclassics.yorku.ca/James/Principles/prin10.htm.

14 S. Ratneshwar, David Glen Mick, and Cynthia Huffman (Eds.), *The Why of Consumption: Contemporary Perspectives on Consumer Motives, Goals, and Desires* (New York, NY: Routledge, 2000), 11.

15 Elizabeth Hirschman, "Attributes of Attributes and Layers of Meaning," *Advances in Consumer Research* 7 (1980), 7–12.

16 Clotaire Rapaille, *The Culture Code: An Ingenious Way to Understand Why People Around the World Live and Buy As They Do* (New York, NY: Broadway Books, 2006), 1–12.

17 *Ibid*, 146–148.

18 Steve Diller, Nathan Shedroff, and Darrel Rhea, *Making Meaning: How Successful Businesses Deliver Meaningful Customer Experiences* (Berkeley, CA: New Riders, 2008), 32–36.

19 Antonio Damasio, *The Feeling of What Happens* (San Diego, CA: Harcourt, 1999), 42. Damasio proposes that the term *feeling* should be reserved for the private mental experience of an emotion, while the term *emotion* should be applied to the physiological characteristics of emotion, many of which are publicly visible (e.g., blushing).

20 Paula M. Niedenthal, Silvia Krauth-Gruber, and Francois Ric, *Psychology of Emotion: Interpersonal, Experiential, and Cognitive Approaches* (New York, NY: Psychology Press, 2006), Chapters 1 & 2. The authors provide a comprehensive introduction to the various views on the nature of emotions and the different ways of classifying them.

21 *Ibid*, 45–46.

22 Damasio, *op. cit.*, 51.

23 Niedenthal et al., *op. cit.*, 77–114. Where Damasio terms these emotions *secondary or social emotions*, Niedenthal refers to them as *self-conscious emotions* and devotes a full chapter to describing them.

24 Damasio, *op. cit.*, 52 & 286.

25 Colin Shaw, *The DNA of Customer Experience: How Emotions Drive Value* (New York, NY: Palgrave Macmillan, 2007)

26 Jeffrey Nevid, "Feeling Your Thoughts," *Psychology Today*, https://www.psychologytoday.com/us/blog/the-minute-therapist/201512/feeling-your-thoughts.

27 Donald A. Norman, *Emotional Design: Why We Love (or Hate) Everyday Things* (New York, NY: Basic Books, 2004), 7.

28 Sadia Najmi, Jennie M. Kuckertz, and Nader Amir, "Attentional impairment in anxiety: inefficiency in expanding the scope of attention," *Depression and Anxiety*, *29* (3), 243–249.

29 Mitsuo Nagamachi and Anitawati Mohd Lokman, *Innovations of Kansei Engineering* (Boca Raton, FL: CRC Press, 2011), 4–5.

30 James Spradley, *The Ethnographic Interview* (Fort Worth, TX: Harcourt Brace Jovanovich, 1979), 111.

31 Barbara Ann Kipfer ed., Roget's International Thesaurus 8th Edition (New York, NY: Harper-Collins, 2019).

32 Joshua Kendall, "Roget's Thesaurus: More than just a collection of related words—Peter Mark Roget intended his Thesaurus to be a classification of all knowledge," *Merriam-Webster website*.https://www.merriam-webster.com/words-at-play/rogets-thesaurus.

33 Ellen Berscheid and Pamela Regan, *The Psychology of Interpersonal Relationships* (Upper Saddle River, NJ: Pearson Education, 2005), 96.

34 *Ibid*, 151.

35 *Ibid*, 224.

36 *Ibid*, 31–62.

37 Nan Lin, *Social Capital: A Theory of Social Structure and Action* (Cambridge, UK: Cambridge University Press, 2001), 19–20.

38 Michael Schrage, *No More Teams! Mastering the Dynamics of Creative Collaboration* (New York, NY: Currency Doubleday), 33.

39 Alex Pentland, *Social Physics: How Social Networks Make Us Smarter* (New York, NY: Penguin Books), 5.

40 *Ibid*, 16.

41 Berscheid and Regan, *op. cit.*, 208–210. The descriptions of trust and assurance are based on this source.

42 North Dakota State University – Agriculture Law and Management, *Overview of Economic Resources,*https://www.ag.ndsu.edu/aglawandmanagement/agmgmt/coursematerials/econresources#:~:text=To%20produce%20a%20product%20(a,(capital)%20and%20other%20resources.

43 *Ibid.*

44 Darrell Mann, *Hands-On Systematic Innovation for Business and Management* 2nd Ed. (Bideford, UK: Lazarus Press, 2007), 396–408.

45 Kalevi Rantanen, David W. Conley, and Ellen R. Domb, *Simplified TRIZ: New Problem Solving Applications for Technical and Business Professionals* 3rd Ed. (Boca Raton, FL: CRC Press – Taylor & Francis Group, 2018), 55–67.

46 Cinzia Parolini, *The Value Net: A Tool for Competitive Strategy* (New York, NY: John Wiley & Sons, 1999), 118.

47 Reducing a customer's monetary costs could just as well be treated as an economic benefit, but for the sake of consistency, I chose to locate it with the other types of cost.

48 IGI Global, *What is Emotional Cost*, https://www.igi-global.com/dictionary/emotional-cost/78169#:~:text=1.,a%20weakening%20of%20emotional%20health.

49 *Webster's New World College Dictionary,* 4th Ed., (Cleveland, OH: Wiley Publishing, Inc., 2004), 1238.

50 N. Kogan and M.A. Wallach, as quoted in Vincent-Wayne Mitchell, "Consumer perceived risk: conceptualizations and models," *European Journal of Marketing 33* Iss ½ (1999), 163–195.

51 Jack Trout with Steve Rivkin, *Differentiate or Die: Survival in Our Era of Killer Competition* 2nd Ed. (Hoboken, NJ: John Wiley & Sons, 2008), 78.

52 Niraj Dawar, *Tilt: Shifting Your Strategy from Products to Customers* (Boston, MA: Harvard Business Review Press, 2013), 60–61,

53 John Spacey, "53 Types of Risk," *Simplicable*, November 29, 2016, https://simplicable.com/new/risks.

4   Functions

A function, as you now know, sits between an offering and a benefit in the offering-function-benefit trilogy, illustrated again in Figure 4.1. The offering performs the function, and the performance of the function produces the desired benefit. Simply put, the function of an offering, or some part of it, is *what it does* to produce the desired benefit. While that sounds simple enough, there's a lot more to functions than initially meets the ear.

What vs. How

Let's start with the definition of a functional class provided by Professors Russell Ackoff and Fred Emery. They declare that a *functional class* is "a set of structurally different individuals, systems or events, each of which is either a potential or actual producer of members (objects or events) of a specified class (Y) of any type …. [T]he function of such a class is Y-production, and each member of the class can be said to have Y-production as its function."[1] In short, the function of something is to produce a kind of object or event. The function of aspirin, for example, is to produce a pain signal blocking event. A bit more formal is to say that aspirin is a member of a functional class of things that produces a pain signal blocking event. The way to state a function is to combine an active verb and a noun to form a verb-noun or an active verb and a short noun phrase to form a verb–noun phrase.[2] So, less formally, we can say that the function of aspirin is the verb–noun phrase *block pain signals*. The fact that aspirin is a member of a functional class—i.e., a set of things that perform the same function—means that it is just one of a number of things that *block pain signals*. Morphine, ibuprofen, and neuromodulation devices also perform this function.

Every offering belongs to a set of things that performs a function. That's why an offering's function statement should say *what* it does, not *how* it does it. Consider, for example, that planes, trains, automobiles, bicycles, and ships are all members of the functional class of things that produce transportation events. The function statement *transport things* states *what* each of these modes of transportation does, whereas each of these modes of transportation is an instance of *how* the function is performed. Another example is the function *buy shirt*. Visiting a store in person, sending someone else to the store, using the store's website, telephoning the store, and emailing the store are all members of the functional class of actions that produce shirt-buying events.[3] The function statement *buy shirt* says *what* is done, not *how* it is done. As you'll later learn, the proper phrasing of function statements is a critical part of finding creative ways to differentiate an offering, so let's dig a little deeper into the *what vs. how* distinction.

A helpful way to understand the distinction between *what* and *how* is to remember that an offering is a physically manifest thing—something you can touch, taste, see, hear, and/or smell. A product is a physically manifest object. A service is an event that occurs in physical space and in which physically manifest objects participate. In contrast, the function of a physically manifest offering is an abstract verb-noun. Consider the physically manifest car,

DOI: 10.4324/9781003271703-5

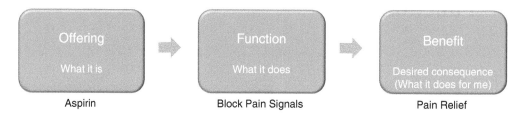

Figure 4.1 Offering–function–benefit trilogy.

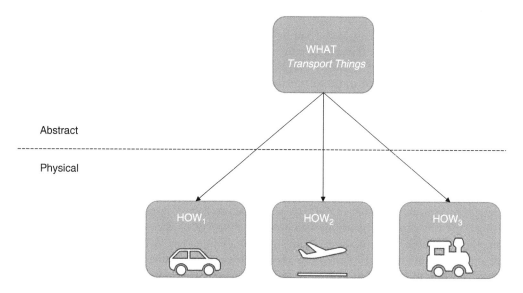

Figure 4.2 An abstract function (the what) can be physically manifested in different ways (the hows).

plane, and train shown in Figure 4.2. Then consider the function statement *transport things* that hovers above them in abstract space. The abstract function statement states *what* the car, plane, and train do. The car, plane, and train are instances of *how* the abstract function is physically manifested.

Just as several types of things can perform the same function, a particular type of thing can perform several functions. The philosopher John Searle serves up the example of a rock, which can be used as a weapon, a paperweight, or an *objet d'art*.[4] This means that the same rock can perform the functions *injure enemy*, *hold down paper*, and *evoke esthetic pleasure*. Searle and others[5] emphasize that people *assign* functions to objects, both naturally occurring objects and artifacts that are created to perform an assigned function. In the case of naturally occurring objects, consider that nature didn't create rocks to perform the functions *injure enemy*, *hold down paper*, *evoke esthetic pleasure*, or anything else. Rather, people assign these functions to rocks. And in the case of artifacts, consider that car manufacturers design cars to perform the function of *transport things*, but some homeless people assign their cars the additional function *provide shelter* and police officers assign their cars the added function *catch bad guys* (Figure 4.3).

One way of differentiating an offering is to incorporate multiple functions in it. For example, the maker of my alarm clock has differentiated it by including a digital clock to perform the function *show time*, a beeper to perform the function *wake people*, a night light to

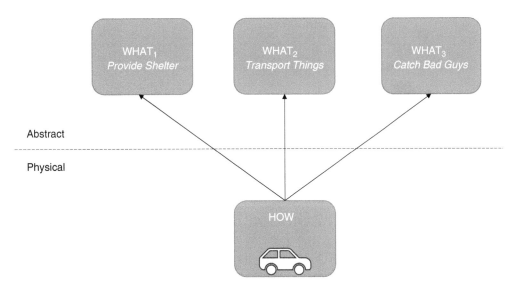

Figure 4.3 A physical manifestation (how) can perform multiple abstract functions (whats).

perform the function *illuminate room*, and a USB port to perform the function *charge mobile phone*. This list of functions describes the *functionality* of my alarm clock.

Production vs. Co-Production

Another nuance of functions is the notion of *production*. Remember that Ackoff and Emery say a thing (member of a class) has Y-production as its function. They go on to explain that Y-production means there is a *producer* and a *product*.[6] The product can be an object or event. We sometimes speak of the producer as if it produces the product in isolation. This is often the case when speaking about functions in the natural world, such as when we say that the function of an animal's camouflage is to produce a detection avoidance event, or *avoid detection* and when we say that the function of the heart is to produce a blood pumping event, or *pump blood*. The same holds true when we view the function of man-made artifacts from a mechanical or engineering perspective, such as when we say that the function of a chair leg is to produce a seat-supporting event, or *support seat*, and that the function of an oil filter is to produce a particle trapping event, or *trap particles*.

But in many cases, Ackoff and Emery point out, it is more accurate to view the user of an artifact as the *producer* and the artifact as the *co-producer*, for it is the user and the artifact together that produce the product rather than the artifact alone.[7] Consider, for example, that by itself a hammer is unable to produce a nail pounding event, or *pound nails*. Rather, as shown in Figure 4.4, the user (producer) swings the hammer (co-producer) to produce the nail-pounding event (product). So it is more accurate to say that the function of a hammer is to *help* or *enable* the user (who swings it) to perform the function *pound nails*. In the same vein, it is more accurate to say that the function of a car is to *help* or *enable* the user (who drives it) to *transport things*, and the function of an aspirin is to *help* or *enable* the user (who ingests it) to *block pain signals*. The idea of co-production adds to the meaning of a *function*. The useability consultants Jeff Johnson and Austin Henderson explain that products and services are tools that *help* or *enable* people to perform a task. Thus, they say, a function can be described as either *what an offering does* (e.g., *support seat*) and *what an offering is used to do*, or *what it's used for* (e.g., *pound nails*).[8]

Figure 4.4. The producer and co-producer of a product.

Sorce: David Holt Design, Adobe.

Enablement and Relief

I italicized the terms *help* and *enable* in the last two paragraphs to call attention to these important but under-appreciated concepts. I also want to call attention to the related concept of *relief*.[9] At base, offerings are tools that either *help* or *enable* users to produce a product (e.g., a nail-pounding event) or *relieve* them of their role in the production altogether. To help is to assist someone produce a product, just as a pair of glasses helps a person *see objects* and a sports commentator helps fans *understand (the) game*. To enable is to make it possible for people to produce a product they would otherwise be unable to produce alone. For example, a bottle opener enables a person to *remove cap* and a shovel enables a person to *dig hole*. Without the bottle opener or the shovel, a person would be unable (vs. enabled) to perform these functions. Some offerings, in contrast, relieve the user of the requirement to participate in the performance of a function, as is the case with a car repair shop that relieves the user of having to play a role in the *repair car* function and a dry cleaner that relieves the user of the obligation to play a role in the *clean clothing* function.[10] Doing a better job relative to your competitors of helping or enabling your customers to perform a function or doing a better job of relieving them of their role in the performance of a function are ways to differentiate your offering.

Performance

Another aspect of functions is the concept of *performance*. Consider again Searle's observation that people often assign different functions to the same thing. He used the example of a rock functioning as a weapon, paperweight, or art object. Searle explains that when people judge how well something performs (i.e., its performance), they do so with respect to one of the functions they have assigned to it. For example, when a person judges the performance of a rock, he bases his judgment on whether he is using the rock to perform the function *injure the enemy*, *hold down paper*, or *evoke esthetic pleasure*. Another example is a party hostess who assigns one of the following functions to a coffee table book: *convey interesting information*, *stimulate conversation*, and *decorate room*. When the party hostess judges the performance of the coffee table book, she will first decide (consciously or subconsciously) whether to judge it on the basis of its *convey interesting information* function, its *stimulate conversation* function, or its *decorate room* function.

How well an offering is perceived to perform a function determines the user's perception of the relative magnitude of the corresponding benefit and, in turn, the relative magnitude of the benefit's cognitive or monetary worth. Our party hostess may perceive that one coffee table book outperforms another with respect to the *stimulate conversation* function and that it therefore provides a greater amount of the social benefit *others view me as an entertaining hostess*, so she will assign more cognitive and monetary worth to the better-performing book. Similarly, if Aspirin-A outperforms Aspirin-B with regard to the *block pain signals* function, the user will perceive that Aspirin-A provides a greater amount of the *pain relief* benefit than Aspirin-B and therefore judge that Aspirin-A has more cognitive and monetary worth.

Function Analysis

Function analysis is a well-established practice that is credited with significant creative potential.[11,12,13] It was originally developed during World War II by Lawrence D. Miles, who was then a purchasing agent for General Electric.[14] Miles noticed that although he was not always able to provide requested items (because of war shortages), he was nearly always able to fulfill a request with a substitute that performed the same function. Oftentimes, the substitute performed the function better and at a lower cost. Miles came to realize that generating creative alternatives is constrained by the fact that people have a hard time seeing past the physical shape or concept of an artifact. Identifying an artifact's abstract function and asking how else it could be performed overcomes the constraint.

A fundamental part of function analysis is the previously described discipline of stating a function as two words—an active verb and a noun. As the value engineering consultant Richard Park explains in his book *Value Engineering: A Plan for Invention*, "The requirement to define a function in two words is a forcing technique that requires consensus among team members, eliminates confusion, creates in-depth understanding of the [design] requirement, clarifies overall knowledge of the project and ultimately breaks down barriers to visualization that will lead to new, outstanding solutions to the project."[15] Park provides an extensive list of function verbs, function nouns, and combinations that apply to various aspects of management.[16]

A system consists of a set of interacting parts. One way of identifying an offering's functions is to first diagram the system of parts that comprise the offering and the system of which the offering is a part and then identify the functions at each level of the system. For example, as shown in Figure 4.5, the parts of a toothbrush are the head, neck, and handle. A part of the head is the bristle, and a part of the handle is the grip. The whole toothbrush interacts with the toothpaste and water that are applied to it, which together comprise the teeth-cleaning system. The teeth-cleaning system interacts with the user's hand and teeth and gums. The assigned functions (remember, people assign functions to artifacts) relate to the parts that exist at each level of analysis. The function of the bristle, for example, is to *dislodge food particles* (sometimes it's impossible to comply with the two-word, verb-noun rule) and to *hold toothpaste*. The function of the grips is to *prevent the hand from slipping*. The function of the neck is to *fasten the handle and head together*. The function of the handle is to *reach teeth, transmit user force*, and *transmit user's up and down motion*. The function of the toothpaste is to *dissolve stains* and *kill bacteria*. The function of the water is to *wet bristles* and *rinse off debris*. And the function of the teeth-cleaning system is to enable the user to *clean teeth and gums*.

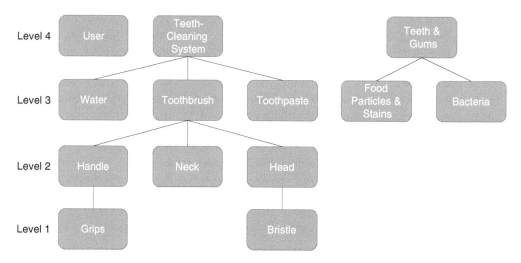

Figure 4.5 Hierarchy of system parts.

There are several methods for identifying the functions of an offering.[17] One way is to do what we've just done—first diagram the parts in the system hierarchy and then identify the function(s) of each of the parts. Charles Bytheway, a mechanical engineer, explains another way of identifying functions in his book *FAST Creativity & Innovation: Rapidly Improving Processes, Product Development and Solving Complex Problems.*[18] FAST, which stands for Function Analysis System Technique, involves using *why-how logic*[19] to build a *function diagram* like the one shown in Figure 4.6. The first step of the FAST method is to identify the offering's *basic function* (aka *user function*). The basic function describes the overall function of the offering. In the case of the teeth-cleaning system (toothbrush-toothpaste-water), the basic or user function is to *clean teeth and gums*. The next step is to ask how the basic function is performed. The answer(s) may reveal a single *subordinate function* or several of them. The subordinate functions are diagrammed beneath the basic function. The same question is asked of each of the subordinate functions, and the answers are diagrammed beneath each of them. The process is repeated until you reach what you believe to be a suitable level of analysis.

The reason for identifying the functions is to generate ideas for improving the way the functions are performed and thereby differentiate the offering. One way of doing so is to ask of each subordinate function, "How could the performance of this function be improved?" and "How else could this function be performed?" Another way is to ask the following of the basic function, "Why is this function performed?" For example, asking this question of the *clean teeth & gums* function would identify functions like *increase attractiveness* and *maintain health*, which could be used to stimulate ideas for complementary products, such as a mouthwash or gum that increases attractiveness and vitamins that contribute to a person's dental health.

The FAST method for developing a function diagram is a top-down method in which you start with the basic function and then decompose it into subordinate functions. An alternative approach is the bottom-up *subtract and operate* method.[20] With this approach, an existing offering is reverse engineered by disassembling it into its smallest isolatable components. Then, each component is physically or mentally removed, one at a time. After the component is removed, the product is operated (again, physically or mentally), and based on the operation, the function(s) of the component is deduced. For example, removing the bristle

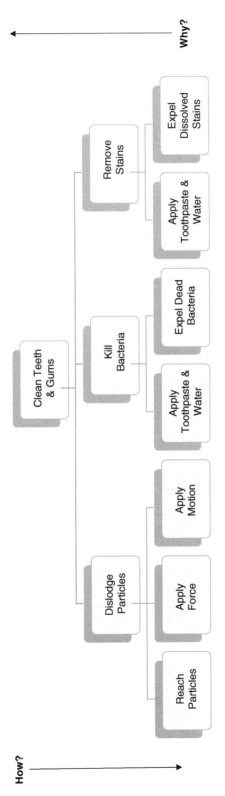

Figure 4.6 Function diagram for the teeth–cleaning system (toothbrush–toothpaste–water).

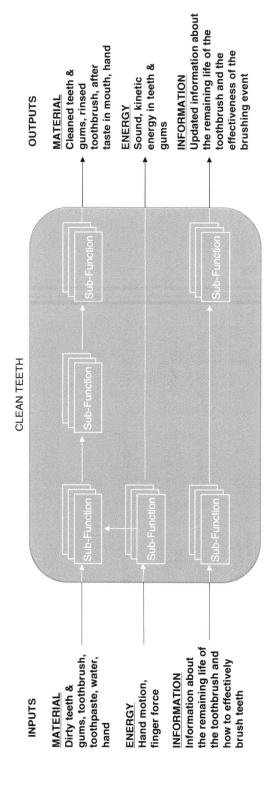

Figure 4.7 Function structure diagram.

assembly from a toothbrush would reveal the *hold toothpaste*, *retain water*, and *dislodge particles* functions performed by the bristle.

Another way of identifying subordinate functions is to create a *function structure* diagram like the one shown in Figure 4.7.[21] A function structure—which is more in keeping with Ackoff and Emery's "Y-production" conception of a function—identifies the basic function of an offering and the set of subordinate functions (and, possibly, sub-subordinate functions) that transform the material, energy, and information inputs into the material, energy, and information outputs. Each subordinate function has its own input(s) and output(s). A way of differentiating an offering is to find ways, or better ways, to perform the sub-functions. For example, to perform the information function in Figure 4.7, the toothbrush might employ bristles that change color when they reach the end of their useful life.

In this chapter, you learned that customers judge the performance of an offering based on the function(s) they assign to it. You can differentiate your offering by having it do a better job of performing the functions than rival offerings, by having it do more functions than rival offerings (i.e., by increasing its functionality), or both. The various function analysis methods enable you to identify the existing and potential functions of your offering. You also learned, again, that the offering-function-benefit trilogy summarizes the idea that offerings perform functions that produce benefits. This time, however, it was explained that offerings can *help* or *enable* the user to perform a function or *relieve* the user of having to play a role in performing a function. Now that we've examined the benefit and function parts of the offering-function-benefit trilogy, it's time to take a closer look at the concept of offerings.

Notes

1 Russell L. Ackoff and Fred E. Emery, *On Purposeful Systems: An Interdisciplinary Analysis of Individual and Social Behavior as a System of Purposeful Events* (New Brunswick, NJ: Aldine Transaction, 2008), 26. Ackoff and Emery provide a detailed and logically formal treatment of the concept of a function in the chapter titled "Structure, Function, and Purpose." My treatment is a less formal adaptation of parts of this chapter.

2 When a verb is active, it indicates that the subject of the sentence is the "doer." For example, when we say "Aspirin blocks signals," aspirin is the subject that is doing the blocking action on the signals. When a verb is passive, the subject undergoes the action described by the verb rather than doing the action, as would be the case if we were to say, "Aspirin is blocked by signals."

3 Ackoff and Emery, *op. cit.*, 26. The examples for "transport things" and "buy shirt" are provided by Ackoff and Emery.

4 John R. Searle, *The Construction of Social Reality* (New York, NY: The Free Press, 1995), 14–15.

5 Derek Bickerton, *Language & Species* (Chicago, IL: The University of Chicago Press, 1990), 35–36. Bickerton explains that words and concepts were initially created for things that had *functional utility*. By way of example, he notes that our ancestors conceived of a *bush* as something that a person could use to hide behind when stalking, or being stalked by, an animal, and they conceived of a *tree* as something that a person could climb to escape animals or to see further when hunting them. But they never created the concept of a *trush* covering both bushes and trees, nor did they create the concept *bree* for things intermediate between a bush and a tree because the two concepts had no functional utility.

6 Ackoff and Emery. *op. cit.*, 22–23.

7 *Ibid*, 23.

8 Jeff Johnson and Austin Henderson, *Conceptual Models: Core to Good Design* (Williston, VT: Morgan & Claypool, 2012), 5–7. Their exact phrasing is, "This valuable service—what the application does and the user employs in getting their work done—is the *function*."

9 Richard Norman and Rafael Ramirez, *Designing Interactive Strategy: From Value Chain to Value Constellation* (West Sussex, UK: John Wiley & Sons, 1994), 39–41. Noman and Ramirez explicate the concepts of *enablement* and *relief*.

10 It's possible to argue that by driving the car to the repair shop and taking the clothing to the dry cleaner, the users are participating in the co-production of the *repair car* and *clean clothing* functions. Nonetheless, it is still insightful to ask after ways to help, enable, or relieve people of their roles in the co-production of an outcome.

11 Charles W. Bytheway, *FAST Creativity and Innovation: Rapidly Improving Processes, Product Development and Solving Complex Problems* (Fort Lauderdale, FL: J. Ross Publishing, 2007).

12 Yoshihiko Sato and J. Jerry Kaufman, *Value Analysis Tear-Down: A New Process for Product Development and Innovation* (New York, NY: Industrial Press, 2005).

13 Richard Park, *Value Engineering: A Plan for Invention* (Boca Raton, FL: CRC Press, 1979).

14 *Ibid*, 74–75.

15 *Ibid*, 77.

16 *Ibid*, 306–321.

17 Here the methods are applied to a physical offering composed of physical parts. The methods apply equally well to service offerings in which the parts are the sequential actions taken to deliver the service.

18 Bytheway, *op. cit.*

19 Why-how logic is equivalent to the purpose-mechanism logic used in *hierarchy theory*, where you are advised to look to the next-higher level of a hierarchical system for purpose and the next-lower level for mechanism.

20 Kevin Otto and Kristin Wood, *Product Design: Techniques in Reverse Engineering and New Product Development* (Upper Saddle River, NJ: Prentice Hall, 2001), 159–162.

21 *Ibid*, 162–177.

5 Offerings

At the start of the 20th century, the architect Louis Sullivan (1856–1924) coined the maxim *form follows function*, by which he meant that the purpose of a building should be the starting point of its design.[1] At the start of his book *Notes on the Synthesis of Form*, Christopher Alexander, also an architect, had something similar to say, "These notes are about the process of design; the process of inventing physical things which display new physical order, organization, form, in response to function."[2] What Sullivan and Alexander had to say about buildings applies equally well to the offerings we call products, services, and companies, for they too are physical things that display order, organization, form in response to function. As Sullivan would have put it: *offering follows function*. In this chapter, we're going to take a closer look at offerings, the first element in the offering–function–benefit trilogy. The chapter provides a detailed explanation of the idea that a company's offering can consist of a core product or service, a combination of products and services, and the other elements of the company that determine a customer's experience of it.

Products and Services

A *product* is a tangible object. A *service* is an intangible event. The main thing that distinguishes objects and events is their location in space and time.[3] An object (say, a chair object) is a material thing that occupies a three-dimensional portion of space. An event (say, a chair repair event) is an immaterial thing that occupies a linear block of time. Objects participate in events, but where the objects continue to exist after the event, the event happens and then it's gone. For example, a chair, a repair person, and his tools participate in a chair repair event. Upon completion of the event, the chair, the person, and the tools continue to exist, but the repair event is done and gone.

In their book *Creativity in Product Innovation*, Jacob Goldenberg and David Mazursky, both business professors at the Hebrew University of Jerusalem, provide a useful framework for describing the composition of products and services.[4] As illustrated in Figures 5.1 and 5.2, their framework shows that, despite the foregoing differences, products (objects) and services (events) are composed of the same kinds of elements:

- Components: A *component* is a part of a whole configuration. (The term configuration is defined below.) The seat, legs, and back are the major components of the whole configuration that is a dining room chair. Greeting a customer, gathering information, repairing the chair, and billing the customer are the major components of a chair repair service. Components can be subdivided into progressively smaller components, which, at each step of the progression, are smaller in size in the case of a product and shorter in duration in the case of a service.
- Properties: Components and configurations are "festooned"[5] with *properties*[6]. For

DOI: 10.4324/9781003271703-6

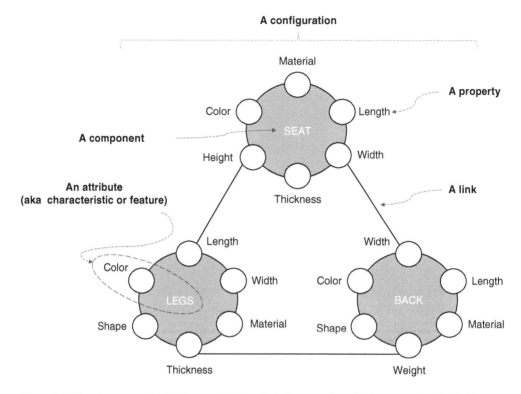

Figure 5.1 The elements of Goldenberg and Mazursky's framework applied to a product (a chair).

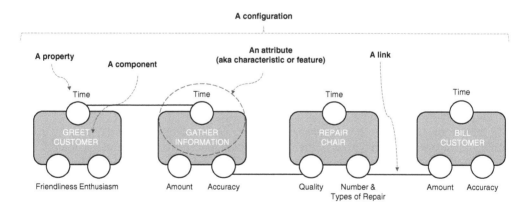

Figure 5.2 The elements of Goldenberg and Mazursky's framework applied to a service (chair repair service).

example, the seat of the chair depicted in Figure 5.1 is festooned with the properties of color, length, width, height, thickness, and so forth. And the greet customer component in Figure 5.2 is festooned with the properties time, friendliness, and enthusiasm. A *property* can be either a constant or a variable. A constant property is considered constant because its value never varies, whereas a variable property is considered variable because its values do vary. For example, the value of the variable property *color* can be black, brown, green, or some other color, and the value of the variable property *friendliness* can be characterized on a scale consisting of not friendly, neutral, and friendly. An *objective property* is one that can be seen, heard, smelled, tasted, or touched. A *subjective property* is one that is inferred from an objective property, such as when people infer that a chair is durable based on its material composition (say, metal vs. plastic) and that a person is friendly based on his facial expression.

Just as a component of an offering is festooned with properties, so too is the configuration that comprises a whole product or service. Scientists explain that properties emerge at different levels of organization, which is why they are referred to as *emergent properties*. Emergence occurs when a level of organization is observed to have properties its parts do not have on their own, which is to say, properties that emerge only when the parts interact to create an integrated whole.[7,8] For example, the *utility* of a chair is a property of the whole chair rather than one of its components, and the *efficacy* of a chair repair service is a property of the entire service, not one of its components.

- Attributes: Products and services are often referred to as "bundles of attributes." An *attribute* (aka *characteristic*[9] or *feature*) is the particular *property value* of a component or configuration. For example, one of the attributes of your dining room chair might be its brown chair legs. Another might be its 20-inch-wide seat. A third attribute of your dining room chair might be its contemporary design. Or maybe your chair has the attributes green chair legs, 24-inch-wide seat, and traditional design. Among the attributes of a chair repair service might be the two-minute average it takes to serve a customer and the good (vs. mediocre or bad) quality of the repair.
- Links: A *link* describes the dependency relationship between two attributes. For example, the height of a chair's seat depends on the length of the chair's legs, the amount of the chair repair bill depends on the number and type of repairs, the customer's perception of the quality of the repair depends on the accuracy of the information that is gathered, and the amount of time it takes to serve a new customer depends on the time required to gather information from an existing customer.
- Configuration: A *configuration*—which is what Sullivan and Alexander refer to as the *order*, *organization*, *form* of a thing—is the complete set of attributes and links that make up a whole product or service.

We can use Goldenberg and Mazursky's framework to flesh out the offering-function-benefit trilogy and the idea that an offering performs a function that provides a benefit. Remember from the last chapter that there are *user (basic) functions* and *structural functions*. Here, we're only concerned with user functions. The configuration of a product or service performs its overall user function(s). For example, the configuration of a chair performs the user functions *hold person off the ground* and *decorate room*. The configuration of the chair repair service performs the user function *repair chair*. The specifics of the configuration determine how, and how well, the function is performed, which, in turn, determines how much of a given benefit is provided by the function.

The relative amount of a given benefit is one way to differentiate a product or service. The relative number of benefits is another way to do it. In this regard, while it's not part of Goldenberg and Mazursky's framework, it's accurate to say that each component is itself a sub-configuration comprised of a set of internal attributes and links and that some of the sub-configurations themselves perform user functions. As shown in Figure 5.3, the more components that perform user functions (i.e., the greater the *functionality* of a product or service), the more benefits are produced. For example, my earlier-described alarm clock has multiple components, each of which performs a different function. It has a digital clock (*component$_1$*) to

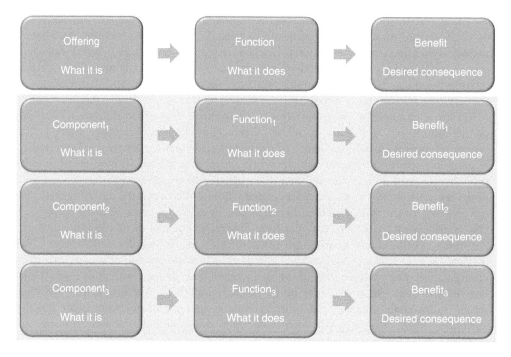

Figure 5.3 An offering can have multiple components, each of which performs a different function and produces a different benefit.

show time (*function₁*) that enables me to know the time (*benefit₁*), a volume-adjustable beeper (*component₂*) to produce an audible sound (*function₂*) that enables me to wake up on time (*benefit₂*), an adjustable night light (*component₃*) to illuminate the room (*function₃*) that keeps me from walking into walls at night (*benefit₃*), and a single USB port (*component₄*) to charge a mobile phone (*function₄*) that prevents my phone battery from going dead (*benefit₄*).

Goldenberg and Mazursky's framework for describing products and services will be helpful to you in Chapter 8, where we will use the concept of attributes to identify differentiation opportunities. It will also be helpful to you in Chapter 11, where we will discuss the fact that many innovations occur at the component level; there, you will learn about a creativity method (Logical Creative Thinking) that describes various ways to think of novel combinations of components.

Bundles and Complements

In the last section, we examined individual products and services. This section moves up a level of organization, order, form to examine the combinations of products and services referred to as *bundles* and *complements*. Where the components of a product are objects that are smaller in size than the entire product, and the components of a service are events that are shorter in duration than the entire service, the components of bundled and complementary offerings are products, services, systems, and/or programs. As you read the following, remember that the idea that many innovations occur at the component level, as novel combinations of components, also applies to the components of bundles and complements.

Bundling is the practice of packaging several products and/or services together as a single combined unit, usually for a lower price than would be charged if they were purchased separately. Common B2C examples are meals (burger, fries, and drink bundle), cable TV (combination of channels bundle), packaged tours (flight, lodging, and ground transportation bundle), and insurance (home and auto bundle). Anderson and his co-authors explain that B2B bundles often take the form of a core product (or service) and one or more supplementary services (or products), systems, and/or programs.[10] Examples of supplementary services are financing, consulting, emergency delivery, and disposal/recycling services. Examples of supplementary systems are ordering systems and inventory management systems. Examples of supplementary programs are joint market research and co-marketing programs. The same kinds of supplements are used in B2C settings. For example, Enterprise Rent-A-Car's pick-up and drop-off service supplements their core car rental service. Harry's automatic razor blade replenishment system supplements their core razor blade product. The loyalty programs offered by the hotel and airline brands supplement their core products and services.

Anderson and his co-authors go on to explain that many B2B companies (this also applies to B2C companies) make the mistake of offering all customers the same bundle of core product and supplementary service(s), system(s), and/or program(s), when it would be better to offer what they term a *naked solution with options*.[11] A *naked solution* is the bare minimum of core product (or service) and supplementary services (or product), systems, and/or programs that will satisfy all the customers in the target market. In other words, the naked solution is the minimally augmented core product (or service). *Options* consist of various combinations of the naked solution and additional services (or products), systems, and/or programs. Each of the options is designed and priced to appeal to a specific subsegment of the target market. Offering naked solutions with options is a way for a company to differentiate itself. Where the company's rivals offer a one-size-and-price-fits-all bundle, the company that offers a naked solution with options can differentiate itself in a particular subsegment of the market by offering a bundle that is appropriately customized and priced for the subsegment.

The components of a bundle may, or may not, be *complementary*. The same goes for products and services that are sold separately, either by the same company or by different companies. Offering A is said to *complement* Offering B when it boosts the demand for Offering B[12], or it increases the willingness to pay for it.[13] Offering A increases the demand and willingness to pay for Offering B by increasing the benefits that are derived from it. The classic example is peanuts and beer. Salty peanuts (Offering A) increase the demand and willingness to pay for a beer (Offering B). The peanuts do so by increasing the thirst-quenching benefit derived from the beer. In some cases, as depicted in Figure 5.4, rather than one offering complementing another, the offerings complement each other. For example, peanuts increase the taste benefit of beer, and beer increases the taste benefit of peanuts. Similarly, smartphones increase the benefits derived from apps, and apps increase the benefits derived from smartphones.

As explained below and illustrated in Figure 5.5, there are four ways products and services can complement one another. Note that the following complementary products and services might, instead, be what Anderson and his co-authors refer to as programs and systems:

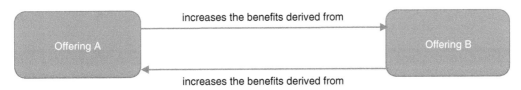

Figure 5.4 Offerings complement one another when one or the other, or both, increase the benefits derived from the other.

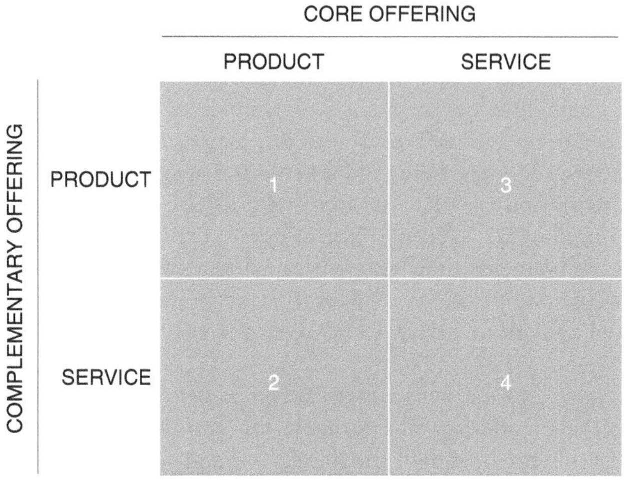

Figure 5.5 Four types of complements.

1   Core Product and Complementary Product(s): This combination combines a core product with one or more complementary products. For example, Gatorade turned around the flagging sales of its core energy drink by adding the complementary 1 2 3 G Series of energy products, including energy shakes, protein shakes, protein bars, and energy chews.[14] A second example is Novo Nordisk's human growth hormone, HGH, and the complementary HGH injection pens that come prefilled with multiple doses, each of which is automatically dispensed in the correct amount.[15] A third example is Mitsubishi Electric Industrial Controls, which combines its controls with a complementary software tool.[16]

2   Core Product and Complementary Service(s): In this case, a core product is combined with one or more complementary services. An oft-cited example is Apple's iPod product and its iTunes service. A second example is the combination of GM's core product, vehicles, and its OnStar in-vehicle safety and security service.[17] A third example is Sunoco's Industrial Containers Division, where the core product is fiber and plastic drums and the complementary service is a factory process-flow analysis service.[18]

3   Core Service and Complementary Product(s): Examples of a core service and complementary products are the optometrist service that sells eyewear and the car wash that sells scented air fresheners and aftermarket car products. Another example is universities, where the core service is teaching and the complementary products are books and educational tools, such as calculators and computers.

4   Core Service and Complementary Service(s): R.R. Donnelly's core service focuses on printing, binding, film preparation, and prepress work, but its management is looking to add complementary services like database management, consulting and training, dimensional and talking ads, and mapping services.[19]

Each of the foregoing is an example of using one or more complements to differentiate a core product or service. A key thing to note is that a complement can be *proprietary* or *non-proprietary*. As the Harvard Business School professor Felix Oberholzer-Gee explains in his book *Better Simpler Strategy: A Value-Based Guide to Exceptional Performance*, a proprietary complement is one that is offered exclusively by the company that offers the core product or service, whereas a non-proprietary complement is one that is offered by companies other than the company that offers the core product or service.[20] He cites the following examples of proprietary complements—Apple's FaceTime app, which works on Apple devices, but not Android devices, Nespresso coffee capsules, which only work on Nespresso coffee machines, and Tesla Supercharge stations that can only be used to charge Tesla's cars. Clearly, a proprietary complement is what you want to use to differentiate your offering and, if you do, your primary concern will be a company that intercedes by offering a non-proprietary alternative.

Company

Most managers think of their offering as consisting of their product and/or service, either alone or as part of a bundle or combination of complements. Few consider that it also consists of the customer's experience of the *company* before, during, and after they use the product and/or service. As is next detailed, the points at which customers experience, or could potentially experience, a company before, during, and after they use its offering are called *touchpoints*.[21]

A company's *sales & marketing* activities touch customers before they use its product or service. The properties of a company's sales effort that customers use to judge the company include the sales team's frequency of contact, appearance, knowledge, helpfulness, responsiveness, presentation skills, and relationship with customers. Superior performance on these properties—which is to say, superior attributes, such as more frequent contact, better appearance, being more knowledgeable, etc.—is a way to differentiate an offering. IBM and Xerox, for example, are known for having sales teams that set the companies apart from their competitors.

The marketing properties that customers use to judge a company include the frequency and timing of its advertising, the media in which the advertising is delivered, and the content of the advertising. More advertising raises recognition and recall (awareness). Customers are going to buy from a brand they remember as compared to one they don't, and they are inclined to prefer a brand they recognize to one they don't. Younger generations may be more responsive to advertising delivered through social media as compared to traditional media. Superior ad content convinces customers the company will do a better job of fulfilling their needs. A good example of the way marketing can differentiate a company is the story of Hitachi and GE televisions. In the mid-1980s, the two companies jointly owned a factory that made identical television sets. The televisions looked the same and cost exactly the same to produce. The only difference was the GE and Hitachi brand names affixed to the front of the televisions and the way the brands were marketed. Because Hitachi did a superior job of marketing, they were able to charge $75 more for their televisions *and* sell twice as many of them. Hitachi's competitive advantage was so large that GE decided to get out of the television business altogether.

Other points at which customers experience a company before they use its offering are the company's *channels of distribution*. A channel of distribution is a conduit through which a company sells its product or service or, in reverse, a conduit through which customers buy the product or service. The major kinds of channels are illustrated in Figure 5.6 and described below.

The sales team is a way for companies to sell their products and services and a way for buyers to buy them. In some cases, the sales team is made of employees and in others, it is comprised of agents. Some of the ways a sales team can differentiate a company were described above.

"Brick & Mortar" outlets include physical facilities like offices, retail stores, supermarkets, restaurants, hotels, fitness clubs, and repair shops. Some outlets are owned and operated by a

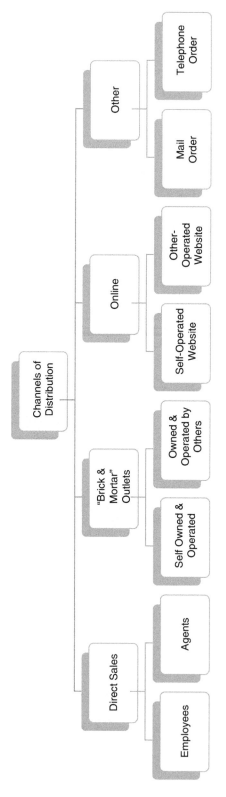

Figure 5.6 Channels of distribution.

company. Others, such as franchised operations and the retail and grocery stores through which manufacturers sell their products, are not. Among the properties that customers use to judge an outlet are its location, design, cleanliness, staffing, hours of operation, and the breadth and depth of inventory. The stock brokerage firm Edward Jones is an example of the way location can be used to differentiate brick and mortar outlets. Where traditional brokerages operate in major cities out of a limited number of Class A office buildings, Edward Jones's offices exist in high-traffic strip malls in some 15,000 locations in North America. This makes it easier for clients to stop by an office to discuss a transaction and to build a personal relationship with their broker. Another example of using a type of location to differentiate an offering is exclusive enclaves. Wealthy customers will oftentimes travel the extra distance to be seen buying, or to be able to say they bought from, a luxury outlet in an exclusive location. Couture clothing, for instance, sets itself apart by distributing through stores located on Rodeo Drive in Beverly Hills, 5th Avenue in New York, Bond Street in London, and Avenue Montaigne in Paris.

Another property of brick and mortar outlets is their geographic coverage and density, i.e., the geographic area in which the outlets are located and the number of outlets that exist in that area. Consider, for example, the way drug store and supermarket chains blanket a city. The benefit is that the more densely distributed competitor will have stores that are closer to customers than the stores of the less densely distributed rival. Another example is Caterpillar, the heavy equipment manufacturer. With more than 2,600 locations in the USA, Caterpillar customers do not have to travel as far to purchase equipment and have it serviced as compared to other heavy equipment brands. Loyalty programs are an additional way in which a large number of locations differentiates an offering. Customers will prefer a hotel loyalty program that offers more, and more types of, locations to one that offers fewer, less varied locations. The same goes for airline frequent flyer programs and the number and variety of flights.

Online channels include self-operated websites and websites that are operated by others. Examples of the former are the websites operated by Barnes & Noble, Walmart, and the hotel and airline brands. Examples of the latter are Amazon and online travel agents like Expedia, Kayak, and Travelocity. One of the properties of websites is their ranking on Google and other search engines. Companies differentiate their websites by using search engine optimization (SEO) methods to elevate their ranking on the search engines. Other properties of websites are their ease of use and content. Amazon's 1-click attribute sets its website apart from rivals by making it easier to purchase an item. Companies differentiate themselves on other-operated websites (e.g., Travelocity) by doing a better job of describing their goods (e.g., superior photographs) and doing a better job of following the website's rules for optimum placement.

Two other kinds of distribution channels are mail order and telephone order. Mail-order pharmacies are an example of the first, where two important properties are the ease of ordering and delivery times. Mail-order pharmacies set themselves apart from their brick and mortar rivals by eliminating the need for customers to drive to the pharmacy, tell the pharmacist (and the person behind them) the drug they need, and then wait 30 minutes for their prescription to be filled. Hotel and airline telephone reservation centers are examples of telephone ordering systems, where differentiation is largely a matter of having reservation agents that answer the phone faster and are friendlier and more knowledgeable. As far as I know, no one has created a phone tree that does anything more than drive their customers mad (in both senses of the term).

The convenience of one-stop shopping is a way to differentiate all the channels of distribution. Amazon, which seemingly sells everything, is the quintessential example. Other examples are large retail locations that offer an extensive variety of goods, a streaming music service that sells many songs from popular and independent artists, a news website that covers a wide variety of stories, a service firm that provides a wide range of services, large entertainment complexes that have entertainment for a range of age groups, and resorts that offer numerous shopping, dining, and entertainment options.[22] A restaurant can offer one-stop shopping by offering sit-down service, pickup service, delivery service, and catering service. Another example of one-stop shopping is law firms that offer multiple types of legal counsel and medical practices that offer a range of medical specialties. With one-stop shopping, customers save the time, money, and effort of having to drive all over town (or the internet) to find what they want. However, in the circumstance where customers want only one or a few commonly bought items, they are willing to forego variety for ease of access. Two common examples are convenience stores vs. supermarkets and small hardware outlets vs. large home improvement centers.

Further along the consumption chain, after customers have made their purchase, is the opportunity to use superior delivery to differentiate an offering. Amazon has gone to great lengths to ensure two-day delivery, including expanding its truck and air fleet and building an estimated 180 warehouses around the world.[23] Compare this to the 7–10 days (or more) that is the norm for most mail-order products. Reliability is another way of using delivery to differentiate an offering. The company that can be relied on to have what the customer wants when the customer wants it sets itself apart from competitors who don't. Best Buy's failure to ship thousands of preordered Christmas items is an infamous example of the latter.[24] Helping with installation is another way to differentiate an offering, be it the installation of a complicated piece of home electronics (smart televisions come to mind) or a complex piece of factory equipment.

After customers find, purchase, and accept delivery of an offering, they move on to the use stage of the consumption chain. One way of differentiating difficult-to-use offerings is to provide more and better training. Ways of presenting the training include self-instruction (manuals and videos), formal classes, and remote and online learning. Innovative ways of presenting the content of the training include superior design,[25] using branching scenarios and gamification,[26] presenting content in bite-sized chunks,[27] and making sure the content is mobile-friendly. Doing a better job of providing help is another way for a company to differentiate itself while customers are using its offering. The traditional way of delivering help is the telephone helpline. New ways of helping customers include email, SMS, and access to online information. Some ways of providing help that differentiate an offering are to provide it when rivals don't (e.g., 24/7 help vs. business-days-and-hours-only help) and providing substantially more help than rivals provide.

Consistent quality across locations and experiences is another way to differentiate offerings during the use stage of the consumption chain. In the hotel industry, Marriott and Hilton, for example, have set their brands apart by consistently franchising high-quality hotels and requiring that their franchisees maintain them to the highest standards. This compares to certain other hotel brands that have sacrificed quality for growth. Delivering consistent high-quality service (e.g., fast, friendly, and responsive service) from one location to the next is another thing that Marriott and Hilton work hard to do. Consistent property and service quality can also be used to differentiate branded retail outlets, restaurants, fitness centers, car dealerships, and other businesses that offer multiple locations under a single brand name. The same applies to airline, train, bus, and taxi companies, which provide multiple service experiences under the same brand name. Similarly, vehicle and equipment manufacturers can use consistent quality (e.g., consistent reliability, durability, conformance to specifications, etc.) to differentiate themselves. Another form of consistency that differentiates an offering at the company level is using the same logo, colors, font, and other elements of a brand's visual identity on the company's signage, stationery, uniforms, and elsewhere. Small- and medium-sized enterprises are especially prone to inconsistencies in visual identity, which is something more brand-savvy competitors can use to set themselves apart.

The final steps of the consumption chain occur after the customer has used the offering. The steps include storing the offering, returning it, maintaining and repairing it, and disposing of it at the end of its lifecycle. Each of these steps presents an opportunity for a company to differentiate itself. Nordstrom, for instance, used to differentiate itself with a no-questions-asked return policy. Ultimately, it had to change the policy because it was abused, but it still sets itself apart with a return policy that is accommodating and easily accomplished. As for the maintenance step of the consumption chain, the sensors that are now a part of the Internet of Things (IoT) provide myriad opportunities to use remote diagnostics to provide innovative maintenance services. For example, Otis Elevators uses remote diagnostics to identify maintenance and repair requirements before their elevators fail and go out of service. At the disposal step of the consumption chain, there are all sorts of opportunities for those who manufacture and sell products to differentiate themselves by offering disposal and recycling services.

Customer relationship management (CRM) activities are a third way in which customers experience an offering at the company level. CRM is often wrongly identified with loyalty programs and customer relationship software, when it should be considered a core business strategy having the objective of creating and delivering customized benefits to targeted customers.[28] In B2C businesses, where the company may have many thousands or millions of customers, the CRM program is more statistical in nature and targets defined populations of customers. In B2B businesses, where the company may have just a few dozen customers, making it difficult to generalize about them, a CRM program may target the unique needs of individual customers.[29] In both cases, as Wharton School professors Nicolaj Siggelkow and Christian Terwiesch explain in *Connected Strategy: Building Continuous Customer Relationships for Competitive Advantage*, the end objective is to turn occasional, sporadic transactions with customers into long-term, continuous relationships.[30]

At the level of individual services, lawyers, accountants, consultants, and other professionals typically work to develop social bonds (positive personal relationships). The bonds are strengthened over time by increasing levels of trust in the competency and honesty of the professional and by personal chemistry. But, as Francis Buttle and Stan Maklan explain in *Customer Relationship Management: Concepts and Technologies*, CRM is much more complex at the company level.[31] In B2C businesses, it involves building a relationship with customers by using blogs, helplines, complaint centers, catalogs, customer clubs, loyalty programs, and sales promotions to interact with and stay in front of them. In B2B businesses, CRM involves both social and structural bonds. The *social bonds* often involve multiple relationships between different people at different levels and in different functions of the customer company. The various functions will have different concerns and the quality of the relationship in one of the customer's functions may influence the quality of the relationship in another function. All the relationships need to be managed in a way that strengthens the social bonds and ensures consistent messaging.

A *structural bond*, Buttle and Maklan elaborate, is created when the company or the customer (or both) commits a resource to the relationship. Types and examples of structural bonds include financial bonds (tenure-related discounts), equity bonds (both parties invest money to create an offer for customers), legal bonds (a contract or common ownership), knowledge-based bonds (the parties grow to know each other better), technological bonds (the technologies of the two organizations are aligned), process bonds (the processes of the two organizations are aligned), values-based bonds (the organizations have common values), geographic bonds (the organizations are located near each other), project bonds (the organizations are engaged in the same project), and multi-product bonds (the customer buys several offerings from the seller). In both B2C and B2B businesses, each of the means of building social and structural bonds is a way to differentiate an offering.

The Offering

As depicted in Figure 5.7, the sum of this chapter is that a company's offering consists of its core product or service, the core plus the supplementary products, services, programs and systems that are a part of its bundles and complements, and the sales & marketing, channels of distribution, and CRM activities that make up the remaining ways in which customers experience the company. Each level (or ring) of the offering provides multiple opportunities for a company to differentiate itself. The second half of this book explains a variety of methods for revealing the opportunities. But before we get into that, the next chapter takes a deeper dive into the concept of differentiation.

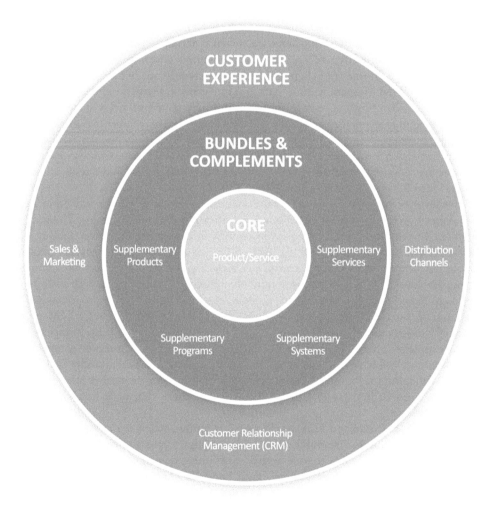

Figure 5.7 A company's offering consists of its core product/service; its bundled and complementary products, services, programs, and systems; and its sales & marketing, distribution channel, and CRM activities.

Source: David Holt Design.

Notes

1 Wikipedia contributors, "Form follows function," *Wikipedia, The Free Encyclopedia*, https://en.wikipedia.org/w/index.php?title=Form_follows_function&oldid=999842686. Sullivan actually wrote "form ever follows function," but the simpler phrase "form follows function" is the one that is most remembered.

2 Christopher Alexander, *Notes on the Synthesis of Form* (Cambridge, MA: Harvard University Press, 1964), 1.

3 Nikk Effingham, *An Introduction to Ontology* (Cambridge, UK: Polity Press, 2013), 2.

4 Jacob Goldenberg and David Mazursky, *Creativity in Product Innovation* (Cambridge, UK: Cambridge University Press, 2002), 168–173. Goldenberg and Mazursky's definitions of these terms go a long way toward clearing up the inconsistent and ill-defined ways in which the terms *components, parts, features, attributes, properties, characteristics, qualities,* and *variables* are used in various business books and journal articles.

5 David Weissman, *A Social Ontology* (New Haven, CT: Yale University Press, 2000), 26. Weissman describes things as being "festooned" with properties.

6 Goldenberg and Mazursky use the term *attribute* instead of *property*. I'm using attribute in the way that it is normally used in business writings.

7 Wikipedia contributors, "Emergence," *Wikipedia, The Free Encyclopedia*, https://en.wikipedia.org/w/index.php?title=Emergence&oldid=1009642293.

8 Harold J. Morowitz, *The Emergence of Everything: How the World Became Complex* (Oxford, UK, Oxford University Press, 2002).

9 Goldenberg and Mazursky here use the term *characteristic.*

10 James C. Anderson, Nirmalya Kumar, and James A. Narus, *Value Merchants: Demonstrating and Documenting Superior Value in Business Markets* (Boston, MA: Harvard Business School Press, 2007), 81–105. The authors provide many more examples of services, systems, and programs on page 83.

11 *Ibid*, 84–85.

12 David Besanko, David Dranove, Mark Stanley, and Scott Schaefer, *Economics of Strategy*, 6th ed. (Hoboken, NJ: John Wiley & Sons, 2013), 262.

13 Felix Oberholzer-Gee, *Better Simpler Strategy: A Value-Based Guide to Exceptional Performance* (Boston, MA: Harvard Business Review Press, 2021), 63. Oberholzer-Gee provides an extensive discussion of complements, including the dynamics of pricing proprietary complements and the difference between complements and substitutes.

14 David C. Robertson with Kent Lineback, *The Power of Little Ideas: A Low-Risk, High-Reward Approach to Innovation* (Boston, MA: Harvard Business Review Press, 2017), 1–9.

15 *Ibid*, 12–13.

16 James C. Anderson and James A. Narus, "Capturing the Value of Supplementary Services," *Harvard Business Review* January-February, 1995, 81. https://hbr.org/1995/01/capturing-the-value-of-supplementary-services.

17 Clayton M. Christensen, Taddy Hall, Karen Dillon, and David S. Duncan, *Competing Against Luck: The Story of Innovation and Customer Choice* (New York, NY: HarperCollins Publishers, 2016), 165–171.

18 Anderson and Narus, *op. cit.*, 80.

19 Anderson et al., *op. cit.*, 99.

20 Oberholzer-Gee, *op. cit.*, 64–65.

21 Jim Kalbach, *Mapping Experiences: A Complete Guide to Creating Value Through Journeys, Blueprints & Diagrams* (Boston, MA: O"Reilly Media, 2016).

22 John Spacey, "Eight Examples of a One Stop Shop," *Simpicable*, https://simplicable.com/new/one-stop-shop.

23 Suman Sarkar, *The Supply Chain Revolution: Innovative Sourcing and Logistics for a Fiercely Competitive World* (New York, NY: AMACOM, 2017), 17.

24 *Ibid*, 18.

25 Julie Dirksen, *Design for How People Learn* 2nd ed. (New York, NY: New Riders, 2016).

26 Clark Aldrich, *Learning by Doing: A Comprehensive Guide to Simulations, Computer Games, and Pedagogy in e-Learning and Other Educational Experiences* (San Francisco, CA: John Wiley & Sons, 2005).

27 James M. Lang, *Small Teaching: Everyday Lessons from the Science of Learning* (San Francisco, CA: Jossey-Bass, 2016).

28 Fancis Buttle and Stan Maklan, *Customer Relationship Management: Concepts and Technologies 3rd ed.* (New York, NY: Routledge, 2015), 22.

29 Don Peppers and Martha Rogers, *One to One B2B: Customer Development Strategies for the Business-to-Business World* (New York, NY: Doubleday, 2011), 8.
30 Nicolaj Siggelkow and Christian Terwiesch, *Connected Strategy: Building Continuous Customer Relationships for Competitive Advantage* (Boston, MA: Harvard Business Review Press, 2019).
31 Buttle and Maklan, *op. cit.*, 90–101.

6 Differentiation

So far, I've had the following to say about differentiation. A competitive strategy is a way of gaining the customers your competitors are trying to gain at the same time. A differentiation strategy is one of two types of competitive strategy, the other being a cost leadership strategy. An offering is differentiated when it's different in a way that causes customers to prefer it to competing offerings. The offering–function–benefit trilogy summarizes the idea that offerings perform functions that deliver benefits. The trilogy helps to explain the difference between a customer wanting an offering and preferring an offering. Customers *want* an offering when it performs a function that delivers a desired benefit. Customers *prefer* an offering when, compared to competing offerings, the offering functions to deliver significantly more of a desired benefit, an additional desired benefit, or both, at a comparable price. Now let's dig a bit deeper into the concept of differentiation.

Different Why?

Why be different? What's the point? I just gave half the answer. Customers will prefer an offering if, and only if, it helps or enables them to obtain significantly more of a desired benefit, an additional desired benefit, or both, at a comparable price. In order to provide more and better benefits, a company must do things differently and do different things. For example, the enormous size of their stores enables IKEA to provide complementary houseware and décor, which saves customers the time and effort that would be required to find these items elsewhere, and IKEA's flat packing feature enables immediate self-delivery, which provides the emotional benefit of instant gratification, a benefit that competing furniture stores do not provide.

The other half of the answer takes us back to the gap diagram discussed in Chapter 1. Remember that a company has a competitive advantage when, and only when, it is more profitable than its competitors. The two ways to be more profitable are (1) to increase customer-perceived value, and thereby increase price or volume, and (2) to lower costs. Doing things differently and doing different things are ways to lower costs. For example, where traditional furniture stores tend to locate closer to the center of a city, IKEA offsets the cost of providing enormous stores by locating in a suburb, where land prices are less. And the company has gone to great lengths to develop a cost-efficient supply chain, where a key part of its cost control is credited to the unique (different) way it communicates with and relates to its suppliers.

So the two reasons for being different are to provide customers with more customer-perceived value than rivals and to be able to do it while achieving a larger gap than rivals between the value and the cost to provide it.

DOI: 10.4324/9781003271703-7

Different Where?

An offering is differentiated when customers *decide* that they *prefer* it to other offerings because it provides them with more of the benefits they *desire*. Preferring, deciding, and desiring are things that occur in the mind, which means that the answer to the "Different where?" question is "Different in the customer's mind." Trout and Rivkin, the authors of the earlier-cited book *Differentiate or Die: Survival in Our Era of Killer Competition*, devote an entire chapter to this idea, appropriately titled "Differentiation Takes Place in the Mind."[1]

Customers use an offering's physical attributes to judge whether it will provide them with the benefit(s) they desire. In other words, they use the things they can see, hear, touch, taste, and smell to infer that the offering will provide them the physical, mental, emotional, social, economic, and/or cost-risk reduction benefit(s) they desire. For example, from the satisfying "thunk" sound (vs. tinny sound) when a car door closes, customers infer that the car is durable; from the advertising materials that cite a certain 0–60 mph time or engine horse-power rating, customers infer that the car will provide them the thrills and chills they desire; and from the car's brand name, they infer others will perceive them as successful (Mercedes-Benz), or adventurous (Porsche), or practical (Honda). From the traditional interior of a stockbroker's office, customers infer that the brokerage is stable; from the stockbroker's Brooks Brothers suit, customers infer that the broker is conservative and professional; and from the brokerage's promotional materials and newsletters, customers infer that the brokerage can provide them with sound advice.

So customers use an offering's physical attributes to judge whether it will provide them the benefits they desire. Actually, it's more accurate to say that customers use an offering's physical attribute plus the function they've assigned to it to judge whether the offering will provide the desired benefit. Remember from Chapter 4 that people judge the performance of something based on the function(s) they assign to it. One of the examples was the party hostess who judges the performance of a coffee table book based on whether it is being used to perform the function *convey interesting information, stimulate conversation,* or *decorate the room.* Thus, when considering how customers judge the performance of an attribute, you must first know the function they have assigned to it.

The properties that customers use to decide whether and from whom to buy an offering are sometimes referred to as their *purchase criteria*. A company differentiates its offering by having an attribute (property value) that outperforms its competitors on a particular purchase criterion (property). For example, one of the properties of cars is fuel efficiency, as measured by miles per gallon (mpg). Say Car A has the attribute (property value) of a 30 mpg fuel efficiency rating and Car B has the attribute (property value) of a 25 mpg rating. Car A is positively differentiated relative to Car B with respect to this purchase criterion. This example makes clear that the attributes of an offering are what differentiate it because customers use them to judge whether they will receive the benefits they desire, which in this case is fuel cost savings. Thus, we can refer to the attributes of an offering that outperform the corresponding attributes of competing offerings as its *differentiators*. I've gone to great lengths, here and in the earlier chapter on offerings, to explain the difference between properties and attributes because it will, in a later chapter, help you create a strategy canvas.

The *strategy canvas*, initially popularized in the international bestseller *Blue Ocean Strategy: How to Create Uncontested Market Space and Make the Competition Irrelevant*,[2] and later modified in the books *Value Innovation Works*[3] (where it's called a *value curve*) and *Better Simpler Strategy: A Value-Based Guide to Exceptional Performance*[4] (where it's called a *value map*), is a helpful way of picturing the differentiation strategy for an offering. A sample strategy canvas for Airbnb, as compared to traditional full-service hotel chains, is shown in Figure 6.1. On the left side of the canvas are the purchase criteria (properties of the offering) that Airbnb's target market

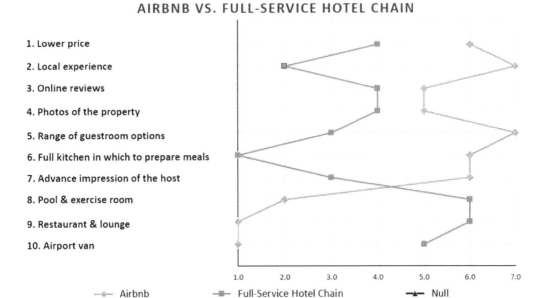

1. Lower price
2. Local experience
3. Online reviews
4. Photos of the property
5. Range of guestroom options
6. Full kitchen in which to prepare meals
7. Advance impression of the host
8. Pool & exercise room
9. Restaurant & lounge
10. Airport van

Figure 6.1 Strategy canvas comparing Airbnb to traditional full-service hotel chains.

considers when deciding from which kind of hotel chain (Airbnb or a traditional full-service hotel chain) to buy, ranked in order of importance. As a matter of convention, price is always listed first. The seven-point scale along the bottom is used to measure the competitors' (i.e., Airbnb and traditional full-service hotel chains) performance on each of the purchase criteria. As just explained, a performance is an attribute (property value) of an offering. The attributes of an offering differentiate it (or not) because customers use them to judge whether they will receive more of the benefits they desire. Note that Airbnb outperforms traditional full-service hotels on the seven most important purchase criteria and underperforms them on the three least important criteria.

The principal value of the strategy canvas is that it enables you to take in your, and your competitor's, differentiation strategy at a glance. Each of your differentiation strategies is illustrated by its graph line on the canvas, which consists of your and your competitor's relative performance on the purchase criteria. As Niraj Dawar explains, "Customers use these criteria not just to decide whether to purchase a brand, but also to organize and make sense of the brands and the marketplace. Whether you know it or not, and whether you like it or not, your brand is positioned [relative to your competitor's brand] along the criteria that customers consider important."[5] Note how Dawar's use of the term "positioned" explains why a *differentiation strategy* is sometimes referred to as a *positioning strategy*. Devising a differentiation strategy is basically about deciding where to position your performance on each of the purchase criteria. We will go into the details of creating a strategy canvas in Chapter 8.

In his book *Compete Smarter, Not Harder: A Process for Developing the Right Priorities Through Strategic Thinking*, William Putsis, a business professor at the University of North Carolina at Chapel Hill, explains that an offering's attributes can be categorized as either *must-have* attributes (elsewhere referred to as *table stakes* or *hygienic* attributes) or *salient differentiator* attributes.[6] A must-have attribute is one that an offering has to have in order to compete, i.e., the offering must have it to get in the game (hence the term *table stakes* attribute). A company can *lose* business by not having a must-have attribute, but it can't *win* business by having it. A hotel, for example, must meet some minimal level of cleanliness for customers to even consider it, but the cleanliness level will not cause customers to prefer it to other hotels because all the competing hotels are expected to be clean. A salient differentiator, in contrast, is an attribute that enables a company to *win* business. A salient differentiator of a hotel, for example, would be the existence of a loyalty program.

Putsis uses the results of a survey to explain the difference between a must-have attribute and a salient differentiator. The survey asked businesspersons flying from London to New York to name the top three reasons why they would choose one airline over another. Collectively, they answered: (1) safety, (2) route, and (3) schedule. Were these answers mapped on the strategy canvas, they would be listed as the top three purchase criteria on the list (after price). But, Putsis explains, equivalent performance on the three purchase criteria is an attribute that every airline *must have* in order to compete. To get in the game, an airline must be safe—who wants to fly on an unsafe airline? And it must fly the desired route—who wants to fly from London to New York with a stopover in Iceland? And it must have frequent departures—who wants to fly an airline that flies from New York to London one time per week? All the airlines that fly from London to New York are safe, fly the non-stop route, and have daily flights because customers consider the three things to be must-have attributes. And because all the airlines offer the three attributes, none of them serve as a point of differentiation, which is to say, none of them serves as a salient differentiator. The salient points of differentiation are attributes like loyalty programs, on-time performance, and flat beds in business class. In short, the must-haves are necessary not to lose business, but they are not sufficient to win it. It is the salient differentiators that cause customers to prefer one airline over another.

While customers don't visualize a strategy canvas in their mind's eye, they do mentally possess the information it contains, and they use that information to decide whether and from whom to buy—with the following two qualifications. The first qualification is that people are only able to remember so much. As Dawar explains, "In any product category, customers find it easier to mentally associate each criterion with a single brand and to associate each brand with a single criterion."[7] The second qualification is that minds don't like to change. The economist John Kenneth Galbraith noted this when he said, "Faced with the choice of changing one's mind and proving that there is no need to do so, almost everyone gets busy on the proof."[8] The upshot of the two qualifications is that a company needs to decide where (i.e., on which purchase criterion) it wants customers to associate its offering with superior performance (preferably the most important criterion). And it needs to be the first one to get customers to make the association because it's nearly impossible to cause customers to change their minds if they already associate superior performance on the purchase criterion with another brand. Walmart, for example, was the first to associate its name with "everyday low prices." Because Walmart was first, competing retailers who try to associate their name with everyday low prices will be viewed as frauds and copycats.

Volvo and other car brands serve as additional examples. Volvo was the first to associate its brand with superior safety. Even now, when other brands have achieved better safety ratings than Volvo, customers continue to think of Volvo as the safest car available. Trout and Rivkin point to other car brands that have successfully associated their names with superior performance on a purchase criterion, such as BMW (drivability), Toyota (reliability), and Jaguar (styling).[9] In the opposite direction, they point to Chevrolet, Nissan, Mercury, and Oldsmobile as examples of brands that are unfocused and don't own an association, which, they note, may help to explain why the Mercury and Oldsmobile brands no longer exist. Other examples are Google, which owns the association with faster, more-exhaustive search results; Apple, which is associated with superior design and useability; Fed-Ex, which owns the association with reliable overnight delivery; and Intel, which is associated with the fastest computer chip processing speeds. By being the first to forge these associations in the customer's mind, each of these brands has made it nigh on impossible for competing brands to usurp their associations. Even Apple failed when, with its PowerPC chip, it attempted to take over Intel's association with the fastest processing speeds.

But what if all the associations with the most important purchase criteria have already been taken by competitors? In some cases, Dawar explains, it makes sense to settle for a me-too strategy.[10] One case is the circumstance where the customers' preference is so centered on a purchase criterion that it's impossible to ignore it. Another case is the situation where a me-too player is satisfied with the returns it is able to achieve by playing second fiddle. An alternative way of dealing with the lack of available associations is to create a new one, so long as the new association is effective.

So, where does differentiation occur? It occurs in the customer's mind. Decisions, desires, preferences, assigned functions, purchase criteria, importance rankings, beliefs about relative performance, and associations are things that exist inside a customer's head. All of which means that an offering isn't differentiated until the customer *thinks* it's differentiated.

Different How?

In his journal article titled "What is Strategy?" Michael Porter declares, "[T]he essence of strategy is in the activities—choosing to perform activities differently or to perform different activities than rivals."[11] Porter's use of the term *activity* is so broad that I interpret him to mean that the essence of a differentiation strategy is to do things differently or to do different things than competitors. What he very clearly does *not* mean is that the essence of strategy is trying to do the same things your competitors are doing, in the same way, only better. If you're going to do the same things your competitors are doing, you need to do them in a different way, a way that enables you to do them significantly better. (The meaning of "significantly better" is explained in the next section.) In addition to doing things differently, you might also do different things, which is to say, things that your competitors are not doing. In both cases, the fundamental message is that differentiation is about being *different*, not the *same*.

By way of example, Porter compares IKEA to traditional furniture stores. Following are some of the ways IKEA performs activities differently (i.e., does things differently):

- Both IKEA and traditional furniture stores display their furniture. But where traditional stores display their furniture in groupings of the same kind of furniture (say, 25 sofas here and 15 coffee tables there), IKEA displays its furniture in room-like settings, so customers can see how the various kinds of furniture in a room fit together.
- Both IKEA and traditional furniture stores have aisles. In a traditional furniture store, the aisles are straight and intersect at right angles, which enables multidirectional movement and makes it possible to see across the store from one furniture grouping to another. In contrast, IKEA's floorplan has customers walk a curvy, unidirectional path through the store, one that requires them to walk past all the room-like settings (all the kitchen settings, then all the living room settings, then all the bedroom settings, etc.). The curvy path heightens their sense of curiosity about what lies around the next bend.
- Both IKEA and traditional furniture stores convey information about their furniture and their store. In a traditional furniture store, a salesperson escorts customers through the store, answering questions and helping them navigate the floorplan. IKEA, in comparison, employs a self-service model, where informative in-store displays and salesperson kiosks are available to answer customer questions. And the unidirectional aisles enable customers to navigate the store themselves.

- Both IKEA and traditional furniture stores make it possible for the furniture to be delivered to the customer's home. Traditional furniture stores require customers to wait weeks or months for the store to deliver their fully assembled furniture. In contrast, IKEA's customers can put IKEA's flat-packed furniture in or on top of their car, take it home with them, and assemble it the same day. Note that furniture assembly is an activity that IKEA does not perform that traditional furniture stores do perform. Not doing an activity that others perform is another way of doing an activity differently.

The foregoing describes ways IKEA performs activities differently. IKEA also performs different activities (i.e., does different things). For example, where IKEA's stores offer kitchenware and other kinds of homeware, traditional furniture stores do not. Where IKEA's stores have a restaurant, traditional furniture stores do not. And where IKEA's stores offer a childcare service, traditional furniture stores do not offer the service. In each case, IKEA is performing activities that are different than those performed by traditional furniture stores.

As explained in the last chapter, offerings exist at the level of individual products and services, at the level of bundles and complementary sets of products, services, systems, and programs, and at the level of the company's sales & marketing activities, channels of distribution, and customer relationship activities. At each of these levels, there are myriad opportunities to do activities differently and do different activities. Or, to put it another way, at each of the levels, there are countless ways to do things differently and do different things. Whichever way you put it, "doing differently" and "different doings" are what differentiation is all about.

How Different?

Relative to the conventional offerings in an industry, the degree of differentiation can range from incremental to radical (Figure 6.2). IKEA is an example of radical differentiation. Almost every attribute of a conventional furniture store is changed. Cirque du Soleil, the Montreal-based producer of contemporary circuses, is another example of radical differentiation. In their offering, almost every attribute of conventional circuses is changed. Where traditional circuses offer three-rings full of star performers, animals, clowns, and trapeze artists, Cirque de Soleil combines live music, beautifully choreographed dance, stunning costumes and makeup, and extraordinary lighting to create an offering that is as much theater as it is a circus. Because they are so different, radical offerings like IKEA and Cirque de Soleil are radically difficult for competitors to copy. But for most companies, radical differentiation is unrealistic because they don't have the time and money required to change every attribute of their offering. Just imagine, for example, what it would take for a conventional furniture store chain to turn itself into an IKEA-like offering. Even if most companies did have the resources to radicalize, few managers would be willing to adopt what amounts to a bet-the-company strategy.

At the opposite pole is incremental differentiation. In the most extreme cases, it amounts to little more than a jar of jellybeans on the reception desk or some similarly trivial difference. Better, but still incremental, is the sort of differentiation described by Harvard Business

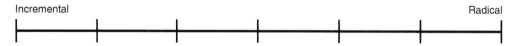

Figure 6.2 Degrees of differentiation.

School professor Youngme Moon in her book *Different: Escaping the Competitive Herd*.[12] In just about every product category, she explains, competitors engage in the sort of competitive copying that causes them to cluster together in an undifferentiated herd. The herding behavior goes like this. One company adds a new attribute, its competitors copy it, then everybody tries to explain how their basically-the-same attribute is different. For example, American Airlines added a frequent flyer program, the other airlines did the same, and now everybody tries to explain why some minor difference in their program makes them different. Hotel beds are another example. Westin Hotels introduced the Heavenly Bed®, its competitors added divinely-inspired beds of their own, and now everyone works to explain why their bed is nearer the hereafter than the others. Toothpaste is yet another example. Colgate added a whitener to its toothpaste, the other brands did the same, and now everyone claims to whiten teeth whiter. And on it goes in one product category after another. As Moon expounds, "The more diligently firms compete with each other, the less differentiated they can become, at least in the eyes of consumers."[13] She elaborates, "[I]n too many cases this is what business has been reduced to: the artful packaging of meaningless distinctions as true differentiation."[14]

So what's a wanna-be differentiator to do? What sort of differentiation strategy avoids the extremes of meaningless incrementalism and bet-the-company radicalism? In his book *Zero to One: Notes on Startups or How to Build the Future*, Peter Thiel, the co-founder of PayPal, proffers a useful rule of thumb.[15] Thiel proposes that to achieve meaningful differentiation, a company must possess a proprietary technology that makes its performance on a differentiator at least 10 times (an order-of-magnitude) better than its closest competitor. He points to Google, PayPal, Amazon, and Apple as examples:

- In the early 2000s, Google's search algorithms returned results that were 10 times better than its competitors, and its short page load times and accurate query autocompletion added to the difference.
- By enabling immediate payment, PayPal made selling on eBay at least 10 times better than waiting 7–10 days for a check to arrive by mail. So did the fact that, unlike checks, sellers knew that the PayPal funds were good.
- Amazon made its first order-of-magnitude improvement by offering 10 times as many books as any other bookstore.
- Apple's iPad, when it first came out, was 10 times more useful and useable than Microsoft Windows XP Tablet PC Edition and Nokia's Internet Tablet.

While these companies do a great job of illustrating Thiel's point, relatively few companies have the technological chops to imitate them. Fortunately, there's more to technology than the high-tech miracles that daily emerge from Silicon Valley. Or perhaps better said, there's less to technology than the high-tech wizardry we normally associate with the term. McKinsey & Company defines technology as *ways of doing things*.[16] The economist Brian Arthur explains that technological ways of doing things include *devices* as well as the methods, processes, and approaches collectively referred to as *practices*.[17] Thus, Thiel's rule of thumb, or some approximation of it, applies to all devices and practices, all of which are ways of doing things. Niraj Dawar provides the following example of a practice.[18] A division of Imperial Chemical Industries (ICI), he explains, sells dynamite and other explosives to quarries. The quarries use the explosives to blast solid rock into pieces of roughly equal size. If a quarry fails to use the correct amount of explosive in the correct places, much of the resulting rock goes to waste because it is too large or too small for the quarry to sell. To overcome this problem, ICI collected and analyzed data (up to 20 variables affect the outcome of a blast) on hundreds of blasts in a range of quarries. They made their offering 10 times better than their competitors' offerings by using the data to guarantee that a certain percentage of rocks will fall within a specified size range. In this way, they made their offering an order-of-magnitude better than their competitor's offering and, Dawar emphasizes, they did it without having to employ a radical, bet-the-company strategy.

The business professors Rita Gunther McGrath and Ian MacMillan provide another example of using a proprietary technology to devise a strategy that lies intermediate between incrementalism and radicalism. CEMEX is a Mexican cement company that grew from a regional player during the 1960s to the global behemoth that it is today.[19] The problem with ready-mix concrete is that it begins to set almost as soon as it's loaded in the cement truck, which means that delays caused by heavy traffic and other factors result in the delivery of a smaller amount of usable cement. This is bad for the cement customers, whose chief concern is having the right amount of usable cement delivered at the right time so they don't have to pay their construction crews extra while they wait for more cement. CEMEX differentiates its offering by guaranteeing a delivery time. Originally, they developed practices that enabled them to guarantee delivery no later than three hours after the customer placed the order, but with improvements in technology and the application of more sophisticated routing methods, they are now able to guarantee that the cement will be delivered in twenty minutes or less. This makes CEMEX's offering an order-of-magnitude better than its competitor's offering without having to resort to a bet-the-company strategy.

Yet another example is provided by David Robertson.[20] Robertson makes a strong case for using proprietary complements to differentiate an offering in a way that lies midway between meaningless incrementalism and bet-the-company radicalism. One of his many examples is Sherwin-Williams. As earlier explained, Sherwin-Williams sells paint to small painting contractors. They set themselves apart from other paint stores by providing their contractors with an end-to-end service that starts with going to the contractor's customer to help with color selection and to inspect the job site. Then they help the contractor develop a plan for the job and estimate how much labor and material will be required at each step. In this way, they help the contractor provide the customer with an accurate estimate of cost and timing, and they ensure that the contractor will earn an acceptable profit. During the job, Sherwin-Williams checks the contractor's daily orders and suggests items the contractor may have forgotten. Then, at the end of the job, Sherwin-Williams helps the contractor prepare estimates for any additional jobs the homeowner decides to do. By pairing their core paint product with a proprietary complementary service, Sherwin-Williams sets itself apart from other paint sellers in a way that is more than incremental and less than radical.

Different for How Long?

Sustainable differentiation is the key to successful differentiation. Being different in a way that competitors can't copy, or don't want to copy, is ideal. Second best, and more realistic, is to sustain the difference long enough to achieve a reasonable return on the cost to create it. Worst—and, unfortunately, most common—are differences of the sort earlier described by Youngme Moon, differences that are easily replicated and cause the herd to take a collective step closer to losing money.

One way to prevent copying is *patent protection*. Infringement penalties and legal fees make patent protection nearly absolute during the usual seventeen-year term. The patent lawyer James Yang explains that an invented product or process is patentable when it is *useful*, *eligible* (meaning it's not an abstract idea, natural phenomenon, or law of nature), *novel*, and *non-obvious*.[21] Patentable products, he elaborates, can be similar products so long as the differences between them are non-obvious. And a combination of existing products is patentable so long as the combination is non-obvious. But the non-obvious requirement appears to stump most companies, for, as Columbia Business School professors Bruce Greenwald and Judd Kahn report, patent-protected positions are relatively rare outside the pharmaceutical industry.[22]

Trade secrets are another way to prevent copying, or at least make it more difficult. Trade secrets are a type of intellectual property that comprise "formulas, practices, processes, designs, instruments, patterns, or compilations of information that have inherent economic value because they are not generally known or readily ascertainable by others, and which the owner takes reasonable measures to keep secret."[23] In contrast to registered intellectual property like a patent, trade secrets are protected by company efforts to prevent their disclosure to competitors. The efforts include special procedures for handling the secrets (e.g., computer firewalls) and using legal protections like non-disclosure and non-compete agreements. But these protections don't always prevent a competitor from learning secrets through lawful methods like reverse engineering and potentially unlawful methods like industrial espionage.

An effective way to discourage competitive copying is to create an offering that is downright difficult to duplicate. It's easier to do this with a complex product or service than with a simple one. The Toyota Production System (TPS), for instance, is a complex sociotechnical system that combines respect for Toyota's people and partners, continuous improvement (Kaizen), and root cause analysis to manufacture vehicles that are differentiated by their reliability and durability.[24] Another example is the Danaher Business System (DBS), which is an adaptation of the TPS that is used to manufacture biomedical and other types of equipment. Danaher expanded on the TPS by applying business practices like sequentially entering niche markets and not entering a market unless they can achieve a market share four times larger than their nearest competitor.[25]

TPS and DBS are, at heart, about finding ways to differentiate an offering by learning more about customers and the internal processes used to serve them. By applying their learning methods, simple offerings can be made more complex and therefore more difficult to copy. A good example is Toyota's employee idea system, which still, after decades of use, generates an average of nine implementable ideas per employee per year, or more than a *million implementable ideas* annually.[26] When first applied in the Clarion Hotel in Stockholm, the idea system generated an average of fifty ideas per employee per year.[27] Most of the ideas were small and straightforward, e.g., train the bartenders to answer questions about local attractions, increase the font size on the coupons, offer organic cocktails, and mix drinks at the tables to give customers a show when things are slow in the bar. None of the ideas alone differentiates the Clarion-Stockholm, but the accumulation of many hundreds of ideas like these—even thousands, over the years—makes the hotel stand apart and makes copying its offering difficult to do. One way to implement an employee idea system is to start simple (e.g., short idea sessions at the start of every shift and an Excel spreadsheet to track the ideas) and then progressively increase the idea system's level of sophistication over the years (e.g., problem-finding and problem-solving training and a computerized idea management system).[28] Continuously improving the idea system is a way to stay ahead of competitors who decide to implement employee idea systems of their own. More information on employee idea systems is provided in Chapter 10.

CEMEX is another example of using learning to sustain differentiation. As noted above, CEMEX originally guaranteed delivery no later than three hours after the customer placed the order, but with improvements in technology and the application of more sophisticated routing methods, they are now able to guarantee the cement will be delivered in 20 minutes or less. In other words, they have applied continuous learning to stay abreast of the technological and routing innovations that enable them to sustain their differentiating delivery promise. ICI is also an example of using continuous learning to sustain a differentiation advantage. The more blast data they accumulate, the more they are able to refine their models and the further they pull ahead of their competitors.

Danaher's niche strategy, mentioned above, is another way to stymie competitive copying. This is an instance of Porter's *differentiation focus* strategy. As earlier explained, this type of strategy entails identifying a group of customers with unique needs and differentiating the offering by doing a significantly better job of satisfying the needs. The objective is to so dominate the chosen segment as to make it difficult or impossible for competitors to compete. In Danaher's case, as noted above, they shoot to have a market share that is four times as large as their nearest competitor in order to build economies of scale.

Opportunities to implement a focused differentiation strategy usually exist because the competitors in an industry have undershot or overshot the needs of a segment of customers. GoPro is a good example of a company that implemented a successful differentiation focus strategy by tailoring its offering to undershot needs. The company's video cameras are designed to appeal to people who want to capture their sports and hobby adventures. GoPro started in 2004 with a waterproof video camera that could be attached to a surfboard. As David Robertson explains, GoPro has since expanded to offer a line of "affordable, rugged, waterproof cameras" and a comprehensive line of the "accessories that make adventure recording possible: portable power packs, smart remotes, hand grips, memory cards, repair kits, and, above all, mounts for nearly all settings and occasions."[29] In addition to the mounts and other accessories, a GoPro camera includes two free software packages. One enables users to use the smart remotes to pan and otherwise remotely control the video camera (like when it's mounted under the wing of an airplane), and another enables users to edit the resulting videos and easily move them from a PC to a smartphone for easy sharing. The GoPro Channel on YouTube also makes it easy to share the videos with others. In these ways, GoPro has made itself the go to source for people who want to record and share their surfing, flying, hiking, biking, scuba diving, skateboard riding, race car driving, and other adventures. And talk about dominating a market. Less than a decade after its start, GoPro outgrew its focus strategy and sold more video cameras (6.6 million) than all the other camera companies combined, including Sony, Canon, JVC, and Panasonic.

The competitors in an industry *overshoot* a group of customers when they satisfy more of their needs than they want to have satisfied. Overshoot is often the result of the sort of competitive arms races described by Youngme Moon, where the competitors collectively copy and add one feature after another to their offerings. Eventually, one of the competitors, or a new competitor, sees the opportunity to stand apart from the herd by eliminating a set of features. This was the case with Southwest Airlines (SWA) at its start. They became the low-cost producer in the airline industry by eliminating food service, first-class service, inter-airline baggage transfer, primary airport operations, and hub connectivity—all things a certain segment of the market did not need and did not want to pay for. These changes, plus other aspects of their operation, such as making maintenance faster and easier by having only one kind of airplane in their fleet and having the flight attendants clean the cabin rather than wait for a crew of cabin cleaners to do it, also enabled them to offer more frequent flights than their competitors. For example, rather than two flights per day between Phoenix and Los Angeles, SWA offered ten flights per day, which was another thing a segment of the market found attractive. The major airlines tried to copy Southwest Airline's business model, but soon discovered that making these sorts of changes to their legacy systems—e.g., a maintenance system centered on a single type of airplane and getting their unions to agree to have the flight attendants clean the cabin—was nearly impossible for them to do.

A superior supply chain is an additional way to make it difficult or impossible for competitors to copy an offering. Here, again, IKEA serves as an example. The company buys products from more than 1,800 suppliers in 50 countries, and it maintains 42 trading service offices around the world to manage existing suppliers and identify new ones.[30] The suppliers enable IKEA to feed superior materials (e.g., superior-quality wood) and components into its furniture manufacturing operations. The clothing store chain Zara is another example. By managing the design, warehousing, distribution, and logistics functions in-house rather than outsourcing them, as most retailers do, Zara is able to get new designs into its stores in 10–15 days, as compared to the 9 to 12 months it takes the Gap and other competitors to update their designs.[31] In an industry in which staying abreast of design trends is a must, Zara's supply chain enables it to achieve sustainable differentiation.

Supply chain advantages don't have to be as dramatic as those implemented by IKEA and Zara. A company can achieve a sustainable advantage by making a serious commitment to attracting and retaining superior employees and continuously enhancing their skills. The customer service consultant Jeff Toister serves up an excellent example.[32] Rackspace is a company that provides a computer hosting service for more than 300,000 customers. The company's employees, who refer to themselves as "Rackers," provide an extraordinary level of customer service—so extraordinary that they've branded it Fanatical Support®. Stories of over-the-top service abound, like the technical support rep who ordered a pizza for a customer during a long troubleshooting session after hearing the customer say he was hungry and an account manager who demonstrated her appreciation for a visiting client by preparing a home-cooked meal. Rackspace's extraordinary service stems, in part, from the way it hires people. Instead of hiring employees with technical backgrounds, many Rackers have backgrounds in hospitality, caregiving, and other professions that attract people who are empathetic.

Different at What Level of Abstraction?

Later you're going to learn how to identify purchase criteria and attributes by interviewing customers and brainstorming with your fellow managers. One of the issues you'll run into is that people refer to purchase criteria and attributes at different levels of abstraction. For example, sometimes they'll say they like a car's antilock brakes, which is a specific, physical attribute. Other times they'll say they like a car because it's safe, which is a more general, abstract attribute. And many times, multiple specific attributes are part of a general attribute. For example, antilock brakes, airbags, adaptive headlights, backup cameras, reinforced bodies, forward collision warning, lane departure warning, and blind-spot detection all contribute to the safety of a car.

There are several reasons why it's important to understand the distinction between specific, physical purchase criteria and attributes and general, abstract purchase criteria and attributes. One reason is to be able to make sense of what customers are talking about when you interview them and what your fellow managers mean when you're brainstorming with them, such as when they conflate an attribute like superior safety with better antilock brakes, airbags, and so forth. Two additional reasons for understanding the concept of abstraction are that we will later be putting abstraction to work when building a strategy canvas and when we use analogy to devise creative offerings.

As it is commonly used, the term *abstract* combines (and confuses) the concepts of generality and physicality. The notion of an *abstraction ladder* helps tease the two concepts apart. The late S. I. Hayakawa (1906–1992), a professor of English and US Senator from California, introduced the idea of an abstraction ladder in his classic book titled *Language in Thought and Action*.[33] An example is shown in Figure 6.3. On the bottom rung of the ladder is *your chair*—the specific, physically manifest chair in your living room that you see and sit on every day. On the next rung of the ladder is the more general concept of a *chair*, which is more general because it includes all the chairs in the world, including the chair in your living room. It is on this rung of the ladder that you have left the world of physical things and entered the abstract world of concepts and ideas. Above this rung is the still-more-general concept of

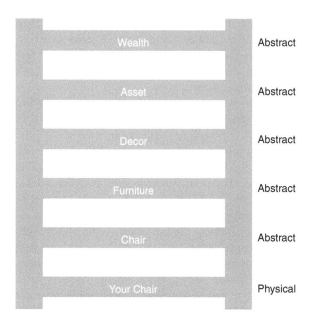

Figure 6.3 The abstraction ladder.

furniture, which includes chairs, couches, lamps, and so forth. And above the furniture rung are the progressively more general, and therefore more abstract, concepts of *décor*, *asset*, and *wealth*.

With each step up the ladder, some of the attributes of the concept on the rung below are subtracted. As the art theorist and perceptual psychologist Rudolf Arnheim explains in his book *Visual Thinking*, "Abstraction removes the more particular attributes of the more specific instances and thereby arrives at the higher concepts, which are poorer in content and broader in range …. These generalizations limit themselves to what all instances of a family of cases have in common and ignore everything else."[34] In the realm of visual art, he talks about the artist "washing away the particulars" to arrive at a piece of abstract art.[35] Things work in reverse when climbing down the ladder. With each step down, attributes are added to the attributes of the rung above, making the concepts richer in content and narrower in range.

In sum, with each step up the ladder, a concept becomes more general and therefore more abstract. And with each step down, the concept becomes more specific and therefore less abstract. Consider, for example, that *your chair* is more specific than the concept of a *chair* because your chair includes the attributes of being a particular type, size, shape, and color, and it has a coffee stain on the right arm and a scratch on the left front leg. Then consider that the concept of a *chair* is more specific than the concept of *furniture* because it includes all the attributes that define a chair, whereas furniture does not.

The mathematician Alfred North Whitehead (1861–1947) said, "We think in generalities, but we live in detail."[36] Figure 6.4 illustrates the idea of climbing up from the detail of the physical world to the abstract world of concepts and ideas, i.e., from the world of *your chair* to the concepts *chair*, *furniture*, *décor*, etc. A helpful way to grasp the difference between the two worlds is to close your eyes and try to imagine a *chair* that is not a physically manifest chair, like *your chair* or some other living room, dining room, or desk chair you've encountered. You'll find that you can't do it. That's because in the world of your mind, there are no chairs for you to see, sit on, or bump into. There is only the abstract idea of a *chair*.

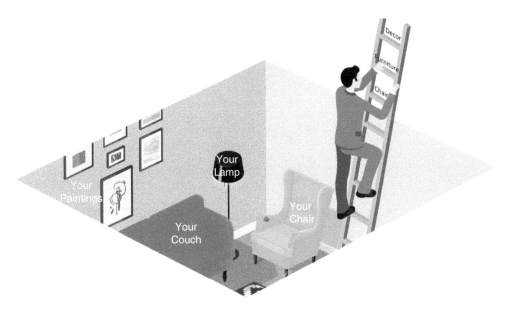

Figure 6.4 Climbing out of the physical world into the world of the abstract, where there is nothing to see.
Source: David Holt Design, Adobe.

Most managers consider discussions of abstraction to be pretty theoretical, verging on navel-gazing and questioning the nature of reality. Which makes this a good place to end the theory part of the book and move on to the practice part. We'll start with the practice of segmentation.

Notes

1 Jack Trout with Steve Rivkin, *Differentiate or Die: Survival in Our Era of Killer Competition* 2nd Ed. (Hoboken, NJ: John Wiley & Sons, 2008), 83–91.
2 W. Chan Kim and Renee Mauborgne, *Blue Ocean Strategy: How to Create Uncontested Market Space and Make the Competition Irrelevant* (Boston, MA: Harvard Business School Press, 2005).
3 Richard K. Lee and Nina E. Goodrich, *Value Innovation Works: Move Mountains…… Drive sustainable, profitable growth! Deliver exceptional value to the most important customers in your value chains. A "How To" guide* (Richard K. Lee, 2012), 66–101.
4 Felix Oberholzer-Gee, *Better Simpler Strategy: A Value-Based Guide to Exceptional Performance* (Boston, MA: Harvard Business Review Press, 2021), 195–218.
5 Niraj Dawar, *Tilt: Shifting Your Strategy from Products to Customers* (Boston, MA: Harvard Business Review Press, 2013), 131.
6 William Putsis, *Compete Smarter, Not Harder: A Process for Developing the Right Priorities Through Strategic Thinking* (Hoboken, NJ: John Wiley & Sons, 2014), 22–25.
7 Dawar, *op. cit.,* 133.
8 John Kenneth Galbraith, as quoted in Trout and Rivkin, *op. cit.,* 89.
9 Trout and Rivkin, *op. cit.,* 106.
10 Dawar, *op. cit.,* 137–141.
11 Michael Porter, "What is Strategy?" *Harvard Business Review*, November-December, 1996, 64.
12 Youngme Moon, *Different: Escaping the Competitive Herd* (New York, NY: Crown Business, 2010).
13 *Ibid*, 43.
14 *Ibid*, 65–66.
15 Peter Thiel, *Zero to One: Notes on Startups, or How to Build the Future* (London, UK: Virgin Books, 2014), 48–50.

16 James Manyika, Michael Chui, Jacques Bughin, Richard Dobbs, Peter Bisson, and Alex Marrs, "Disruptive technologies: Advances that will transform life, business, and the global economy," *McKinsey Global Institute Report*, May, 2013, https://www.mckinsey.com/~/media/McKinsey/Business%20Functions/McKinsey%20Digital/Our%20Insights/Disruptive%20technologies/MGI_Disruptive_technologies_Full_report_May2013.pdf.

17 W. Brian Arthur, *The Nature of Technology: What It Is and How It Evolves*, (New York, NY: Free Press, 2009), 28–29.

18 Dawar, *op. cit.*, 81–84.

19 Rita Gunther McGrath and Ian MacMillan, *The Entrepreneurial Mindset: Strategies for Continuously Creating Opportunity in an Age of Uncertainty* (Boston, MA: Harvard Business School Press, 2000), 86–89.

20 David C. Robertson with Kent Lineback, *The Power of Little Ideas: A Low-Risk, High-Reward Approach to Innovation* (Boston, MA: Harvard Business Review Press, 2017), ix-xi.

21 James Yang, *OC Patent Lawyer*, https://ocpatentlawyer.com/can-you-get-patent/.

22 Bruce Greenwald and Judd Kahn, *Competition Demystified: A Radically Simplified Approach to Business Strategy* (New York, NY: Penguin Group, 2005), 28.

23 Wikipedia contributors, "Trade secret," *Wikipedia, The Free Encyclopedia*, https://en.wikipedia.org/w/index.php?title=Trade_secret&oldid=998104562.

24 Wikipedia contributors, "Toyota Production System," *Wikipedia, The Free Encyclopedia*, https://en.wikipedia.org/w/index.php?title=Toyota_Production_System&oldid=1001544236.

25 Bharat Anand, David J. Collis, and Sophie Hood, "Danaher Corporation," *Harvard Business School Case Studies*, https://www.hbs.edu/faculty/Pages/item.aspx?num=35531.

26 Matthew May, *The Elegant Solution: Toyota's Formula for Mastering Innovation* (New York, NY: Simon & Schuster, 2007), xi.

27 Alan G. Robinson and Dean M. Schoeder, *The Idea-Driven Organization: Unlocking the Power of Bottom-up Ideas* (San Francisco, CA: Berrett-Koehler, 2014), 3–6.

28 John Besant, *High-Involvement Innovation: Building and Sustaining Competitive Advantage Through Continuous Change* (West Sussex, UK: John Wiley & Sons, 2003).

29 Robertson and Lineback, *op. cit.*, 103.

30 "IKEA supply chain: How does IKEA manage its inventory?" *Quickbooks Commerce*, https://www.tradegecko.com/blog/supply-chain-management/ikeas-inventory-management-strategy-ikea.

31 Suman Sarkar, *The Supply Chain Revolution: Innovative Sourcing and Logistics for a Fiercely Competitive World* (New York, NY: AMACOM, 2017), 3–4.

32 Jeff Toister, *The Service Culture Handbook: A Step-by-Step Guide to Getting Your Employees Obsessed with Customer Service* (Jeff Toister, 2017), 3–11.

33 S. I. Hayakawa and Alan R. Hayakawa, *Language in Thought and Action* 5th Ed. (New York, NY: Harcourt Brace Jovanovich, 1990), 84–86.

34 Rudolf Arnheim, *Visual Thinking* (Berkeley, CA: University of California Press, 1969), 9.

35 For an excellent example, see Pablo Picasso's 1945 painting titled "The Bull," where he progressively washes away more and more of the particulars of a fully-fleshed-out bull until nothing more than the bull's essential features remain.

36 Alfred North Whitehead, "The Education of an Englishman," *The Atlantic Monthly*, Vol. 138, 1926, 192.

7   Segmentation

The expression "be all things to all people" originated with the Apostle Paul, who said, "I am made all things to all men, that I might by all means save some."[1] In corporate-speak this translates to, "We make all things for all people, that we might by all means serve them." But what worked for Paul won't work for you. It's simply impossible to be all things to all the people in the market you serve, which means your differentiation strategy must target just those segments of the market you're capable of serving. This chapter explains how to identify the segments.

Supply Chain Segments

The first step in identifying a target market segment is deciding which *supply chain segment* to target. Different industries have different supply chains, some long and some short. Consider the examples shown in Figure 7.1 and explained below:

- *Figure 7.1a*: Manufacturing industries have relatively long supply chains. If you were the product manufacturer in this industry, you would need to decide whether to target your strategy at the wholesaler segment, the retailer segment, or the end-user segment, each of which desires different benefits. In this case, deciding which supply chain segment to target is more a matter of deciding where to start. You would eventually want to devise differentiation strategies for all the downstream segments. However, it's usually best to start with the end-user segment based on the logic that the retailer segment won't prefer your products if the end users don't prefer them, and the wholesalers won't prefer your products if the retailers don't prefer them.
- *Figure 7.1b*: In this case, if you were an aftermarket auto parts manufacturer selling to auto repair shops, your priority would *not* be the end users (the customers of the repair shops). Rather, it would be the auto repair shops themselves because they are the ones who make the decision to purchase the parts. In most circumstances, car owners don't know or care about the parts used to repair their cars so long as the car works after it's repaired. However, that's not always the case. NAPA Auto Parts promotes its car parts to end users as a way for repair shops to signal the quality of the parts they use. Intel employs a similar strategy with the "Intel Inside" campaign, which enables PC makers to signal the quality of the processor inside their computers.
- *Figure 7.1c*: Restaurant, hotel, retail, and other franchisors should first be concerned with devising an effective differentiation strategy for the end users of their offering. If the end users don't prefer the franchisor's brand, neither will prospective franchisees. However, it's fair to say that franchisors should be equally concerned about differentiating their brand among prospective franchisees, for it is they who make the decision to choose one franchisor rather than another.

DOI: 10.4324/9781003271703-8

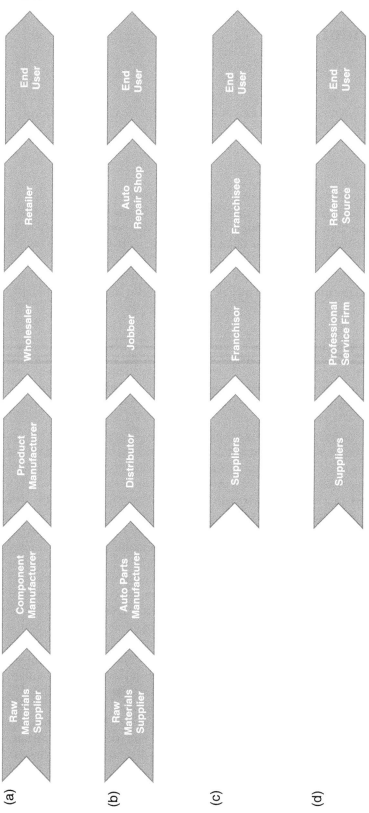

Figure 7.1 Supply chain segments.

- *Figure 7.1d*: Architects, lawyers, accountants, and most other professional service firms sell directly to the client (end user), so it makes sense to first focus on devising a differentiation strategy for prospective clients. Oftentimes, however, someone refers the client to the professional, so it makes sense to create a differentiation strategy for the referral sources, as well. But there are exceptions. Specialist physicians, for instance, usually rely on referrals from general practitioners, which means their primary concern should be with differentiating themselves among the general practitioners rather than the patients. And anesthesiologists are almost always chosen by surgeons, so anesthesiologists should target their differentiation strategy at the surgeons rather than the people they put to sleep.

Market Segments

It's rarely the case that you'll want to target all the customers in the chosen supply chain segment because, again, you can't be all things to all people. So you'll need to subdivide the supply chain segment into parts and choose one or more parts to focus on. A market—in this case, the chosen supply chain segment—consists of a group of customers. The market can be subdivided into smaller segments called *market segments*. All the customers in a market

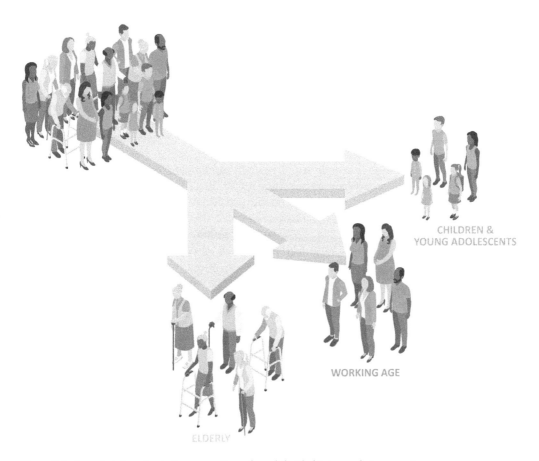

Figure 7.2 A market (supply chain segment) can be subdivided into market segments.
Source: David Holt Design, Adobe

Table 7.1 Commonly used segmentation variables for consumer and business markets

Consumer variables	Business variables
• Demographic	• Firmographic
• Geographic location	• Geographic location
• Socio-economic class	• Size of company
• Lifestyle	• Technology used
• User status	• User status
• Usage rate	• End-use application
• Purchase location	• Volume used
• Price paid	• Price paid
• Attitude	• Purchasing policy
• Purchase/use/situation occasion	• Purchase/use/situation occasion
• Brand loyalty	• Relationship with seller
• Benefit(s) sought	• Benefit(s) sought

segment have one or more characteristics in common. Consider the example shown in Figure 7.2, where the customers in the end-user market are segmented by age into three groups: children and young adolescents (all are under 15 years old), working age (all are 15–64 years old), and elderly (all are 65 years and older). Variables that are commonly used to segment consumer and business markets are listed in Table 7.1.

Target Market Segment

It's best to start by devising a differentiation strategy for the largest market segment you're able to serve, provided you can serve it profitably. We'll call that the *target market segment*. In every case, a company's target market segment will involve the geographic variable. For example, the target market segment for a flower shop might be all the end users in the city in which it is located or all the end users in the part of the city that surrounds the shop. Oftentimes, a company's target market segment is defined by the geographic variable and one or more other variables. An example is Curves, a health and fitness club chain that targets women who prefer not to exercise in the company of men. The target market segment for each club consists of health- and weight-conscious women (which is the value of the de-mographic variable) who live or work in the geographic area surrounding the club (which is the value of the geographic variable). A frequent combination of variables involves geo-graphic location and the price customers are willing to pay (referred to as *price paid* in Table 7.1). Imagine, for example, that the end users of a company's offering are located throughout the world and that there are end users who are willing to pay for low-, medium-, or high-priced offerings. As depicted at the end of the down arrow in Figure 7.3, the end-user supply chain segment can be segmented into six segments on the basis of geography and price. As depicted at the end of the up arrow, the company might decide that its target market segment should be medium-price customers located in the United States.

So far, the segmentation process I've described is as follows. The first step is to break the industry into supply chain segments. Then, one of the supply chain segments (in Figure 7.3, the end-user segment) is selected as the target of the differentiation strategy. The next step is to use one or more segmentation variables to subdivide the selected supply chain segment into market segments and choose one of the market segments as the target of your differ-entiation strategy, which, in Figure 7.3, are the end users located in the United States who are willing to pay medium-level prices. At this point, you'll need to rely on your knowledge of the target market segment to determine if (a) its members desire the attributes (and corresponding benefits) you are able to deliver and (b) you can achieve a competitive

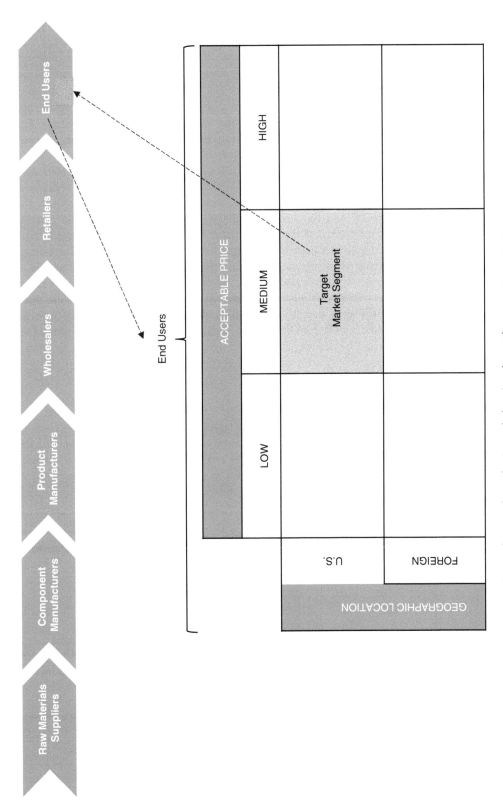

Figure 7.3 Segmenting the end users on the bases of geography and price and choosing the market segment to target.

advantage in the segment. Later, as explained in Chapter 10, you'll perform research to verify your determination and to elaborate on it. If it turns out you're wrong, you'll need to find a different market segment to target.

Roles

After identifying the target market segment, you may want to take the further step of sub-dividing it into the roles played by the people in the segment. As shown in Figure 7.4, a common way to subdivide a target market segment is to use the roles of *decision-maker, support team,* and *users,* although other roles may be appropriate in some industries.

Targeting a differentiation strategy at the three roles is more often done with B2B customers, where there is a purchasing department or a department head that makes the decision to buy the offering, a maintenance department or other team of people that support the offering after it is purchased, and the people who use the offering. An example is a car manufacturer that sells to companies that operate a large fleet of vans. These companies will typically have a purchasing department that makes the decision to purchase the vans, a maintenance department that maintains the vans, and drivers that use the vans. The people in each role will desire different attributes and benefits, all of which the car manufacturer needs to take into consideration when devising a differentiation strategy. In B2C settings, the three roles are often played by the same person, such as the consumer who makes the decision to buy a car, maintains it, and drives it. Nonetheless, in each role, the consumer has a unique set of attributes and benefits that he desires, all of which need to be considered when devising a differentiation strategy.

Smaller Market Segments

After you've devised a differentiation strategy for the target market segment, it's a good idea to devise specialized strategies for the smaller market segments that make up the target market segment. The first step of the process is to specify the target market segment using a sentence like, "The target market consists of customers located _____ who desire _____." For example,

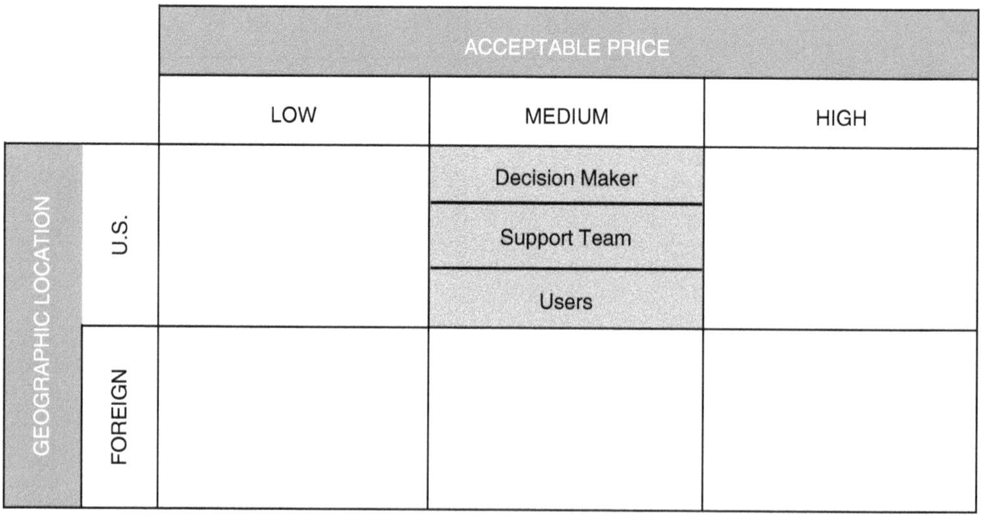

		ACCEPTABLE PRICE		
		LOW	MEDIUM	HIGH
GEOGRAPHIC LOCATION	U.S.		Decision Maker	
			Support Team	
			Users	
	FOREIGN			

Figure 7.4 The target market segment can be divided into the decision-maker, support team, and user roles.

"The target market consists of customers located in the USA who desire lodging in mid-price, full-service hotels" or "The target market is middle-aged women who live or work in the vicinity of our health and fitness clubs who don't want to work out in the company of men."

The second step, illustrated in Figure 7.5, is to use the segmentation variables in Table 7.1 to subdivide the target market segment into progressively smaller segments (subsegments, sub-subsegments, etc.). You might want to start with the traditional way of segmenting the market in your industry, then use other segmentation variables to subdivide each of those segments into progressively smaller segments. For example, Figure 7.5 shows that the usual way of segmenting hotel guests is by purchase occasion—there are guests who are traveling for the purpose of *business*, for the purpose of participating in a *group* function at the hotel, and for the purpose of *leisure*. Each of the segments can be divided into progressively smaller segments. Group travelers, for example, can be divided into business and association groups and social groups. Social groups can be divided into wedding groups and reunion groups. Reunion groups can be divided into high school reunions and military reunions. And so on. You should continue the process until you reach segments that you can visualize and talk about.

The third and last step is to identify the unique attributes desired by each of the smallest segments, i.e., by each of the segments in the bottom row of the hierarchy. (You'll do that by performing interview and observation research, as explained in Chapter 10.) Then ask *why* they desire each attribute. The answers reveal the benefits they want to derive from the attributes. The point of this exercise is to gain insights into ways to differentiate your offering by providing the attributes and benefits desired by each of the smallest segments.

The smaller the segments you examine (i.e., the lower you go in the hierarchy of segments), the more likely you are to identify attributes and benefits that are not already recognized and provided by the competitors in your industry. In other words, the lowest parts of the hierarchy are where you are most likely to find useful insights. Two of my favorite examples in the hotel industry are these:

- The Monaco Hotel in Chicago identified a segment consisting of tall athletes traveling with sports teams who would benefit from the comfort and convenience of larger-than-normal accommodations. They responded by adding 86-inch-long beds and touting the fact that their hotel rooms have ten-foot-tall ceilings, both of which differentiated their hotel with regard to the tall athlete segment. Were he made aware of this example, Michael Porter would be quick to point out that the hotel differentiated itself not by trying to do what competing hotels do, only better, e.g., by being cleaner, friendlier, and so forth. Instead, the Monaco Hotel differentiated itself by offering something different.
- Tokyo's Imperial Hotel identified a segment consisting of high school class reunion organizers who wanted to be relieved of the time-consuming responsibility of planning the class reunion. The hotel responded by offering a class reunion organizing service, thereby getting the beleaguered organizers to steer their reunions to the hotel. Here, again, Porter would explain that the Imperial Hotel differentiates itself by doing something different instead of trying to do what its rivals are doing, only better.

In the B2B sector, where companies have far fewer customers than their B2C brethren, the smallest target market segment may be a segment of one, which is to say, a single company and the individuals within it who play the roles of decision-maker, support team, and users. This is especially true in circumstances where a handful of customers account for a significant share of a company's business. Here, again, the objective should be to determine the unique attributes that each company and each role within the company desires and the benefits that

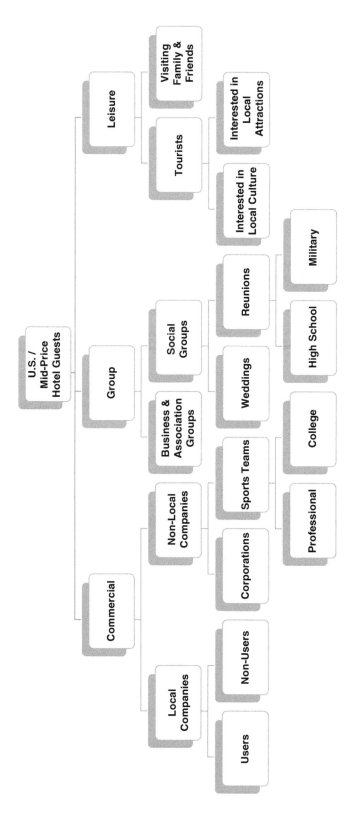

Figure 7.5 The target market segment can be divided into progressively smaller segments.

correspond to the attributes, then create ways of providing more of the desired attributes and benefits.

In their book *The Entrepreneurial Mindset: Strategies for Continuously Creating Opportunity in an Age of Uncertainty*, Rita Gunther McGrath and Ian MacMillan provide an example that illustrates the benefit of segmenting a target market into progressively smaller segments.[2] Blyth Industries manufactures candles and accessories. As a "hobby," Bob Goergen purchased the company in the late 1980s for $200,000. By 1996, he had grown the company from a $3 million maker of religious candles to a global candle and accessories company that achieved nearly $500 million in sales. How? As shown in Figure 7.6, he did it by segmenting the candle market into progressively smaller niche markets and then creating candles and accessories specifically designed for each segment. (Note that his segmentation scheme was far more extensive and detailed than the one that is shown in Figure 7.6. For example, it includes the holidays for different countries and religions.)

There are five important take-home lessons in the Blyth Industries example. The first lesson is the efficacy of using what is variously referred to as the *purchase occasion variable* (as it is termed in Table 7.1), the *use occasion variable*, or the *situation variable*. The idea is that customers purchase or use an offering on particular occasions or in particular situations. In the foregoing hotel example, the purchase occasions were traveling for the purpose of business, group events, and leisure. In the candle example shown in Figure 7.6, people use candles on the occasion of being in a home, a restaurant, a church, and so on. The home use is subdivided into using candles in the various rooms of the home, and the dining room situation is further divided into the situations of using candles for celebration and for mood. Then each of these is divided into specific celebration situations and mood situations. Common purchase occasions in B2B markets are situations in which customers have different levels of urgency (e.g., emergency and stock out situations), situations in which customers use a product for different applications, and situations in which customers need different order sizes or a different size of some part of an order. In all these examples, customers buy or use an offering on different occasions or, said differently, when they are in different situations.

The second lesson to be learned from the Blythe Industries example is the value of the earlier-mentioned practice of progressively segmenting down to the level of segments you can visualize and talk about. In Figure 7.6, for example, it's much easier to think of candles and accessories for Easter than it is for Religious Holidays. (Note that to keep the size of Figure 7.6 manageable, not all the candle segments are identified and not all the segments in the figure have been progressively divided into visualizable segments.)

The third lesson is the value of adopting a niche-market differentiation strategy, or what Michael Porter refers to as a *focus* differentiation strategy. The strategy starts by identifying niche segments that rivals have yet to identify, or that they are ignoring, or that they are doing a poor job of serving. The next step is to understand the attributes and benefits desired by each segment and use that understanding to create differentiated offerings for each of them. The final step of a niche-market differentiation strategy is to dominate many small niches in rapid succession to build economies of scale and scope. Remember the earlier example of Danaher Corporation, which uses this strategy and works to achieve a market share that is four times the size of its closest competitor.

The fourth lesson relates to the first three.[3] While purchase occasions or use occasions or situations, however you care to characterize them, are a useful and under-appreciated way to segment a market, there are many other variables for doing so, as Table 7.1 makes clear. Experimenting with the different variables will result in many different segmentation schemes. Even more schemes are made possible by applying different variables at the different levels of a segmentation hierarchy. That there are many segmentation variables and combinations of variables you can use makes it difficult to decide which variable to start with and

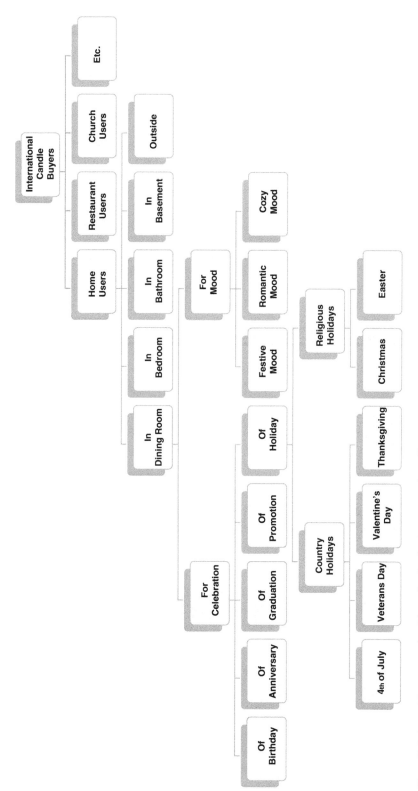

Figure 7.6 A partial segmentation hierarchy for the international candle market.

which ones to use at subsequent levels. Unfortunately, there's no way around this. The only thing you can do is take the time to experiment with various ways of segmenting the target market and learn to live with the fact that many of the experiments will fail to bear fruit. Living with that fact is made easier by the knowledge that the successful segmentation schemes (you may find more than one useful scheme) will reward you with exclusive insights into segments and niches. In many cases, you can use the insights to build an overwhelming competitive advantage in the segments and niches before your competitors catch on to your insight.

The fifth lesson is to remember that your goal is to apply the offering–function–benefit trilogy to the lowest segments in the hierarchy. For each of the segments, you want to know what attributes the segment desires, the function(s) the members of the segment have assigned to the attribute, and the benefits that are produced by the functions. These are the insights you should be seeking, for they are the ones that will enable you to differentiate your offering.

While a management team will benefit from performing the segmentation process on its own, the process will be far more insightful if it includes the interview, observation, and other forms of customer research explained in Chapter 10. The Tokyo Imperial Hotel is a good example of the insights to be gained by doing customer research, which in their case took the form of observation and an employee idea system. A waiter in one of its restaurants overheard (observed) a high school reunion organizer bemoaning the fact that arranging the reunion had consumed a burdensome amount of her time. The waiter relayed the information to the employee idea group, and the hotel responded with the class reunion organizing service. Without the employee idea system, it's likely the waiter's observation would have been missed by the hotel.

If you're interested in learning about more-sophisticated segmentation methods, a good resource is the book *Market Segmentation: How to do it and how to profit from it*, written by Malcolm McDonald and Ian Dunbar, principals of the Market Segmentation Company.[4] They describe a process for subdividing the target market segment into what they call *micro-segments*. Their method includes the use of visual and mathematical methods for performing what is known as *cluster analysis*.

Bottom-up Segmentation

So far, we've looked at top-down ways of identifying market segments. Other methods employ a bottom-up approach. Rather than starting at the top with a large market segment and working down to identify progressively smaller segments, bottom-up methods work by first interviewing and observing a collection of customers and then working up to identify the market segments of which they are a part. In the social sciences, this approach is described as working up from the data to arrive at a *grounded theory*, i.e., a theory that is grounded in the data.[5] With bottom-up segmentation methods, the theory that is grounded in the data is that some set of market segments exist, each of which seeks a different set of attributes and benefits.

In his book *Laddering: Unlocking the Potential of Consumer Behavior*, the consumer researcher Eric Holtzclaw explains that the laddering method involves interviewing and observing a collection of customers and then analyzing the interviews and observations to identify the more general themes that connect or summarize the interview data.[6] The themes are analogous to the way the more general concept *furniture* connects or summarizes the more specific concepts *couch*, *chair*, *table*, and *lamp*, except that in this case, a general market segment (theme) connects a number of the more specific comments and observations in the interview and observation transcripts (the data). In the grounded theory process, finding themes in the data is called *coding*. The team method for doing it is called *formal indication*.[7] The processes for performing the coding and the formal indication methods are explained in later chapters.

One of Holtzclaw's laddering case studies concerns female baby boomers, the demographic segment consisting of women born between the years 1946 and 1964. The laddering process was applied to discern their motives for going on a cruise. The interviewees were asked very general questions about their lives before being asked more specific questions about their attitudes toward cruise travel. The analysis of the interview transcripts revealed three market segments—destination, party, and leisure. The *destination segment* chooses a cruise based on its destination. This segment doesn't much care about the ship so long as it has food and a place to sleep. They never want to travel to the same place twice, and they want their passport stamped with as many exotic locales as possible. The *party segment* cruises for the party. They want the ship to be as new as possible and offer a variety of dance venues, bars, casinos, and onboard activities. The *leisure segment* wants to be pampered. They want poolside lounging, spas, hot tubs, and a variety of fine dining options, and they prefer to spend their time with a select few people. Knowing the attributes and corresponding benefits sought by the three segments enables a cruise line to create more and better ways to differentiate its cruise ship offerings.

An extreme, but potentially useful, application of bottom-up segmentation is to start with an observation of, or a conversation with, a single person or company, i.e., to start with a single piece of data. The idea is to understand the attributes and benefits that are desired by the person or company and then do research to determine if the attributes and benefits are desired by a group of people or companies that is large enough to constitute a segment. For example, the high school reunion service at the Tokyo Imperial Hotel started with overhearing a single reunion organizer and then asking if there were enough high school reunion organizers, or other kinds of reunion organizers, to justify a reunion organizing service. And the 86-inch-long beds at the Monaco Hotel may have been prompted by a single observation of some tall basketball players checking into the hotel.

In this chapter, you learned how to do segmentation and the two reasons for doing it. The first reason is to identify the market segment(s) that will be the target of your differentiation strategy. The second reason is to identify ways to differentiate your offering within each segment. Attribute methods are another way to identify differentiation opportunities. We'll take a look at them next.

Notes

1 New International Version of the Bible, 1 Corinthians 9:22: "To the weak became I as weak, that I might gain the weak: I am made all things to all men, that I might by all means save some," https://www.biblegateway.com/passage/?search=I+Corinthians+9%3A22&version=NIV.

2 Rita Gunther McGrath and Ian MacMillan, *The Entrepreneurial Mindset: Strategies for Continuously Creating Opportunity in an Age of Uncertainty* (Boston, MA: Harvard Business School Press, 2000), 52–56. The authors describe the subsegments in much more detail than is provided here.

3 Thomas V. Bonoma and Benson P. Shapiro, *Segmenting the Industrial Market* (Lexington, MA: Lexington Books, 1983), 15–23. The content of this paragraph is based on insights provided by Bonoma and Shapiro.

4 Malcolm McDonald and Ian Dubar, *Market Segmentation: How to do it and how to profit from it* Revised 4th ed. (West Sussex, UK: John Wiley & Sons, 2012).

5 Anslem L. Strauss, *Qualitative Analysis For Social Scientists* (Cambridge, UK: Cambridge University Press, 1987), 22–39.

6 Eric Holtzclaw, *Laddering: Unlocking the Potential of Consumer Behavior* (Hoboken, NJ: John Wiley & Sons, 2013).

7 Christian Madsbjerg and Mikkel B. Rasmussen, *The Moment of Clarity: Using the Human Sciences to Solve Your Toughest Business Problems* (Boston, MA: Harvard Business Review Press, 2014), 115–118.

8 Attributes

In this chapter, we're going to examine three more ways of identifying differentiation opportunities, each of which centers on the concept of *attributes*. The first method involves the earlier-described *strategy canvas*. The second method pertains to *attribute maps* and the third to *attribute lines*. Remember that an attribute is a property value of an offering or one of its components. Also remember that offerings exist at three levels—the level of individual products and services, where objects and events are the components, the level of bundles and complements, where the components are the core and supplementary products, services, programs, and systems, and the company level, where the sales and marketing activities, the channels of distribution, and the customer relationship activities are the components.

Strategy Canvas

In 2005, INSEAD professors W. Chan Kim and Renee Mauborgne published *Blue Ocean Strategy: How to Create Uncontested Market Space and Make the Competition Irrelevant*.[1] It went on to become an international bestseller. Amazon reports that the book has sold more than 4 million copies and is being published in a record-breaking 46 languages on 5 continents.[2] In 2017, Kim and Mauborgne followed with the publication of *Blue Ocean Shift Beyond Competing: Proven Steps to Inspire Confidence and Seize New Growth*.[3] The term *blue ocean* is used to evoke the image of competing alone in a blue area of the ocean instead of an area that is red with your blood and that of your competitors as you battle each other for the same customers. The idea is to stand apart (swim apart, actually) from your competitors by differentiating your offering.

Both books describe a method that centers on the concept of a strategy canvas similar to the one illustrated and explained in Chapter 6 and reproduced in Figure 8.1. (You may want to review the explanation in Chapter 6 before you go on.) If you're familiar with the form of strategy canvas used by Kim and Mauborgne, you'll notice the following differences in Figure 8.1. Kim and Mauborgne list the industry's purchase criteria on the horizontal axis rather than the vertical axis, they don't rank the purchase criteria in order of importance, and they use a five-point rather than a seven-point performance scale to indicate how well an offering's attribute performs on a purchase criterion. Another way in which Kim and Mauborgne's strategy canvas differs is that they refer to the purchase criteria as *factors of competition*, where I refer to them as *purchase criteria* and others refer to them as *value elements*[4] or *value drivers*[5].

A second strategy canvas, this one comparing the strategies of IKEA and the high-end contemporary furniture store chain Copenhagen, is shown in Figure 8.2. There are a number of things to note about the Airbnb and IKEA strategy canvases. Knowing these things will make it much easier for you to create your own strategy canvas.

DOI: 10.4324/9781003271703-9

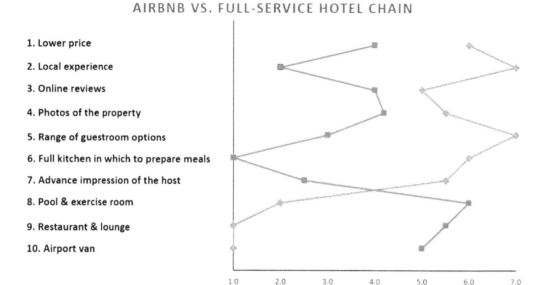

Figure 8.1 Strategy canvas comparing Airbnb to traditional full-service hotel chains.

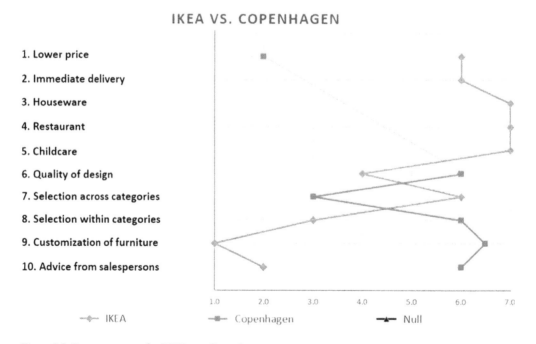

Figure 8.2 Strategy canvas for IKEA vs. Copenhagen.

- The first thing is that a company's differentiation strategy can be compared to a class of competitors (e.g., traditional full-service hotels on the Airbnb canvas) or to a single competitor (e.g., Copenhagen on the IKEA canvas).
- Second, recall from Chapter 5 that offerings are "festooned" with properties. Customers use some of those properties as purchase criteria. The purchase criteria shown on the left side of the two strategy canvases are the properties that the target market (Airbnb's target market in the first case and IKEA's target market in the second) consider when deciding from whom to buy. The purchase criteria are listed in order of importance to the target market. As a matter of convention, price is always listed first.
- Third, remember that a purchase criterion (property) is a variable. A variable is called a variable because its values vary. The values of the purchase criteria variables are what we refer to as attributes. For example, in the case of the IKEA strategy canvas, one of the purchase criteria is houseware. IKEA has the attribute of offering houseware, whereas Copenhagen has the attribute of not offering houseware. Another purchase criterion is customization of the furniture, such as the ability to customize fabrics and colors. An attribute of Copenhagen is that it offers a high amount of customization, whereas IKEA has the attribute of offering very little customization.
- The fourth thing to note is that purchase criteria and attributes can exist at any of the three levels of an offering—the product or service level (e.g., the amount of selection across categories in a retail outlet), the bundle and complements level (e.g., whether a home and auto insurance bundle is offered), and the company level (e.g., the amount of advertising that is conducted).
- The fifth thing worthy of note is the way the strategy canvas shows where the competitors have positioned themselves relative to each other with respect to their performance on each purchase criterion, i.e., with respect to their attributes. As explained in Chapter 6, the graph line on the strategy canvas enables you to easily compare your differentiation strategy with your competitor's.
- The sixth thing to note requires that you compare the Airbnb and IKEA strategy canvases. Note how Airbnb and its competitors are using their performance on the same purchase criteria to differentiate themselves (or not). In other words, they are all trying to be different in the same way. Being different in the same way isn't necessarily a bad thing, so long as the offering significantly outperforms its competitors on a purchase criterion. Remember Peter Thiel's advice that a company should have as its objective to be an order-of-magnitude (10X) better than its competitors, which usually requires that the difference be driven by a superior technology. Even better, however, is to do what IKEA has done, which is to create some entirely new attributes to differentiate itself—immediate delivery, houseware, a restaurant, and childcare. Rather than trying to be different on the purchase criteria everyone else is competing on, IKEA has created four entirely different ways to be different.
- The last thing to note is that Airbnb and IKEA have chosen to underperform their competitors on the less important purchase criteria. Why would they do that? Why not outperform their competitors on all the criteria? The answer takes us all the way back to the gap diagrams in Chapter 1, where you learned that a company has a competitive advantage when, and only when, it makes more money than its competitors. Outperforming competitors on the most important purchase criteria usually requires a company to spend more money on those criteria. To spend that money and still achieve a higher profit, the company must reduce the amount of money it spends on the less important purchase criteria.

As explained in the last chapter, the first step in creating a differentiation strategy is to segment the market and choose a segment to target. Once you've identified a target market segment, you can create a strategy canvas for it. The first step in creating the strategy canvas is to identify your customer's *next-best alternative*.[6] The next-best alternative is the entity with whom you want to compare yourself on the strategy canvas. As previously explained, most of the time the customer's next-best alternative is your closest competitor(s). But in some circumstances, the next-best alternative is the do-it-yourself option, the status quo option, or the previous version option. Going forward, I'll assume the customer's next-best alternative is the company's closest competitor(s).

The second part of completing the strategy canvas is to identify the purchase criteria, which, again, are the properties customers consider when deciding from whom to buy in your industry. Kim and Mauborgne suggest that you list between 5 and 12 purchase criteria—5 to get your team members to think about more than price and 12 to keep them focused on the most important criteria. While this sounds simple enough, I've yet to work with a management team that could easily create a complete and accurate list of the purchase criteria in their industry, much less their order of importance. As it turns out, this isn't unusual. In her book titled *The Strategist: Be the Leader Your Business Needs*, Professor Cynthia Montgomery, who teaches Harvard Business School's executive education strategy courses, explains that many executive teams are unable to identify the needs their businesses fill or the attributes that distinguish them from their competitors.[7] She goes on to note the confusion this must cause in their companies.

To get around this problem, before facilitating a strategy workshop, it's a good practice to capture the purchase criteria and attributes that are touted in your and your competitors' marketing materials. Then have the list available to jump-start the conversation during the workshop. Another useful practice is to tell your management team to imagine themselves as your customers and have them list the purchase criteria they would consider when deciding whether to buy your offering or a competing offering.

Remember that customers and managers tend to talk about purchase criteria and attributes at different levels of abstraction. Earlier I used the example of a car. Sometimes people talk about a car's antilock brakes, which is a specific, physical attribute. Other times they talk about safety, which is a general, abstract attribute. Multiple specific attributes are oftentimes part of a more general, abstract attribute. For example, antilock brakes, airbags, adaptive headlights, backup cameras, reinforced bodies, forward collision warning, lane departure warning, and blind-spot detection all contribute to the safety of a car. When placing the purchase criteria on the strategy canvas, you and your team should keep in mind that some criteria are better described using slightly abstract classifications of multiple specific criteria (e.g., safety rather than antilock brakes and all the rest). And, again, you should also remember that purchase criteria can pertain to the level of individual products and services, to the level of bundles and complements, and to the company level.

The third step in completing the strategy canvas is to rank the purchase criteria in order of importance to the customer. When a team of managers is ranking the criteria, you'll need to use a voting method and tally all the votes. Following are three ways of voting. The methods are best carried out with a voting software tool:

- Simple Voting Methods: The first way is to have the management team use one of several simple voting methods for rank ordering a list. One method is to have everyone list the purchase criteria from most important to least important. If there are 10 criteria on the list, the top-ranked criterion is assigned 10 points, the next-highest criterion is assigned 9 points, and so on. For each criterion, all the voters' points are added together and the vote totals are used to rank the purchase criteria. Another method is to assign everyone some number of points (say, 100) and have them distribute the points among the purchase criteria according to their level of importance. Then, for each criterion, add the points together to determine where the group thinks it is located on the list. A third method is to have everyone rate each criterion on an importance scale (say, a 1–9 scale), and then add together the voters' ratings to determine the group's ranking.

- Pairwise Comparison: Pairwise comparison is a more sophisticated way of ranking the purchase criteria. This involves comparing one purchase criterion with another and deciding which one is more important. The criterion that wins is assigned one point and the one that loses is assigned zero points. In the event of a tie, each criterion is assigned one-half point. After comparing all the purchase criteria with one another, they are listed in order of the total points they were assigned. While more accurate and insightful than simple voting, pairwise comparison is more time-consuming because of the large number of comparisons that are required to complete the vote. You can use the formula $n(n-1)/2$ to calculate the number of pairwise comparisons that are necessary. For example, for a list of 10 purchase criteria, $10(10-1)/2 = 45$ comparisons are necessary.

- Analytical Hierarchy Process: A third, more sophisticated, and even more time-consuming way of ranking the purchase criteria is the analytical hierarchy process (AHP). Without going into the details, the AHP process involves creating a hierarchy of progressively more specific choice criteria, weighting the criteria, and then using the criteria to make pairwise choices among the purchase criteria. A comprehensive description of the analytic hierarchy process is available at this reference.[8]

The fourth step in completing the strategy canvas is to judge your performance and your competitor's performance (or some other next-best alternative's performance) on each of the purchase criteria. I use a 7-point Likert scale, but you can use a 5-point or 9-point scale or any other odd-numbered scale you prefer. The two principal ways of measuring performance are *natural measures* and *constructed measures*.[9] The performance on some kinds of purchase criteria can be measured or counted using a *natural form of measurement*, like miles per gallon, store hours, number of locations, advertising impressions, and so on. Once you've measured or counted the level of performance, you'll need to convert the natural measure to the Likert scale you are using, as explained in this endnote.[10] Other kinds of purchase criteria, like image and attractiveness, do not have a natural way of measuring them, so it's necessary to *construct a form of measurement* using a Likert scale, then have your management team (and later, customers) judge where your offering and the competing offerings fall on the scale. It's a good practice to create a verbal description for each point on the scale to make it easier for people to judge where a performance should fall on the scale.

You should first prepare a strategy canvas that compares your current performance on the purchase criteria with your competitors' performances. This is your "as is" or "current" strategy canvas.[11] In order to "step out of the box" (create a new differentiation strategy), you first need to understand the box you plan to exit. That means, as just explained, understanding who your competitors are, the customer's purchase criteria for your kind of offering, their order of importance to customers, and your relative performance on the criteria. A veridical understanding of these things creates a solid foundation for building your new differentiation strategy. That's why, before you start to build your "to be" or "new" strategy canvas, it's best to perform the customer interview and other research described in Chapter 10 to make sure the "as is" strategy canvas you've created coincides with what customers think, i.e., that it is veridical.

Once you're satisfied that the "as is" strategy canvas is veridical, you should create the "to be" or "new" strategy canvas. The "to be" canvas maps your strategy as you want it to be, which is to say, it maps your new differentiation strategy. The "to be" canvas is created by examining the "as is" canvas and answering the following four questions, which Kim and

Mauborgne refer to as the *Four Actions Framework*.[12] (Kim and Mauborgne use the term *factors of competition* in the questions instead of *purchase criteria*.)

1   On which purchase criteria should our performance be *raised well above* the industry's standard? Note, for example, that in Figure 8.1 Airbnb has chosen to raise its performance on *local experience* well above the industry standard. And here again, it's important to remember that you should shoot for a performance that is an order-of-magnitude better.

2   Which attributes should we *create* that the industry has never offered? This is about creating altogether new ways of competing by offering new attributes at one or more of the three levels of an offering. As shown in Figure 8.2, IKEA created the attributes of *immediate delivery*, *houseware*, *restaurant*, and *childcare*.

3   On which purchase criteria should our performance be *reduced well below* the industry's standard? This is about minding Pietersen's gap in order to achieve or maintain the superior profitability that is required to have a competitive advantage, as both Airbnb and IKEA have done with the least important purchase criteria.

4   Which of the purchase criteria the industry takes for granted should we *eliminate?* The same mind-the-gap logic applies to choosing not to compete on certain purchase criteria. This usually applies to purchase criteria the industry continues to compete on because they fail to realize the criteria are no longer important to customers.

How do you generate ideas for new attributes (question #2 above)? The short answers are *segmentation, attribute maps and lines, action frameworks, customer research*, and *creative problem-solving*. In Chapter 7, you saw how segmentation can uncover ideas for new attributes (e.g., a reunion organizing service). Later in this chapter, you're going to learn how attribute maps and lines can stimulate ideas for new attributes. In Chapter 9, you'll learn how action frameworks like the *consumption chain* and *jobs-to-be-done* methods are used to generate ideas for new attributes. Chapter 10 explains how customer research reveals ideas for new attributes. And in Chapter 11, we'll look at how you can create new attributes by using creative thinking methods to solve the problems your customers encounter.

How do you generate ideas for improving your performance on a given purchase criterion (question #1 above)? Here, the short answers are *creative problem-solving* and *activity systems*. Most business problems are performance improvement problems that take one of two forms. The first form is *How can we increase X?*, where X might be prices, market share, employee retention, and so forth. The second form is *"How can we decrease Y?"*, where Y might be expenses, customer churn, liability lawsuits, and so on. In our case, the performance improvement problem has to do with increasing your performance on a given purchase criterion. Here, again, creative problem-solving comes to the rescue, including the problem-solving method employed by the management consulting firm McKinsey & Company and the design thinking method employed by design firms like IDEO. Both methods are explained in Chapter 11. Another way of improving performance is to create a dependency diagram for the activity system that generates the attributes, as will be explained in Chapter 13.

Attribute Maps

The strategy canvas is one way of mapping your offering's attributes. Rita Gunther McGrath and Ian MacMillan explain another way in their earlier referenced book *The Entrepreneurial Mindset: Strategies for Continuously Creating Opportunity in an Age of Uncertainty*.[13] As detailed below, their *attribute map* consists of a nine-cell, three-by-three matrix in which the first row consists of three kinds of positive attributes, the second row consists of three types of negative attributes, and the third row consists of two types of neutral attributes (one of the cells in this row is null). As with the strategy canvas, the first step in creating an attribute map is to identify your target market segment and your principal competitor(s). The next step is to assign your offering's attributes to the eight cells in the matrix.

The three cells in the first row all have to do with positive attributes. The three cells are progressively more positive.

- Nonnegotiable: Customers expect nonnegotiable attributes to perform at least as well as the competing attributes. This is what was previously described as a *must-have* attribute, a *table stakes* attribute, or a *hygienic* attribute. You will lose a competitive battle if you don't have the attribute but having it won't help you win the battle. As earlier noted, the cleanliness of a hotel is a non-negotiable attribute. Customers expect that a hotel will be clean and that it will be no less clean than its competitors. A clean hotel gets you in the game, but cleanliness doesn't determine who wins the game. The objective here should be to reduce the cost of the nonnegotiables, if possible.
- Differentiator: A differentiator attribute causes customers to prefer your offering because you offer it and your competitors don't, or because you do a significantly better job of offering the attribute. IKEA'S performance on *immediate delivery* is an example of a differentiating attribute. Here the objectives are to improve your performance on existing differentiators and introduce meaningful new ones. As earlier explained, differentiators are usually driven by technologies that enable a 10X improvement.
- Exciters: An exciter attribute is one that is so overwhelmingly positive that it becomes the primary reason why customers purchase the offering. An example is Novo Nordisk's previously mentioned injection pen, which comes prefilled with multiple pre-measured doses of insulin and other drugs, thereby relieving users of the arduous task of filling the syringes themselves, sometimes when their illness causes their hands to shake. As with differentiators, the objective is to improve your performance on existing exciters and introduce new ones. Meaningful performance improvements are usually driven by technologies that enable an order-of-magnitude improvement.

The second row of the attribute map contains negative attributes. In this case, the three cells are progressively more negative. McGrath and MacDonald point out that fixing negative attributes that your competitors have failed to fix is an often-overlooked opportunity, and they note that good sources of insight into negative attributes are salespeople, complaint handlers, and return processors:

- Tolerables: Tolerables are attributes that customers don't like but are willing to tolerate. An example is the way people used to tolerate not knowing exactly when their taxi or bus would arrive. Then along came the Uber app and similar apps that enable people to know the precise location of their taxi or bus and exactly when it will arrive. Another example is the grips on kitchen utensils that make it difficult for arthritic hands to hold them. OXO responded with its Good Grips® line of large, easy-to-grip handles for potato peelers, spatulas, can openers, and other kitchen utensils. With tolerables, the objective is to be the first, or only, one to see and solve them.
- Dissatisfiers: These are attributes that differentiate an offering, but in the wrong direction. It is much easier to convince customers to switch from a competitor's offering to your offering if you can convince them they can avoid dealing with the dissatisfier by making the move. For example, online used car dealers like Carvana are

having great success with convincing customers they can avoid the haggling and high-pressure sales tactics of traditional used car dealers. CarMax, with its large inventory, no-haggle pricing, and generous return policy, is also pulling business away from traditional used car dealers. Here, the strategy is to identify and eliminate dissatisfiers, including those that are exclusively yours as well as any you share with your competitors.

- Enragers: Enragers amp up dissatisfaction to the level of fury or disgust. Netflix owes its start to its founder being enraged by Blockbuster's late fees. Considering that Blockbuster went bankrupt while Netflix prospered, it appears that a lot of Blockbuster's customers felt the same way. As with dissatisfiers, the objective is to identify and eliminate enragers.

The third row of the attribute map contains two types of neutral attributes, classified as "So Whats?" and "Parallels." So Whats? are attributes that do not influence the customer's purchase decision. Parallels influence the decision indirectly.

- So Whats?: These are attributes that evoke responses like "So What?" and "Who cares?" One sort of neutral attribute adds cost without adding value. Another sort of neutral attribute is an attribute that people like, but not enough to pay for it. It's usually a good idea to eliminate neutrals.
- Parallels: Parallels are attributes that differentiate an offering but are offered in parallel with its primary attributes. Frequent flyer mileage, for example, is an attribute that is offered in parallel with an airline's flights. In many cases, it's necessary to offer a parallel in order to remain competitive.

Note that by including negative and neutral attributes, the attribute map often reveals attributes that are missed by the strategy canvas, which tends to focus on positive attributes. As with the strategy canvas, you should conduct customer research to ensure your attribute map is veridical. Also, you can use the above-described methods to generate ideas for adding attributes and improving attribute performance. McGrath and MacMillan provide multiple examples of attribute maps in their book. The examples are worth reviewing because they serve to stimulate ideas for adding attributes and improving attribute performance.

Attribute Lines

Harold Hotelling (1895–1973) was a statistician and economist. He is known, in part, for what are termed (what else?) Hotelling lines. An example of a Hotelling line is shown in Figure 8.3. The line shows two businesses, labeled X and Y, located at opposite ends of the line—say, for example, two ice cream stands located at opposite ends of a beach. Customers are assumed to be evenly distributed along the line/beach. Hotelling's law holds that, all else being equal, customers located to the left of the vertical line will prefer the shorter walk to ice cream stand X, and customers located to the right of the vertical line will prefer the shorter walk to ice cream stand Y. The location of the vertical line is determined by the price difference. If the two ice cream stands have the same price, the line is located midway

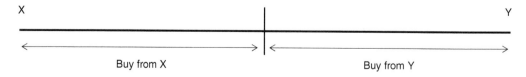

Figure 8.3 A Hotelling line.

between them. If ice cream stand X drops its price relative to ice cream stand Y, the vertical line moves to the right of the center, meaning more customers want to buy from X. Alternatively, if ice cream stand Y has a lower price than ice cream stand X, the line moves to the left of the center, meaning that more customers want to buy from Y.

In his book *Competitive Solutions: The Strategist's Toolkit*, Preston McAfee notes that Hotelling lines are a fundamental tool for analyzing product differentiation because many types of differentiation can be analyzed using line segments. "When the differentiator is not physical space, but some characteristic of the product," he explains, "the line is used to represent the product characteristics and to represent consumer preferences."[14] Among the examples McAfee points to are low-sugar breakfast cereals located on the left pole of the line and high-sugar breakfast cereals located on the right pole of the line, low-fat potato chips on the left and high-fat ones on the right, and lightweight laptop computers occupying the left pole and heavy ones occupying the right pole. Other examples are the purchase criteria listed on the strategy canvases shown in Figures 8.1 and 8.2, where each of the criteria has a corresponding performance line that is, in fact, a Hotelling line on which a 1–7 scale is used to identify the low- and high-performance values for the criterion. Since *attribute line* is a friendlier term than *Hotelling line*, we'll use the former term going forward (with apologies to Dr. Hotelling).

Gary Hamel is a prolific author, management consultant, and former business school professor. In his book *Leading the Revolution*, he designs a hypothetical cyber business school MBA program[15] by first describing the salient attributes of a traditional business school and then describing their polar opposites.[16] The two poles are shown in Table 8.1. The combination of his cyber school example and the idea of attribute lines points to another way of using attributes to identify differentiation opportunities. The process is to first list the properties (variables) of an offering (listed in the middle column in Table 8.1), then identify the traditional value of each attribute (in the left column), then specify the polar opposite value (in the right column), and finally decide where you want your offering to fall on the resulting attribute line. One of Youngme Moon's many insights is especially relevant here. She says, "What we consider to be different depends on what we consider to be the norm …. In fact, trying to define what is different is like trying to define what is opposite[.]"[17] And here, yet again, it's worth remembering Michael Porter's insight that differentiation is about doing activities differently and doing different activities.

We don't have to look far for additional examples of doing the polar opposite. Consider IKEA again. Where traditional furniture stores deliver their furniture, IKEA's customers must deliver it themselves. Where traditional stores take months to deliver, IKEA's self-delivery is immediate. Where traditional furniture is delivered fully assembled, IKEA's customers must assemble the furniture themselves. Where traditional stores group their furniture by type of furniture, IKEA groups their furniture by room type. Where the aisles in traditional stores are straight, the aisles in IKEA's stores are curved. Where traditional stores have salespeople trail customers around the store, IKEA employs salesperson kiosks. And where IKEA offers housewares, a restaurant, and childcare, traditional stores do not. This last example suggests that in addition to listing the attributes that exist, you should list attributes that don't exist, but possibly could.

Hidden in Plain View

So in the last section, I said to *first list the properties (variables) of an offering*. That sounds simple enough. In fact, it's not. Why? Two reasons. In some cases, the properties are there for everyone to see (or hear, taste, smell, or feel), but like Poe's purloined letter, they're hidden in plain view. We are sometimes like fish who have become so accustomed to the water that

Table 8.1 Attributes of a traditional B-school vs. a cyber B-school

Traditional B-school attribute (value)	Property (variable)	Cyber B-school attribute (value)
Faculty and students live within 20 miles of campus	Geography	Faculty and students live hundreds to thousands of miles away from one another
Admission requires honor student GPA and high score on GMAT	Admission	Students are only required to submit three letters from non-family members—the first describing an "against the odds accomplishment," the second describing the applicant in a leadership role, however humble, and the third describing a contribution the applicant has made to the community
Classes held in a classroom; with 1 professor for 80 students	Classroom	Classes are held online; there is 1 professor for the 100,000 students in the class + tutors recruited from second-tier universities; students are able to interact via chat rooms
The courses are discipline-based, e.g., accounting, finance, marketing, etc.	Courses	The courses are issue-based and cross-disciplinary, e.g., courses titled "Profiting From Strategic Alliances," "Unleashing Innovation," and "Accessing Global Capital Markets," etc.
20% of the faculty have world-class reputations; 90% of their income is from outside teaching and consulting	Faculty	The school recruits 2–3 stars from the 10 best business schools plus 10 or more of the most cerebral consultants in the leading consulting companies
The salary difference between the stars and newly hired professors is 3:1	Pay structure	Faculty are given equity in the school and guaranteed a salary of $1 million per year, which is made possible by the large number of students paying tuition
Publish or perish - promotion rests on publishing within a narrowly defined discipline; little or no multi-disciplinary research or teaching exists; most research never gets applied	Academic research	50% gross margins and recorded webinars enable the school to free faculty from the burden of repetitive teaching and surround themselves with a first-rate, multi-disciplinary research team, thereby increasing the quantity and applicability of their research
Most students are college graduates, 25–30 years of age, with 3–4 years of experience	Student demographics	Online access and flexible, asynchronous courses make it possible for older students to attend
Admit 200 students per year	Student numbers	Admit hundreds of thousands of students
Tuition is as much as $20,000 per year	Tuition	Tuition is $2,000 per year, irrespective of how quickly a student progresses through the program
Two-year program, 20 classroom hours per week, classes held at set times	Program of study	Dedicated students can finish the program in three years; they must pass a demanding "exit" exam; those who don't pass are awarded a certificate outlining their educational accomplishments

Source: Created from the textual descriptions set forth in *Leading the Revolution*, pp. 62–65.

surrounds them, they no longer see it. As Daniel Kahneman, the Nobel Prize-winning economist explains in his book *Thinking, Fast and Slow*, "[We] can be blind to the obvious, and we are also blind to our blindness."[18]

The hotel industry provides a great example of industry executives becoming so habituated to a property that they stopped seeing it. Why do people stay in hotels? To have a place to sleep. And where do they sleep? In beds. So why did it take decades (centuries, actually) for the industry to get serious about the comfort of its beds? Because it was hidden in plain view. That is, until 1999, when the founder of Starwood Hotels & Resorts, Barry Sternlicht, a relative newcomer to the industry, introduced the Westin Heavenly Bed®. At Sternlicht's direction, Westin Hotels spent more than a year and $30 million to design a bed so luxurious that Youngme Moon jokingly claims to have caught a glimpse of the hereafter the first time she slept in it.[19] After a round of forehead slaps, the competing hotel brands followed suit.

Sternlicht got the idea for the Heavenly Bed® after comparing the comfort of his own bed with the beds he experienced in hotels. Saul Wurman, creator of the TED conference and author of the book *Information Anxiety*, underlines the benefit of comparison.[20] He notes that he loves collecting things and that he tends to buy things in threes. The reason, he explains, is that "you understand much more about each of them by seeing the variations between them, the variations on a theme."[21] Or, as the Germans put it, he elaborates, *Einmal ist keinmal*, meaning *Once is nothing*. See for yourself. Compare the chairs in Figure 8.4, then consider how the comparison enabled you to notice properties you might otherwise have missed by looking at a single chair. Then imagine the value of comparing all the elements of a more complex offering. For example, imagine comparing the lobby, restaurant, lounge, exercise room, etc. in a hotel with those same elements in other hotels and wherever else the elements exist.

In their book *Value-Analysis Tear-Down: A New Process for Product Development and Innovation*, Yoshihiko Sato and Jerry Kaufman explain a way of comparing complex offerings called *product tear-down*, or simply *tear-down*.[22] The tear-down process involves dissecting a company's offerings and its competitors' offerings and then comparing them, with the goal being to uncover, analyze, improve, and incorporate the attributes that customers value. The major steps in the process are selection, disassembly, analysis, display, and examination. You can use the process to identify the attributes of your and your competitors' offerings by disassembling them physically or on paper and then comparing them side by side. While the tear-down process is usually applied to physical products, it can just as well be applied to services by observing competing services and using *service blueprints* to dissect them into their individual steps.[23] It can also be used to compare the bundles and complements that exist at

Figure 8.4 Notice the different properties of a chair by comparing the different instances of a chair.

Source: David Holt Design, freepik.

the next-higher level of analysis and the components of the company (i.e., sales and marketing activities, distribution channels, and CRM programs) that exist at the level above that.

The second reason why properties are sometimes difficult to see is that you literally can't see or otherwise sense them because they're abstract. With abstract properties, you have only words to compare. (To remind yourself of why this is so, look again at Figure 6.4 and re-read the accompanying text.) In this case, a useful approach is the previously mentioned practice of identifying and comparing the verbiage used in your and your competitors' sales pitches, marketing materials, annual reports, websites, and so forth. Another useful practice, also previously suggested, is to have your management team think of themselves as customers and have them list the properties they would consider when choosing between your offering and competing offerings.

In the last chapter, I described how segments can be used to identify differentiation opportunities. In this chapter, we looked at ways of using attributes to do the same. The next chapter is devoted to describing how the concept of *actions* can be used to identify new ways to differentiate your offering.

Notes

1 W. Chan Kim and Renee Mauborgne, *Blue Ocean Strategy: How to Create Uncontested Market Space and Make the Competition Irrelevant* (Boston, MA: Harvard Business School Press, 2005).
2 Blue Ocean Strategy. *Amazon.* https://www.amazon.com/Blue-Ocean-Strategy-Uncontested-Competition/dp/1591396190#:~:text=Blue%20Ocean%20Strategy%20has%20sold,a%20bestseller%20across%20five%20continents.
3 W. Chan Kim and Renee Mauborgne, *Blue Ocean Shift Beyond Competing: Proven Steps to Inspire Confidence and Seize New Growth* (New York, NY: Hachette Books, 2017).
4 Richard K. Lee and Nina E. Goodrich, *Value Innovation Works: Move Mountains...... Drive sustainable, profitable growth! Deliver exceptional value to the most important customers in your value chains. A "How To" guide.* (Richard K. Lee, 2012).
5 Felix Oberholzer-Gee, *Better Simpler Strategy: A Value-Based Guide to Exceptional Performance* (Boston, MA: Harvard Business Review Press, 2021).
6 James C. Anderson, Nirmalya Kumar, and James A. Narus, *Value Merchants: Demonstrating and Documenting Superior Value in Business Markets* (Boston, MA: Harvard Business School Press, 2007), 25.
7 Cynthia Montgomery, *The Strategist: Be The Leader Your Business Needs* (New York, NY: Harper Business, 2012), 11.
8 Thomas L. Saaty, *The Analytic Hierarchy Process* (New York, NY: McGraw-Hill, 1980).
9 Ralph L. Keeney, *Value-Focused Thinking: A Path to Creative Decisionmaking* (Cambridge, MA: Harvard University Press), 101–103. Keeney explains natural and constructed measures as well as a third type of measure called proxy measures.
10 You convert a natural measure to the scale on your strategy canvas in the following way. By way of example, assume that the factor you are measuring is average miles-per-gallon (mpg), the high and low measures are 30 mpg and 10 mpg, your offering averages 25 mpg, and you are using a 5-point scale. First, subtract the high and low measures from each other (30 mpg − 10 mpg = 20 mpg). Then subtract the high and low points of your scale (5 − 1 = 4). Next divide the first difference by the second difference (20 mpg ÷ 4 = 5), which equates to the mpg increments on your 5-point scale (1 = 10, 2 = 15, 3 = 20, 4 = 25, and 5 = 30). So you can see that a 25 mpg rating would translate to a 4 on the 1–5 scale and a 23 mpg rating would have a rating between 3 and 4 on the rating scale. The exact number, 3.45, is calculated as follows: 3 ÷ 20 = x ÷ 23, so x = (3 × 23)/20 = 3.45.
11 You might wonder how you can map your current strategy before having created one. The fact is that whatever you're now doing to cause customers to prefer your offering is your current differentiation strategy—even if you never explicitly planned the strategy or refer to it as such.
12 Kim and Mauborgne, *op. cit.*, 29.
13 Rita Gunther McGrath and Ian MacMillan, *The Entrepreneurial Mindset: Strategies for Continuously Creating Opportunity in an Age of Uncertainty* (Boston, MA: Harvard Business School Press, 2000), 23–48.
14 R. Preston McAfee, *Competitive Solutions: The Strategist's Toolkit* (Princeton, NJ: Princeton University Press, 2002), 64.

15 Bear in mind that Hamel (presciently) wrote this in the year 2000, well before online education had taken off.

16 Gary Hamel, *Leading the Revolution* (Boston, MA: Harvard Business School Press, 2000), 62–65.

17 Youngme Moon, *Different: Escaping the Competitive Herd* (New York, NY: Crown Business, 2010), 194.

18 Daniel Kahneman, *Thinking, Fast and Slow* (New York, NY: Penguin Books, 2011), 24.

19 Moon, *op. cit.*, 56.

20 Richard Saul Wurman, *Information Anxiety* (New York, NY: Doubleday, 1989), 170.

21 *Ibid*

22 Yoshihiko Sato and J. Jerry Kaufman, *Value Analysis Tear-Down: A New Process for Product Development and Innovation* (New York, NY: Industrial Press, 2005).

23 Andy Polaine, Lavrans Lovlie, and Ben Reason, *Service Design: From Insight to Implementation* (Brooklyn, NY: Rosenfeld Media, 2013), 91–108.

9 Actions

In this chapter, we're going to examine how the consumption chain, jobs-to-be-done, mental model, and journey mapping methods can be used to identify differentiation opportunities. The first method centers on what customers are *doing* at each step of the consumption chain, the second on the *jobs* people are trying to get done at each step of the job map, the third on the *tasks* people perform as they work through a process, and the fourth on the benefits customers *expect* at each step of a journey map. I'm using *actions* as an umbrella term for the physical and mental doings, jobs, tasks, and expectations.

Consumption Chain

Ian MacMillan and Rita Gunther McGrath first introduced the concept of a consumption chain in their *Harvard Business Review* article titled "Discovering New Points of Differentiation."[1] They explained it again in their book *Market Busters: 40 Strategic Moves That Drive Exceptional Growth.*[2] A summary version of the consumption chain is illustrated in Figure 9.1. As shown in the figure, the map shows the chain of steps customers take before, during, and after they use your offering. The sequence of steps in MacMillan and McGrath's generic consumption chain is only intended to serve as a guide. Its actual length and the identity of the steps will vary depending on the type of offering. An example of the consumption chain for hotel customers is diagrammed in Figure 9.2.

MacMillan and McGrath's method for identifying differentiation opportunities starts with mapping the steps in the consumption chain. The next part of the process is to understand the customer's context at each of the steps by asking the journalist's questions—*who, where, when, what,* and *how*. Who is the customer at this step? Who is the customer with at this step? Where is the customer during this step? When (clock, calendar, purchase occasion, frequency) does the customer perform this step? What is the customer doing during this step? How does the customer perform this step? After you're done answering these questions (and more like them), you should have enough information to visualize the customer's context at each step of the consumption chain.

Once you've detailed the customer's context, you should ask about the customer's problems, concerns, wishes, and desired benefits. What problems does the customer encounter at this step? What concerns does the customer have at this step? What does the customer wish would happen at this step? What benefits (physical, mental, emotional, social, economic, and cost/risk reduction) does the customer desire at this step? For ease of analysis, it's a good idea to place the answers to these questions in a matrix like the one illustrated in Table 9.1.

MacMillan and McGrath use the example of buying gasoline, which I've amended a bit.[3] Their example focuses on the *purchase* step of the consumption chain. The *who* could be a man, a woman, an elderly person, a person who is alone or with a colleague, spouse, baby, adolescents, youth sports team, or pet. *Where* could be on a major street, on the highway, in

DOI: 10.4324/9781003271703-10

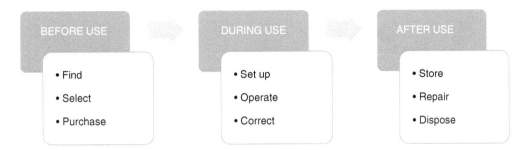

Figure 9.1 Summary version of the consumption chain.

an unfamiliar area, or in a dangerous area. Possible *whens* are when commuting to and from work, when on vacation, when shopping, when buying gas for a lawn mower, during the early morning, late at night, and during the winter. *What* customers are doing at this step includes filling their car with gas, cleaning their car windows, adding air to their tires, checking their oil level, using the restroom, and paying for the purchase, either at the pump or in the store. They may also buy coffee, food, cigarettes, or some other item. The *how* could be pumping the gasoline themselves or having an attendant pump the gasoline, using the wash buckets to clean the car windows or using their own cleaning materials, going into the store while the gas is pumping or waiting until the pumping is completed, using the store's coffee cup or their own coffee cup, buying healthy or unhealthy food, and so on. These variables and values (and many more) make for myriad combinations, each of which will involve different problems, concerns, wishes, and desired benefits. Consider, for example, a lone male executive commuting to work in the morning on a major street. His principal concerns might be the availability of a particular kind of coffee and breakfast food and the length of time it takes to purchase them. When commuting home during the evening, he may need to pick up some milk for the family. And on a hot summer weekend, this same executive, when getting gas for his lawnmower, may need a gas can, four-cycle engine oil, oil funnels, a pan in which to drain the oil, extra line for the grass trimmer, and something cold to drink.

There are two important things to note about the foregoing options and examples. First is the fact that *context is king* when it comes to understanding customers' problems, concerns, wishes, and desired benefits. Second is the importance of describing the context in a way you can visualize and otherwise sense. The more detail you provide about the context, the easier it is to imagine the customer's problems, concerns, wishes, and desired benefits. A good way to dig down to the visualizable detail is to repeatedly ask: *What kind of X?* For example, if the customer is traveling with a group, ask: *What kind of group?* Is it a group of business colleagues, a family, a youth soccer team, or what? If the *when* is a summer day, is it a hot summer day, a rainy summer day, a balmy summer day, a holiday summer day, or some other kind of summer day?

And now I'm going to (seemingly) contradict myself by saying that another important thing to understand about context is the fact that it can be more general than most people think. People typically take context to mean something like their immediate physical environment. But in the 1970s, as part of developing the field of information science, two Stanford University mathematicians, Jon Barwise and John Perry, proposed the opposite. The British mathematician and popular science writer Keith Devlin explains in his book *InfoSense: Turning Information into Knowledge* that as part of their *situation theory*, Barwise and Perry proposed that we "think about environments, or contexts, *in the most general possible*

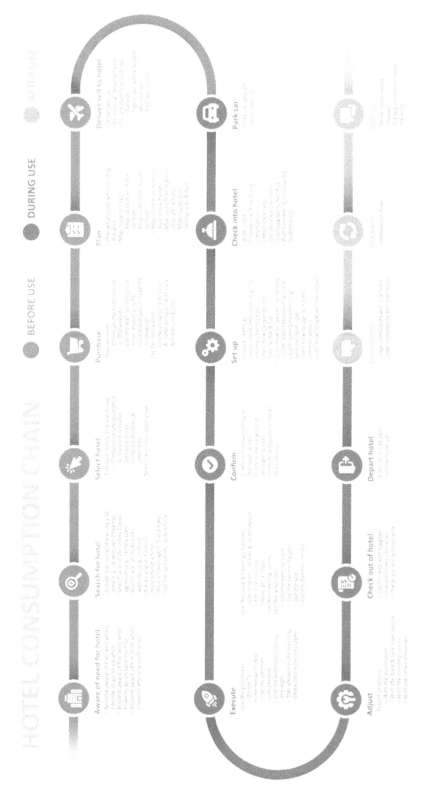

Figure 9.2 Consumption chain showing the steps a customer takes before, during, and after using a hotel.

Source: David Holt Design.

Table 9.1 Determine the context by asking who, where, when, what, and how; then identify the problems, concerns, wishes, and desired benefits

	Before use			During use			After use		
	Step 1	*Step 2*	*Step 3*	*Step 4*	*Step 5*	*Step 6*	*Step 7*	*Step 8*	*Step 9*
Who?									
Where?									
When?									
What?									
How?									
Problems?									
Concerns?									
Wishes?									
Desired benefits?									

way. Forget all the particulars, they [Barwise and Perry] said. Just work with 'environments' in a very general sense."[4] Devlin goes on to explain that in order to think about contexts in the simplest possible way, "Barwise introduced the term 'situation' to refer to any possible environment or context (of and for anything whatsoever)."[5]

Barwise and Perry used situation theory to examine the way that situations give rise to the creation, storage, and transmission of information. We're going to use it to make the point that customers live their lives from one moment to the next in a countless number of situations. Some situations are physical, like the situation of driving through an intersection or the situation of making a sales presentation. And other situations are abstract, like a political or economic situation, or the situation of being 40 years old, or the situation of needing something in a hurry. Whether physical or abstract, each situation gives rise to problems, concerns, wishes, and/or desired benefits. So one way of finding differentiation opportunities is to identify the situations in which your customers find themselves at each step of the consumption chain and, in each situation, identify the ways your offering can help or enable them to solve their problems, address their concerns, fulfill their wishes, and deliver the benefits they desire. And finally, so as not to contradict myself, remember that with abstract situations, it's far more effective to climb back down the abstraction ladder, like the one shown in Figure 6.4, to the point where you can visualize the who, where, when, what, and how of the situation.

MacMillan and McGrath's consumption chain applies to both B2C and B2B customers. With B2B customers, however, there is an additional framework you can use to identify differentiation opportunities—Michael Porter's value chain.[6] The value chain, illustrated in Figure 9.3, shows the generic activities that a business engages in during the process of transforming inputs into the output that comprises its offering. The *primary activities* are listed in sequence along the bottom of the value chain, and the *support activities* rest on top of the primary activities. The activities vary by industry and type of business, as does the name that some attach to this value-creating system.[7] *Value chain* firms, such as Ford Motor Company, are manufacturers that create value by transforming inputs into an output. *Value network* firms like Amazon, eBay, and Uber create value by mediating between networks of buyers and sellers.

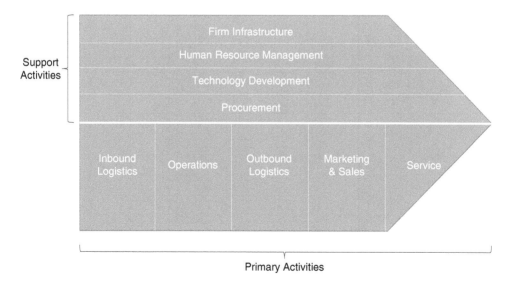

Figure 9.3 The value chain.

Source: Adapted from *Competitive Advantage: Creating and Sustaining Superior Performance*, Figure 2.2, page 37.

Value shops, like architecture and management consulting firms, create value by using competencies and processes to solve unique problems for their customers. Whatever the case, you can differentiate your offering by helping or enabling business customers to do a better job of performing the activities in their value chain/network/shop or by relieving them of having to perform the activities themselves. Here, it is important to remember that B2B customers are most interested in offerings that increase their bottom line, lower their risk, or both.

The final step of the consumption chain or the value chain/network/shop process is to generate creative solutions that eliminate or mitigate the customer's problems and concerns and that fulfill the customer's wishes and desired benefits. We'll talk about the methods for doing so in Chapter 11.

Jobs-To-Be-Done

The *jobs-to-be-done* method is largely attributed to the late Harvard Business School professor Clayton Christensen (1952–2020) and to Tony Ulwick, the founder and CEO of Strategyn, which specializes in jobs-to-be-done consulting. Surprisingly, considering how long the method has been around, there doesn't appear to be a universally accepted definition of the term *job*. Christensen and co-author Michael Raynor first made a tangential pass at defining the term in their book *The Innovator's Solution: Creating and Sustaining Successful Growth*, where they said, "Customers—people and companies—have 'jobs' that arise regularly and need to get done …. [T]hey look around for a product or service that they can 'hire' to get the job done."[8] In a later book titled *Competing Against Luck: The Story of Innovation and Customer Choice*, Christensen and his co-authors defined a job as "the progress a person is trying to make in a particular circumstance."[9] Meanwhile, Ulwick, in his book *Jobs To Be Done: Theory to Practice*, defines a job as, "A task, goal or objective a person is trying to accomplish or a problem they are trying to resolve."[10] Ulwick adds the idea of a *desired outcome*, which he defines as, "A metric that customers use to measure the successful execution of a functional job or a consumption chain job. Synonymous with customer need."[11]

Lance Bettencourt, a business professor at Texas Christian University, and formerly a strategy adviser with Strategyn, is the author of *Service Innovation: How to Go from Customer Needs to Breakthrough Services*.[12] He explains the way jobs and desired outcomes should be stated. For a job statement, he uses the example: *Determine where my car is parked when at a public event, e.g., theme park, sporting event, etc.* The components of the job statement are an *action verb* (determine) and a phrase that describes the *object of the action* (where my car is parked), a *contextual qualifier* (when at a public event), and *optional examples* (e.g., theme park, sporting event, etc.).

Bettencourt also explains the proper format of a desired outcome statement, such as: *Minimize the time it takes to determine where my car is parked when at a public event, e.g., theme park, sporting event,* etc. The first part is the *direction of improvement*, which is typically stated as minimize or increase. (I prefer the terms minimize or maximize.) The second part, the *unit of measure*, is the thing that is to be maximized or minimized. In her book *The Social Innovation Imperative: Create Winning Products, Services, and Programs That Solve Society's Most Pressing Challenges,* Sandra Bates, the co-founder and formally the executive director of the Strategyn Institute, notes that the unit of measure frequently pertains to time, quality, or reliability.[13] And as with the job statement, the desired outcome statement contains the *object of control* (to determine where my car is parked), the *contextual qualifier* (when at a public event) and *optional examples* of the context (e.g., theme park, sporting event, etc.).

Notice how the notions of jobs and desired outcomes track with the six kinds of benefits described in Chapter 3. (In what follows, I skip the job statement and use the short form of the desired outcome statements.) There are the desired outcomes associated with physical jobs, such as *minimize the effort required to jack up my car* and *maximize my ability to see clearly*. Mental jobs and associated outcomes include things like *minimize the difficulty of understanding the material in this book* and *maximize my ability to remember the material*. Emotional outcomes include things like *maximize my sense of wonder* and *minimize my sense of embarrassment*. Examples of social outcomes are *maximize the chance of finding a compatible partner* and *minimize the risk of divorce*. An example of an economic outcome is *maximize the revenue of Widget A*. And, finally, there are cost/risk reduction outcomes like *minimize the cost of producing Widget A* and *minimize the physical risk of jacking up my car*.

Now that you understand the concepts of jobs and desired outcomes, let's talk about how the jobs-to-be-done method can be applied to differentiation. This brings us back to the ideas of *enablement* and *relief* discussed in Chapter 4, where it was explained that offerings are tools that *help* or *enable* people to produce an object or event or that *relieve* them of their role in the production. This is similar to saying that offerings are tools that help or enable people to perform a job-to-be-done--such as the job *pound a nail* (Figure 4.4) and the job *determine where my car is parked when at a public event*--or that offerings are tools that *relieve* people of having to play a role in performing a job. Offerings are differentiated (a) when they help/enable/relieve customers with regard to performing jobs that competing offerings don't help or enable them perform or relieve them of performing, or (b) when they help/enable/relieve customers with regard to more jobs than do competing offerings, or (c) when they are significantly better at helping/enabling/relieving customers with regard to a job as compared to competing offerings.

Strategyn's jobs-to-be-done process, here described in substantially abbreviated form,[14] starts with identifying the core job your offering helps or enables customers to do. The core job is the overriding reason your offering exists, which is to say, the main reason why customers buy your offering. There may be many jobs your offering helps or enables customers to do or many jobs your offering relieves customers of having to do, but all of them are subordinate to the overriding core job. The next step of the process is to map the steps the customer takes to get the core job done. Bettencourt and Ulwick explain that in nearly all cases, the generic steps are similar or the same, which gives rise to what they call the *universal job map*.[15] The universal job map—which should not be confused with the consumption chain map—is used to identify what the customer does immediately before, during, and after executing the core job. Pre-execution steps are to *define* what must be done, *locate* the things required to do it, *prepare* those things, and *confirm* that everything is properly prepared. The next step is to *execute* the core job. Post-execution steps are to *monitor* that the job is being performed correctly, *modify* the execution, if necessary, and *resolve* any problems associated with the modification. The final post-execution step is to *conclude* the job. As shown in Table 9.2, at each of the nine steps, the customer may have to perform one or more sub-jobs to complete the step. The total number of sub-jobs typically totals 15–25. Table 9.2 also shows that each sub-job has one or more desired outcomes and that the total number of desired outcomes is typically100–150.

Consider, for example, a paint contractor performing the core job *paint the interior of my customer's house*. To perform the core job, the contractor must *define* the paint color(s) and the interior parts of the house that need to be painted, determine what materials are needed, and establish the price he will charge. Next, the contractor must *locate* the paint, brushes, tape, drop cloths, ladders, and other things that are required to do the job. Then the contractor has to *prepare* the items, e.g., mix the paint, select the brushes, attach the rollers, and set up the drop cloths and ladder. Following that, he needs to *confirm* that everything is properly prepared—for example, confirm that there is enough paint, that the paint is the correct color, that the drop cloths are properly placed, and that the ladder is tall enough. Once everything is located, prepared, and confirmed, the contractor *executes* the paint job. During the execution, he *monitors* for painting problems like paint runs, drops, and overruns, and he makes sure he

Table 9.2 The core job, job steps, sub-jobs, and desired outcomes

| Job steps | Core job | |
	Sub-jobs	Desired outcomes
Define	Sub-job 1	Desired outcome 1
		Desired outcome 2
		Desired outcome 3
	Sub-job 2	Desired outcome 4
		Desired outcome 5
	Sub-job 3	Desired outcome 6
		Desired outcome 7
Locate	Sub-job 4	Desired outcome 8
		Desired outcome 9
		Desired outcome 10
		Desired outcome 11
	Sub-job 5	Desired outcome 12
		Desired outcome 13
	Sub-job 6	Desired outcome 14
		Desired outcome 15
		Desired outcome 16
	Sub-job 7	Desired outcome 17
		Desired outcome 18
		Desired outcome 19
		Desired outcome 20
Prepare	Etc.	Etc.
Confirm	Etc.	Etc.
Execute	Etc.	Etc.
Monitor	Etc.	Etc.
Modify	Etc.	Etc.
Resolve	Etc.	Etc.
Conclude	Etc.	Etc.
9	15–25	100–150

has enough paint to complete the job. If there are problems, he *modifies* his process and *resolves* any problems. Finally, he *concludes* the core job by removing and stowing the paint and materials and billing the customer.

As just noted, each of the sub-jobs has one or more (usually more) desired outcomes (see the right-most column in Table 9.2). The desired outcomes for the sub-job *bill the customer*, for instance, may include *minimize the time it takes to create the bill*, *minimize the chance of making a mistake on the bill*, and *maximize the customer's understanding of the fairness of the bill*. Most core jobs have a total of 100–150 desired outcomes, each of which is a potential opportunity to differentiate your offering by helping or enabling customers to optimize the desired outcome. For example, as earlier explained, Sherwin-Williams sells paint to small painting contractors. To set themselves apart from other paint providers, Sherwin-Williams offers contractors an end-to-end service that starts with helping the contractor's customer with color selection and helping the contractor estimate how much labor and material will be required. Each day during the job, Sherwin-Williams checks the contractor's orders and suggests items the contractor may have forgotten. Then, at the end of the job, Sherwin-Williams provides an accurate accounting of the paint and materials the contractor used to complete the job, and they help the customer estimate additional jobs the homeowner decides to do. Note how providing the contractor with an accurate accounting of the paint and materials helps the contractor optimize the desired outcomes *minimize the time it takes to create*

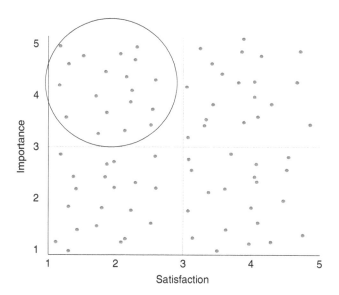

Figure 9.4 Rate the 100–150 desired outcomes on importance and satisfaction; focus first on those that customers consider most important and least well satisfied (the circled outcomes).

the bill, minimize the chance of making a mistake on the bill, and *maximize the customer's understanding of the fairness of the bill.* Helping the contractor optimize these desired outcomes is just one of many ways Sherwin-Williams' differentiates its offering.

Finding ways to optimize 100–150 desired outcomes will probably require more time than you have to devote to the effort (at least to start), so you'll want to pare down and/or prioritize the list. As shown in Figure 9.4, you can do this by performing a multicriteria rating exercise in which one of the criteria is the desired outcome's importance to the customer and the other is the customer's belief as to how well the desired outcome is satisfied by existing offerings. Both are rated on a 1–5 scale. In this way, you can target your efforts at the desired outcomes that customers consider highly important and poorly satisfied by the existing offerings. In other words, you can target the desired outcomes in the upper left quadrant of Figure 9.4, starting with those that are the most up and to the left in the quadrant.

Ideally, you should interview customers in your target market to identify the core job, sub-jobs, and desired outcomes that exist at each step of the universal job map. You should also survey a statistically valid number of customers to identify the desired outcomes that are the most important and least well satisfied by existing offerings. (We'll talk about interviews and surveys in Chapter 10.) If, however, you are unable to interview the customers and conduct the survey, your next-best alternative is to rely on your team's knowledge of your customers by interviewing and surveying the team members. In both cases, however, you may find it difficult to get the survey participants to sit still long enough to reliably rate the level of importance and satisfaction of 100–150 desired outcomes. Sandra Bates proposes the alternative of having people rate the much smaller number of sub-jobs (say, 15–25) for importance and satisfaction and then focus on the desired outcomes for the most important and least-well-satisfied sub-jobs.[16]

Another way to identify differentiation opportunities is to identify job constraints. A constraint, as I conceive of it, is something that does or does not exist that prevents customers from completing a physical, mental, emotional, social, or economic sub-job, or that makes the sub-job costly or risky to do, or that prevents customers from optimizing the desired outcome. Constraints are sometimes referred to as "hassles" or "pain points." For example, customers may not have the time, money, knowledge, equipment, or technology that is required to do a sub-job. Paint contractors, for instance, don't have the time to travel halfway across town to complete the sub-job *pick up paint and materials*, so Sherwin-Williams differentiates itself by having more locations than its competitors in order to minimize the time paint contractors have to spend driving to their stores. In other situations, a physical constraint may prevent customers from doing the sub-job, such as the shaky hands that make it hard for diabetics to draw the correct amount of insulin into a syringe and inject themselves. Recall that Novo Nordisk's injection pens overcome this constraint by coming pre-loaded with the correct amount of insulin. Non-physical constraints can also stand in the way of doing a sub-job or optimizing a desired outcome. They include things like regulatory, psychological, cultural, political, and social prohibitions. For example, most people are psychologically opposed to waiting in line for a cup of coffee while suffering an embarrassingly bad hangover. Starbuck's drive-thru service makes it possible for them to get their curative cup of coffee without having to stand in line.

Figure 9.5 shows that the universal job steps are part of just one step (the *use* step) of the customer's consumption chain. It also illustrates that the steps in the consumption chain are just some of the steps in a commercial (B2B) customer's value chain (or value network or value shop, as the case may be). The jobs, desired outcomes, and constraints that exist at each of the three levels are potential ways for you to differentiate your offering by helping or enabling your customers to perform the jobs, optimize the desired outcomes, and overcome the constraints. Consider the following example.

As just explained, when painting a house, a paint contractor performs the following steps in the *universal job map*—define the paint and materials needed to paint the house, then locate, prepare, and confirm that they are correct, then execute and conclude the paint job. All these steps occur as part of the *use step* of the contractor's consumption chain. However, before the use step, the contractor must find a place to buy the paint and materials, consummate the purchase, and deliver them to the job site. And after the use step, he needs to store his tools, return any unused paint to the paint store, and dispose of the paint and

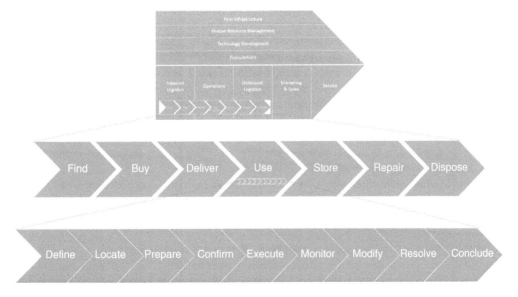

Figure 9.5 Customers have jobs that are part of their universal job map, consumption chain, and value chain.

materials that can't be stored. Then there are the *value chain* activities associated with running his paint contracting business, such as marketing and sales, financing, accounting, hiring and training employees, buying office supplies and equipment, managing multiple paint jobs, and so on. All the jobs, desired outcomes, and constraints that exist at each of these levels of analysis are potential sources of differentiation.

Sherwin-Williams exemplifies the strategy of looking at the universal job map, the consumption chain, and the value chain/network/shop for jobs, desired outcomes, and constraints, then treating each as an opportunity to differentiate an offering. In the *define* step of the universal job map, for example, Sherwin-Williams helps their paint contractor customers select colors and prepare job estimates. Moving up a level to the consumption chain, Sherwin-Williams makes it easier for the contractors to *find* their stores by building more stores than their competitors. And at the value chain level, Sherwin-Williams could identify opportunities to help paint contractors with the accounting, financing, hiring, training, and other jobs the contractors perform at this level. Each level contains opportunities to help or enable (or relieve) their customers do the jobs they are trying to do, optimize the desired outcomes, and overcome constraints. The same strategy can work for you.

Clayton Christensen and his co-authors (hereafter simply referred to as Christensen) take a different approach to the jobs-to-be-done process.[17] Instead of identifying a *core job*, Christensen works to identify the *real job* customers hire an offering to do. And instead of working from the top-down by subdividing the core job into universal job steps and sub-jobs, Christensen works from the bottom-up by using the many jobs for which an offering is hired to identify the overriding *real job* customers are trying to get done. He cites the example of OnStar, GM's in-vehicle emergency service, which performs jobs like *alert emergency services in the event of an accident*, *obtain roadside assistance when my car breaks down*, and *help me navigate in an unfamiliar area*. All these jobs are part of the more abstract real job *provide peace of mind while driving*. (Note that this is another application of the concept of abstraction.)

Christensen goes on to explain that it's not easy to get the real job right. In OnStar's case, Chet Huber, the former CEO of OnStar, and his three-hundred-person team spent months struggling to pin down the real job customers are hiring OnStar to do. Ultimately, Huber had every person on the team spend an hour in the call center listening in on customer calls (which, you should note, is a form of customer research). After hearing the OnStar customers' emotional pleas for an ambulance after a violent collision, for roadside assistance on a dark lonely highway, for help navigating out of an unsafe neighborhood, and for other types of aid in similarly stressful circumstances, the team determined that *provide peace of mind while driving* was the best way to define the real job OnStar is hired to do. In turn, they realized that defining the real job at the right level of abstraction pointed to numerous other ways to do it, like *perform a remote diagnosis when the check engine light comes on* and *unlock my car doors remotely when I lock my keys in the car*. They also grasped that their operational processes—ranging from training call center agents to helping GM salespeople explain OnStar to prospective customers—should center on the real job *provide peace of mind while driving*. As Huber put it, the real job is "… crazy powerful, if you get it right."[18]

So how do you know when you've got the real job right? How do you know when you're at the right level of abstraction? Christensen, who cautions that this is more art than science, proposes the following rule of thumb: "*[I]f the architecture of the system or product can only be met by products within the same product class, the concept of the Job to Be Done does not apply. If only products in the same class can solve the problem, you're not uncovering a job*."[19] In addition to using Christensen's rule of thumb, I suggest you reacquaint yourself with the idea of generalized abstraction, as explained in Chapter 6 and illustrated in Figure 6.3 and Figure 6.4. Then figure out how to identify the abstract theme that is common to the multiple jobs customers want your offering to perform. For help, you can look to the methods for identifying themes (e.g., coding) described in Chapter 10 and Crawford's slip-writing method, described below.

In my view, one of the best ways to identify abstract themes is the slip-writing method developed by Claude Crawford (1897–1992), who for many years was a professor at the University of Southern California. Crawford's method is detailed in William Dettmer's book titled *Brainpower Networking: Using the Crawford Slip Method*.[20] The essence of the method is to write down each statement that is obtained in a brainstorming session, or from customer interviews, on a separate index card. In our case, the statements express the various jobs customers are trying to do. Each statement should be in the form of a whole sentence containing a subject, verb, and object. In the case of OnStar, the statements would be *OnStar, call me an ambulance after I've been in a collision, OnStar, call me roadside assistance when I have a flat tire on a dark lonely highway, OnStar, help me navigate out of an unsafe neighborhood, OnStar, perform a remote diagnosis for me when the check engine light comes on,* and *OnStar, unlock my car doors remotely when I lock my keys in the car.*

The next step is to decide whether it is the subject, verb, or object of each sentence that captures the essence of the idea. In each of the sample statements, OnStar is the subject that is doing the "verbing," i.e., calling, helping, performing, and unlocking. In none of the statements does the subject or verb seem to capture the essence of the idea, which leaves the sentence objects as the essences. Once the essence's location in the sentences is identified, the next step is to decide what abstract idea the essences have in common. One way to do that is to complete the sentence, "These _____ go together because they all _____." In the OnStar example, one way to complete the sentence would be to say, "These sentence objects go together because they all have to do with scary or otherwise upsetting situations." The final step is to use the completed sentence to stimulate ideas for your offering's *real job*. The thought process might go something like this: "Our customers want OnStar to help them when they find themselves in scary or otherwise upsetting situations. They don't want to be scared or upset. They would rather have peace of mind. So, one way to state the real job that customers are hiring us to do is to say *provide peace of mind while driving*."

As Christensen said, identifying the real job is more art than science. You should expect to go through numerous iterations of the process before you land on a *real job* statement that feels right. And as we'll talk about in the forthcoming chapter on creativity, it's best to give everyone's subconscious sufficient time to think about it between iterations. One way to do that is to use a team process called *formal indication*.[21] The first step of the process is for the team members to immerse themselves in the statements by engaging in an intense period of conversation during which they dig deep into what the customers are saying. In the case of OnStar, the team might ask each other questions like: Is the person a man or a woman? How old is the person? What kind of accident and where? What are all the reasons the check engine light comes on? What's the scariest thing about having car trouble on a dark lonely highway? What time of year is the person having the car trouble? What's the weather like? In what situations do people lock their keys in their car? And so on. When the discussion is completed, the team members should step away for a time, ideally overnight, to let their subconscious think about the real job their offering is hired to do. Then the team should regroup and work together to decide what the real job should be. Subjecting your team to all this mental mishigas might seem a bit over the top but remember what OnStar's CEO had to say. The real job is "… crazy powerful, if you get it right."

Mental Models

Indi Young is a consultant in interaction and navigation design and a founding partner of the service and experience design firm Adaptive Path. In her book titled *Mental Models: Aligning*

Design Strategy with Human Behavior, she describes a method for visualizing the tasks people are trying to get done as they work through a process and for visualizing ways of helping them perform the tasks.[22] The visualization is called a *mental model.* A generic example of a portion of a mental model is illustrated in Figure 9.6. The process visualized in the model can be anything from getting ready for work in the morning, to going to a movie, to looking up a part number online. Young defines a task as "... actions, thoughts, feelings, philosophies, and motivations—everything that comes up when a person accomplishes something, sets something in motion, or achieves a certain state."[23] The fundamental reason for building a mental model is to understand how a segment of customers performs the focal process and the way your offering could help or enable them to perform the tasks that are part of the process.

In summary form, the mental model method involves interviewing customers[24] to understand what they're doing during the focal process; analyzing the interview transcripts to identify the tasks they perform; looking for themes in the tasks; using a bottom-up approach to organize the themes (i.e., from sub-subtask, to sub-task, to task) in the top half of the model; and placing existing and potential solutions that correspond with each subtask and sub-subtask in the bottom half of the model. Young uses the example of building a mental model of the process film buffs use when going to a movie.[25] Let's say that one of their major tasks—say, Task 3 in Figure 9.6—is to *identify with the movie,* and one of Task 3's subtasks is to *collect film-related stuff,* and one of the sub-subtasks of this subtask is to *collect film artwork.* Three ways of enabling film buffs to collect film artwork are a kiosk in the theater lobby, a website devoted to film artwork, and artists who specialize in creating custom-designed film artwork. Each of these solutions is a way for a movie theater to differentiate itself.

In actual practice, a mental model printed in 12 font type can run the length of a conference room wall, which is why Young says that a detailed mental model can be used to direct user-centered design for ten or more years.[26] Or, to put it in our terms, a detailed mental model can be used to identify differentiation opportunities for many years. You can find a variety of Young's mental model case studies at this link: https://rosenfeldmedia.com/books/mental-models/details/case-studies/.

Journey Maps

Customer journey maps diagram the chronological order of the steps customers take as they experience an offering, which means that the consumption chain, universal job map, and mental model are different ways of creating a journey map.[27] As Jim Kalbach explains in his book titled *Mapping Experiences: A Complete Guide to Creating Value Through Journeys, Blueprints, and Diagrams,* there are various ways to diagram the customer's journey.[28] One of the ways that Kalbach describes is to map the steps that customers take as part of completing some process (e.g., checking into a hotel or being seated in a restaurant) and then identify the following things at each step: the customer's expectations, the things that threaten to prevent the expectations from being met, opportunities to exceed physical expectations, opportunities to exceed emotional expectations, and the emotion evoked.[29] As shown in Table 9.3, a modified version of this approach is to identify, at each step of the journey, the benefits the customer expects (using the six-benefit typology explained in Chapter 3), the things that threaten to prevent the expectations from being met, and the opportunities to exceed the expectations. As with the other methods, this journey mapping method has the potential to reveal multiple ways of differentiating an offering.

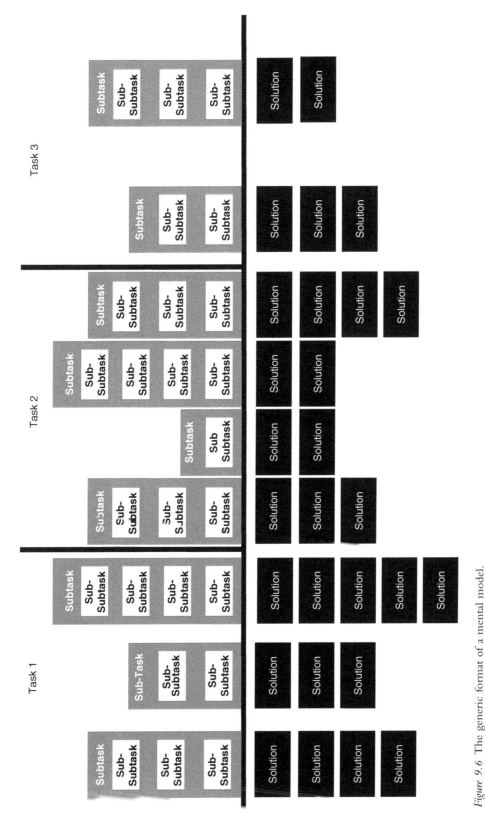

Figure 9.6 The generic format of a mental model.

Source: Adapted from *Mental Models: Aligning Design Strategy with Human Behavior*, various figures. Reproduced with permission.

Table 9.3 A journey map that incorporates the six kinds of benefits

	STEP 1	STEP 2	STEP 3	ETC.
PHYSICAL BENEFITS				
Expected physical benefits				
Threats				
Opportunities to exceed expectations				
MENTAL BENEFITS				
Expected mental benefits				
Threats				
Opportunities to exceed expectations				
EMOTIONAL BENEFITS				
Expected emotional benefits				
Threats				
Opportunities to exceed expectations				
SOCIAL BENEFITS				
Expected social benefits				
Threats				
Opportunities to exceed expectations				
ECONOMIC BENEFITS				
Expected economic benefits				
Threats				
Opportunities to exceed expectations				
COST/RISK REDUCTION BENEFITS				
Expected C/R reduction benefits				
Threats				
Opportunities to exceed expectations				

In this chapter, we examined various ways of identifying the actions customers take before, during, and after they use an offering. Each action at each step is a potential opportunity to differentiate your offering. Actions are the third place where we've looked for differentiation opportunities. The first two were segments and attributes. But knowing *where* to look is only half the battle. The other half is knowing *how* to look, which brings us to the next topic—research.

Notes

1 Ian C. MacMillan and Rita Gunther MacGrath, "Discovering New Points of Differentiation," *Harvard Business Review* July-August, 1997, 133–145. Elsewhere the consumption chain is sometimes referred to as the *customer value chain* or the *customer journey map*.

2 Rita Gunther McGrath and Ian C. MacMillan, *Market Busters: 40 Strategic Moves That Drive Exceptional Business Growth* (Boston, MA: Harvard Business School Press, 2005), 15–25.

3 MacMillan and McGrath, *op. cit.*, 144.

4 Keith Devlin, *InfoSense: Turning Information into Knowledge* (New York, NY: W. H. Freeman and Company, 2001), 38.

5 *Ibid*, 39.

6 Michael Porter. *Competitive Advantage: Creating and Sustaining Superior Performance* (New York, NY: The Free Press, 1985), 33–61.

7 Francesco Ricciotti, "From value chain to value network: a systematic literature review," *Management Review Quarterly* (2020) 70, 191–212.

8 Clayton M. Christensen and Michael E. Raynor, *The Innovator's Solution: Creating and Sustaining Successful Growth* (Boston, MA: Harvard Business School Press, 2003), 75.

9 Clayton M. Christensen, Taddy Hall, Karen Dillon, and David S. Duncan, *Competing Against Luck: The Story of Innovation and Customer Choice* (New York, NY: HarperCollins Publishers, 2016), 27.

10 Anthony W. Ulwick, *Jobs To Be Done: Theory to Practice* (Idea Bite Press, 2016), 189. See also Anthony W. Ulwick, *What Customers Want: Using Outcome-Driven Innovation to Create Breakthrough Products and Services* (New York, NY: McGraw-Hill, 2005).

11 *Ibid*, 187.

12 Lance A. Bettencourt, *Service Innovation: How to Go from Customer Needs to Breakthrough Services* (New York, NY: McGraw-Hill, 2010), 18–21.

13 Sandra M. Bates, *The Social Innovation Imperative: Create Winning Products, Services, and Programs That Solve Society's Most Pressing Challenges* (New York, NY: McGraw-Hill, 2012), 29.

14 In *Jobs To Be Done: Theory to Practice* Ulwick provides a detailed, step-by-step description of the jobs-to-be-done process (84 steps, in all); Bettencourt's treatment, which focuses on service innovation, fleshes out many of the steps, including the questions to ask at each point in the framework; Bates also provides a well-elaborated description of the process, with the focus being its application to social innovation.

15 Lance A. Bettencourt and Anthony W. Ulwick, "The Customer-Centered Innovation Map," *Harvard Business Review* 86, no 5 (May 2008), 109–114.

16 Bates, *op. cit.*, 228–229.

17 Christensen et al., *op. cit.*, 165–172.

18 *Ibid*, 204

19 *Ibid*, 225.

20 H. William Dettmer, *Brainpower Networking: Using the Crawford Slip Method* (New Bern, NC: Trafford Publishing, 2003).

21 Christian Madsbjerg and Mikkel B. Rasmussen, *The Moment of Clarity: Using the Human Sciences to Solve Your Toughest Business Problems* (Boston, MA: Harvard Business Review Press, 2014), 115.

22 Indi Young, *Mental Models: Aligning Design Strategy with Human Behavior* (Brooklyn, NY: Rosenfeld Media, 2008).

23 *Ibid*, 133.

24 Young does an exceptionally good job of describing the interview process and the subsequent process of analyzing the interview transcripts to identify themes.

25 *Ibid*, 206. You can download the entire movie process at this URL: https://rosenfeldmedia.com/mental-models/moviegoer-alignment-diagram/.

26 *Ibid*, 7.

27 Actually, the mental model method is less concerned with capturing the chronological order of the steps and more concerned with capturing the tasks that are performed during a process.

28 Jim Kalbach, *Mapping Experiences: A Complete Guide to Creating Value Through Journeys, Blueprints & Diagrams* (Boston, MA: O"Reilly Media, 2016), 249–270.

29 *Ibid*, 251.

10 Research

Superior strategies stem from superior insights. "Seeing them first and understanding them better than competitors is the name of the game," says Willie Pietersen.[1] Superior insights stem, in turn, from superior research, from working harder to understand the types of customers that exist, the attributes they want, the actions they take, and the benefits they desire. The three most common kinds of customer research are interviews, observation, and surveys. In this chapter, we're going to concentrate on interview and observation research, then take brief looks at survey research and two alternative forms of research—employee idea systems and living labs.

Research Objectives

To start, let's talk about the objectives of customer research. The overall objective is to discover the insights required to design an effective differentiation strategy. The sub-objectives depend on how the research will be used to support the methods described in the last three chapters:

- Segmentation: Here, the research is used to identify the market segments that exist, the attributes they desire, and why they desire the attributes. Remember how the Monaco Hotel *observed* that some of their customers were tall athletes (a niche market segment) and deduced that they would prefer guestrooms with tall ceilings and extra-long beds. And recall how the Tokyo Imperial Hotel *observed* the organizer of a high school reunion complaining about the amount of work that goes into organizing a reunion and inferred reunion organizers (a niche market segment) would prefer a hotel that relieves them of this responsibility. Finally, consider again the example of the researcher who *interviewed* female baby boomers to identify the cruise ship market segments (destination, party, and leisure) and the attributes they desire.
- Attributes: With the strategy canvas method, it's necessary to *interview* customers to identify their next-best alternative to your offering and the purchase criteria they consider when deciding whether and from whom to buy. Interviews are also used to gain insight into which attributes should be raised, reduced, or eliminated and possible new attributes for your offering. *Survey* research is used to rank the order of importance of the purchase criteria and the relative performance of the competitors on each of them. To prepare an attribute map, customers are *interviewed* to determine the categories to which attributes should be assigned. And with attribute lines, customers are *interviewed* to obtain ideas about attributes that fall between the two poles of each line.
- Actions: In the consumption chain method, *interviews* and *observations* are used to identify the steps in the consumption chain and to understand the context of each step. *Interviews* and *observations* are also used in the jobs-to-be-done method to identify the core job the

DOI: 10.4324/9781003271703-11

customer is trying to do, the steps in the universal job map for the core job, the sub-jobs performed at each step, and the desired outcomes and constraints for each sub-job. *Interviews* and *observations* are also used to identify the activities in the customer's value chain, value network, or value shop. A *survey* is used to judge the degree of importance and level of satisfaction of the desired outcomes. In Christensen's alternative way of implementing the jobs-to-be-done method, OnStar listened in on (*observed*) their customers' calls as part of identifying the real job that OnStar is hired to do. The mental model and journey map methods also rely on *interviews* to identify the steps and tasks that occur when customers perform a process, such as going to a movie or returning a part to a manufacturer.

Interviews

The three major parts of doing an interview are *recruiting* the interviewees, *conducting* the interviews, and *analyzing* the outcomes.

The recruiting process starts with deciding how many people to interview. While every research project is different, in my experience, interviewing a dozen people for an hour is usually sufficient. You can do six two-person interviews, or twelve one-person interviews, or some combination of one- and two-person interviews. I prefer not to do focus groups,[2] but if you decide to do them, each focus group should be treated as a single interview. Whatever number of interviews you decide to do, you'll know you've done enough of them when you stop hearing new answers to your questions or, said differently, when you keep hearing the same answers to your questions.

The second step of the recruiting process is to create the screener. The screener is the document that you or your research firm will use to screen the interview candidates. The parts of the screener are the user instructions, the verbiage that introduces the interviewer and the purpose of the interview, the questions regarding the prospect's demographic qualifications and willingness to participate, an explanation of the gift that will be given to the interviewees (I use a $100 Amazon gift card), the ask, and the scheduling. Having a research firm recruit a dozen people typically costs $3,000–$5,000, although the cost varies widely depending on the type of people being recruited. If you can't afford to hire a research firm, you'll have to do the recruiting yourself. Ideally, you should recruit a combination of existing customers, past customers, and competitor customers. One option is to directly identify and approach prospective interviewees. Another option is to use your network(s) to identify and approach prospects. You can also ask, at the end of each interview, if the interviewee can suggest other people to interview.

The sad fact is that it's hard to get people to agree to do a one-hour interview. If you can't recruit enough people to do one-hour interviews, then try for half-hour interviews. Something is better than nothing. Another under-appreciated approach is for you and the other people in your company, especially the members of your sales team, to gather the desired information in snippets over time. In every interaction with your customers and prospective customers, you should ask some of the questions you want to be answered (e.g., What things do you consider when making a purchase decision?) and then contribute the answers to a centralized system for storing and coalescing the information. This is a good practice to use on an ongoing basis, even if you're successful in completing a full set of interviews.

The second step of the interview process is to conduct the interviews. As just mentioned, you can interview people individually or in pairs. The advantage of interviewing people individually is that it's easier to schedule the interview, and you can dig deeper into the person's thoughts. Two-person interviews, in comparison, are more difficult to schedule, and they don't dig as deep into the interviewees' minds. But they have the advantage that the two interviewees find the interview to be less like an hour-long interrogation and more like a conversation in which they stimulate each other to think of things they might not otherwise have thought of.

You can do the interviews in person, via a telephone call, or via a video call. Doing the interviews in person is more expensive, but it has the advantage of enabling you to observe the interviewee and his or her context. Whether you do the interviews in person or remotely, you should always do them in pairs, with one person asking the questions and the other taking notes. Because it's impossible to capture everything when taking notes, you should record, or better, videotape the interviews. Just make sure to obtain the interviewees' written agreement to be recorded or videotaped before you conduct the interview. Also, make sure your telephone or video call provider enables you to record the call and download an MP3 digital file of the recording afterward. You'll also want to ensure that your call provider offers toll-free telephone numbers. I don't recommend using voice-over-internet-protocol (VoIP) because the calls occasionally freeze, which is annoying for you and the interviewees.

You should develop an interview guide for conducting the interviews. The guide has three sections—the opening, the questions, and the closing. In the opening of the interview, you should thank the interviewees for participating, explain the objectives of the interview, and describe the gift they'll receive at the end of the interview. The next section contains the questions you're going to ask. The questions will depend on which of the methods you're using, i.e., whether you're using one of the segmentation methods, attribute methods, or action methods. Whatever the case, remember that your job as an interviewer is to ask follow-on questions that get the interviewee to elaborate on the answers to the questions you have in your interview guide. The closing is where you thank the interviewees for participating and give them their gift or tell them you will be emailing the gift shortly.

In the question part of the interview, it's best to start an interview with a business interviewee by asking "big picture" questions pertaining to the nature of the interviewee's business, the role the interviewee plays in the business, and the interviewee's and company's major problems and concerns, now and in the future. Consumer interviews are best started by asking general questions about the interviewee's life. In both cases, you should also ask what the interviewee likes and dislikes about your offering and your competitors' offerings. When asking follow-on questions, remember that what you ultimately want to know are the benefits that customers desire. Attributes exist to deliver benefits to customers. There's no point in adding, removing, or modifying an attribute unless it provides the targeted customers with a physical, mental, emotional, social, economic, or cost/risk reduction benefit that they desire. In this regard, note how the questions in Table 10.1 progress from a question about a feature (attribute) to its function to its benefits.

Table 10.1 Feature, function, and benefits

Questions regarding a potato peeler	Answer
What feature do you like best? [attribute]	I like the wide handle.
What does the feature do? [function]	It enables me to grip the handle easier.
How does the feature benefit you? [benefit]	It means my hand doesn't get sore.
What does that benefit do for you? [benefit]	It enables me to make a nice meal for my guests.
What does that benefit do for you? [benefit]	It means my guests view me as a good host.

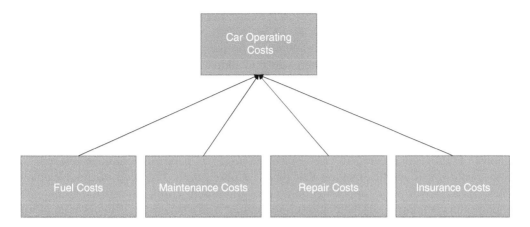

Figure 10.1 Car Operating Costs captures the theme of the four statements.

The third and last step of the interview process is analyzing the content of the interviews to identify the items of interest, i.e., the market segments, attributes, actions, desired outcomes, and so forth. Toward that end, you should download the recording from your call provider or digital device and forward it to a transcription service. The transcription service will translate the audio recording into a written transcript. The cost is typically in the range of $100–$150 per conversation hour. After you receive the transcripts, you and your team should review them to identify the themes in the answers to your questions. A theme is an abstract word or short phrase used to label a category. When analyzing the transcripts, the objective is to identify and label the categories into which the interviewees' comments should be sorted. A useful strategy for identifying the label is to say, "These all have to do with ___" or "These go together because ___." For example, the four comments illustrated in Figure 10.1 go together because they all have to do with *car operating costs*.

As mentioned in Chapter 6, finding themes in qualitative data is referred to as *coding* in the grounded theory method.[3] Claude Crawford's slip method, explained in Chapter 9, is one way of identifying themes. But when dealing with voluminous interview transcripts, a more efficient way to do the coding is to use a qualitative data analysis software program, such as NVivo or Dedoose.[4] These software tools enable you to highlight a word, phrase, or larger portion of an interview transcript and label it with a theme name, i.e., code it. Then, when you're through coding all the transcripts, all the portions of the transcripts that have been labeled with that theme, or any one of the other themes you've created, can be called up for examination. The alternative to using a software tool is to use different marker colors to highlight different themes. Whatever the case, it takes about 1 to 1½ hours to code each transcript, so you might want to split up the work among several people.

Observation

Sometimes people don't tell you the things you want to know because, as Peter Thiel explains, "they are things that people don't know about themselves or things they hide because they don't want others to know."[5] The distinction between *stated preferences* and *revealed preferences* provides another perspective on this behavior. Economic theory holds that what people tell researchers they want (a stated preference) is often different from what they choose in the market (a revealed preference). In other words, "There's a difference between what people *say* and what they *do*," explains the customer experience consultant Mark Hurst in his book *Customers Included: How to Transform Products, Companies, and the World—With a Single Step*.[6] Hurst gives the example of Walmart (in the post–Sam Walton era), where in a massive customer survey their customers said they didn't like the aisles crammed and cluttered with products. Yet, when Walmart decluttered the aisles, customers abandoned their stores in droves.[7] Walmart's customers said one thing. And did another.

So is the moral of the story to disregard everything I just said about interviews? No. The moral is to, whenever possible, add observation to your interviews. *Ethnography*, sometimes referred to as *observational research*, is a branch of anthropology that uses observation to study cultures. Ethnographic methods are sometimes used to perform consumer research.[8,9] *Contextual design* is another method that practices observation.[10,11] Both methods employ systematic frameworks for conducting observational research. Using a systematic framework to guide and discipline your observations is something well worth doing. However, as Hurst notes, it isn't always necessary, "[G]ood research does not require a complicated method with esoteric terminology, practiced with scientific rigor. Simply spending time with customers—observing and listening to them—can often allow insights to emerge."[12] Examples of this "lesser" sort of observational research abound:

- Sony's founder, Akio Morita, was considered a master of observation.[13] Between 1950 and 1982, the insights he gained from watching people work, play, and otherwise go about their daily lives resulted in 12 disruptive new-market growth businesses, ranging from the original battery-powered transistor radio released in 1955 to the iconic Walkman portable cassette tape player introduced in 1979.
- Sam Walton was well-known for observing and talking to customers and staff in Walmart stores and in competitors' stores.[14] (His wife said he seemed to spend as much time in competitors' stores as he did in his own.) He captured what he observed and heard in a spiral-bound notebook.
- Walt Disney had his Disneyland office placed to overlook the entrance to the park so he could observe the visitors' comings and goings, and he constantly roamed the park to observe and talk to them. He once chastised his managers for going off-site to eat lunch rather than observing and conversing with visitors while standing in line with them at the Disneyland food outlets.
- Richard Branson, founder and CEO of Virgin Group, the parent of Virgin Airlines, is constantly observing and talking to customers and cabin crews. He jots down everything he learns in a notebook or on a scrap of paper when the notebook is out of reach.
- Reed Hastings, the co-founder of Netflix, developed the idea for the company based on the simple observation that people, including himself, hated paying the late fees charged by video stores.
- Similarly, Scott Cook, the founder of Intuit, got the idea for the company's Quicken personal accounting software while sitting at the kitchen table with his wife, observing her pay the bills and balance the checkbook by hand and hearing her grumble about how it was all so tedious.[15]

Hurst cites the research that preceded the creation of the OXO measuring cup to elaborate on the benefit of pairing interview and observation research.[16] OXO, which makes easy-to-use kitchenware, retained a research firm to study the problems with traditional glass measurement cups. When asked to say what's wrong with their existing measuring cups, the research participants cited problems like greasy hands make the handle slippery and the glass cup shatters when it's dropped. Then the researchers had the participants demonstrate how they use their existing measurement cups. Among the things they observed is that the participants would pour water into the cup, then bend down to look at the measuring lines on the side of the cup to make sure the water was at the desired level. If it wasn't, they would repeat the pour-bend-check process until they got it right. None of the participants had mentioned this issue when asked to say what was wrong with the measurement cups because they themselves didn't recognize it as a problem. It was only by observing the participants that the researchers were able to detect the pour-bend-check problem. OXO used this insight to design a measuring cup that enables users to read the measurement without having to bend over.

Now ask yourself this. Had you been one of the OXO researchers, do you think you would have noticed the pour-bend-check behavior as a problem? Or would the problem have remained hidden in plain sight? Similarly, imagine yourself in the shoes of Reed Hastings and Scott Cook. Do you think you would have noticed the problems they noticed? Or would they have remained hidden in plain view? The point is that there's more to observation than meets the eye, as Sherlock Holmes famously pointed out to Dr. Watson when he said, "You see, but you do not observe." Amy Herman elaborates on this anecdote in her book *Visual Intelligence: Sharpen Your Perception, Change Your Life.*[17] She explains that in Arthur Conan Doyle's short story "A Scandal in Bohemia," Dr. Watson claimed he could see just as well as Sherlock Holmes, to which Holmes responded, "You see, but you do not observe. The distinction is clear. For example, you frequently see the steps which lead up from the hall to this room."

"Frequently."
"How often?"
"Well. Some hundreds of times."
"Then how many are there?"
"How many? I don't know."
"Quite so. You have not observed. And yet you have seen. That is just my point. Now, I know that there are seventeen steps, because I have both seen and observed."

Herman, a lawyer and art historian by training, uses art to teach professionals (e.g., the New York City Police Department, FBI, and Department of Defense) how to improve their observation skills. She explains the difference between seeing and observing in this way, "Although we frequently use the terms interchangeably, seeing can be thought of as the automatic, involuntary recording of images. Observing is seeing, but consciously, carefully, and thoughtfully."[18] The last three terms deserve elaboration.

To see *consciously* is to be mindful of the fact that you are looking at something. Buddhists say we spend most of our life "asleep," lost in our thoughts about the past and the future rather than being mindful of what we are experiencing in the present moment. Hence the dictum to *be here now*—to *be* fully aware of all that you are experiencing, right *here*, right *now*. Where Watson was too lost in thought to notice the number of steps, Holmes was fully present and counted them. While other entrepreneurs were sleepwalking through their video stores, Reed Hasting was wide awake and paying attention to how he and the other customers felt about late fees. And instead of reflecting on some past event or worrying about the future, Scott Cook was right there in his kitchen, right then, fully aware of what his wife had to say about paying the bills and balancing the checkbook.

By seeing *carefully* Herman means taking the time to look long enough and thoroughly enough to notice the details of the thing you are attending to. The exercises in her book do a wonderful job of revealing the large amount of detail we miss when we don't take the time to look at something carefully. Shari Tishman, a Senior Research Associate at Harvard's Project Zero educational research center, also explains how to practice slow looking in her aptly titled book *Slow Looking: The Art and Practice of Learning Through Observation.*[19] Both authors explain a variety of practices for noticing details, such as examining the focal object at different scales and from different vantage points and describing what you are looking at verbally and pictorially. I doubt that Quicken and Netflix would have come into being if Reed Hastings and Scott Cook hadn't slowed down long enough to notice the things they did.

The notion of *noticing* itself requires a longer look. What exactly does it mean to notice something? In his book *The Mind's Best Work*, D. N. Perkins, the Co-Director of Harvard's Project Zero, explains, "We say 'notice' only when we're not looking directly *for* or *at* whatever we find."[20] He gives the example of walking into your garage and noticing that your car has a flat tire. In that circumstance, you would think it correct to say that you noticed that your tire is flat. If, however, you walked into your garage with the express purpose of inspecting your tires and found one of them to be flat, it wouldn't sound right to say you noticed your tire is flat. Reed Hasting didn't walk into the video store intending to observe the late fee issue, and Scott Cook didn't sit down at his kitchen table for the express purpose of observing bookkeeping hassles. In both cases, they noticed these things because they, like Sherlock Holmes, were in the habit of seeing and hearing consciously and carefully.

While you may not set out to notice some particular thing, there are habits of mind that dramatically increase your chances of noticing something of interest. In her book *Rapt: Attention and the Focused Life*, the writer Winifred Gallagher explains that the skillful management of attention is about "*choosing* [italics mine] the material objects and mental subjects to pay attention to or ignore."[21] Herman teaches her students to skillfully manage their attention by consciously and carefully attending to every aspect and every detail of the paintings they are made to observe. She urges them to consciously choose to look at the who, what, where, and when of the thing they are observing, to ask themselves what they are tuning out and what they are taking for granted, and to observe the thing from various physical and mental perspectives. Similarly, you should train yourself to look for attributes, problems, jobs-to-be-done, desired benefits, and the other things we talked about in the last two chapters.

Choosing what to look for is one of the many mental acts we equate with thinking, which brings us to Herman's third aspect of observation—seeing *thoughtfully*. Skillfully managing our attention by choosing what to look for is a form of thinking that occurs consciously. But some seeing and thinking occurs subconsciously unless we make ourselves aware of it. In our everyday experience of the world, it seems as though we look at something and perceive it directly; an object enters our visual field and a sort of mirror image of it is thrust onto our mind's eye. But what actually happens is that our brains employ a complex manufacturing process to build the images that we seem to experience so easily and directly.[22] The manufacturing processes of perception occur below the threshold of consciousness. Only the products of perception, the images that we experience, are accessible to consciousness. Mental images are not so much mirror images as they are manufactured appearances.[23] Rather than directly-given pictures of the world, our images are *interpreted experiences* of it. As was first explained by the philosopher Ludwig Wittgenstein, we do not simply *see*. Instead, we *see as*. You can experience this for yourself by looking at Figure 10.2 and naming what you see.

Now, answer the following questions. Did you *see* the drawing *as* a duck or *as* a rabbit? What did you *see* it *as*? Were you in any way aware of the manufacturing process underlying the interpreted appearance that popped into your mind's eye? Or did you simply experience the product of the process? Now take a moment to look around the room you're sitting in.

Figure 10.2 What do you see?

Shutterstock, as modified

Do you simply see things? Or do you *see* things *as* things—doors, windows, desks, lamps, chairs, and so forth. Look again and try to see the things in the room in a neutral way; try not to *see* the things *as* things. Are you able to do it? Your answers should make clear to you that, without ever being aware of it, you interpret the things you see and label them accordingly. In other words, you *see* them *as* a kind of thing.

The reason for explaining all this is to make you aware of the fact that while doing observational research, you label every one of the objects and behaviors you observe with a concept, i.e., you *see* everything *as* a kind of thing. The labeling, the *seeing as*, occurs below the threshold of awareness unless you constantly and consciously *think* about how you are interpreting things, i.e., observe *thoughtfully*. The further point is that you can interpret the same thing as different things (e.g., as a duck or as a rabbit), and the way that you interpret something will determine whether you do or don't see what you are looking for. For example, had you seen the tall athlete checking into the Monaco Hotel, you might have seen him *as* a tall person or *as* someone in need of a longer bed. Had you slept on a bed in the hotel, you might have experienced it *as* just a bed or *as* a bed that could be made more pleasurable. And had you been a member of the OXO research team, you might have seen the pour-bend-check behavior *as* nothing out of the ordinary or *as* a problem in need of a solution.

Albert Szent-Gyorgyi (1893–1986), a Hungarian biochemist and winner of the Nobel Prize, once said, "Discovery consists of seeing what everybody has seen and thinking what nobody has thought."[24] Hundreds of hotel managers have seen tall athletes check into their hotels, but only the managers of the Monaco Hotel saw them as people in need of a longer bed. Countless hotel industry executives have slept on guestroom beds, but only Barry Sternlicht thought of the beds as a guestroom attribute that could be made more pleasurable. Hundreds of measuring cup managers have witnessed the pour-bend-check behavior, but only the OXO researchers thought of it as a problem in need of a solution. The offerings they ultimately created—the Monaco Hotel's longer bed, Westin's Heavenly Bed®, and OXO's measuring cup—all started with seeing *thoughtfully*.

In sum, the royal road to being a better observer is to see consciously, carefully, and thoughtfully. But that's easier said than done. Remembering to do all these things in real time is nigh on impossible unless you practice doing them until they become automatic. A great way to start is to buy a copy of Herman's book and practice her exercises. Then, rather than close the book and go back to doing what you've always done (sound familiar?), you need to take what you've learned and make a habit of applying it in your life, always and everywhere. When it comes to learning how to make (and break) habits, an excellent resource is the book *Tiny Habits: The Small Changes That Change Everything*, written by BJ Fogg, the founder of the Behavior Design Lab at Stanford University.[25]

Two final thoughts about observational research. First, wherever and whenever possible, you should photograph and videotape what you observe so that you can later take a slow (or slower) look at it. Most of the qualitative data analysis software tools (e.g., NVivo and Dedoose) enable you to upload photo and video data and to code that data. Second, if you are unable to conduct observational research with customers, your team can always observe itself using your offering. If, for example, you sell tire changing kits, take turns observing each other using the kits to change a tire. The data won't be as insightful as observing customers, but it's better than no data at all.

Surveys

You need to do a survey when you want a statistically valid answer for a population of customers. The strategy canvas and jobs-to-be-done methods are the two circumstances where you would want to conduct survey research. With the strategy canvas, you want to survey customers to determine the order of importance of the purchase criteria and your relative performance on them. In the jobs-to-be-done method, you should do a survey to identify the desired outcomes (or, using Bate's approach, the sub-jobs) that customers consider to be most important and least well satisfied.

Most statisticians say that to obtain a statistically valid result for a basic survey, the minimum sample size should be 100. The maximum sample size should be the lesser of 10% of the customer population or 1,000. Most small- and medium-size companies lack the resources needed to recruit 100–1,000 survey participants, especially if they want to survey non-customers, which they should want to do. As a result, companies usually outsource their survey research. While it's not possible to say the cost of outsourced survey research without knowing the details, suffice it to say that the price is often more than a small- or medium-size company wants to pay. With regard to ranking the purchase criteria on the strategy canvas, an alternative is to rely on what you hear in the customer interviews. You can do this by tracking the number of times each purchase criterion is mentioned in the interview transcripts and then use the number of mentions to infer the order of importance.[26] For example, if purchase criterion A is mentioned 70 times and purchase criterion B is mentioned 50 times and purchase criterion C is mentioned 30 times, the order of importance of the purchase criteria is A, B, and C. The last, and worst, option is for your team to rely on their collective judgment to rank the purchase criteria and to judge your relative performance on each of them.

Survey research is an extensive topic, one that is well beyond the scope of this book. Louis Rea and Richard Parker's book titled *Designing and Conducting Survey Research: A Comprehensive Guide* is a good resource for those who want to learn more about doing surveys.[27]

Employee Idea Systems

As explained in Chapter 6, employee idea systems are a way to learn about customers and the processes used to serve them, which means they are a way to perform customer research. But with employee idea systems it is frontline employees rather than managers who are doing the research. In their book titled *The Idea-Driven Organization: Unlocking the Power of Bottom-Up*

Ideas, the business professors and consultants Alan Robinson and Dean Schroeder explain what they call the *80/20 Principle of Improvement*.[28] This is the idea that 80% of an organization's performance improvement potential lies in frontline-driven approaches to improvement and only 20% in management-driven initiatives. This stands to reason when you consider how much more frontline employees see while doing their daily work as compared to the amount managers see while sitting in their offices. Consider, for example, all the things that the frontline employees of a hotel—the front desk staff, housekeepers, wait staff in the restaurant, bartenders, salespersons, etc.—see and hear as compared to a General Manager who spends most of the day in his office.

Sadly, most of the frontline seeing and hearing is lost because there is no system for capturing it. Creating such a system means more than installing a simple suggestion box. Much more. Designing and implementing a high-performance employee idea system requires a lot of hard work and an ongoing commitment to continuously improving it. But it's worth the effort. Because employee idea systems are a little-used, under-appreciated form of research, they are a great way to gain insights that your competitors have not gained. Accumulating and acting on the dozens, hundreds, or even thousands of insights is a way to differentiate your offering in a way that is impossible for your competitors to copy. Two useful and extensive guides are Robinson and Schroeder's book and John Bessant's book titled *High-Involvement Innovation: Building and Sustaining Competitive Advantage Through Continuous Change*.[29]

Living Labs

Living laboratories—or *living labs*, for short—are another under-appreciated research method. The primary distinction between a living lab and other business laboratories has to do with the difference between "real" and "artificial," or what is known in biology as the difference between conducting experiments *in vivo* (in a living organism) and *in vitro* (in a test tube or on a petri dish). In living labs, customers and concepts are studied *in vivo*, in real, live environments. In traditional business laboratories, customers and concepts are studied *in vitro*, in artificially constructed settings. For example, some hotel brands now obtain feedback from customers who have stayed overnight in a test guestroom in a hotel (a living lab) rather than the traditional practice of obtaining customer feedback on a model guestroom constructed in a warehouse (an artificial lab).

Why use a living lab rather than an artificial one? A good way to answer this question is to imagine yourself as the "guinea pig" in the foregoing settings. In the first setting, you stay overnight in a test guestroom in a hotel. In the second one, you spend time touring a model guestroom in a warehouse. Which laboratory do you think would enable you to give more, and more insightful, feedback? My guess is you will say the living lab rather than the artificial lab. And insightful feedback is what it's all about. Living labs have become an effective instrument in a new paradigm that is variously referred to as *open innovation* or *co-innovation*, which is short for collaborative innovation. The co-innovation paradigm includes the practice of obtaining insightful feedback from users during all phases of the innovation process, which is to say, during initial research, concept development and design, and implementation.

Living labs can be far more extensive than just a hotel guestroom. In Europe, where the concept is being applied with vigor, there are hundreds of applications, including making living labs of homes, retail establishments, museums, theaters, airports, farms, fishing villages, streets, neighborhoods, industrial districts, and even an entire city of 60,000 people. You can find more information on the website of the European Network of Living Labs (ENoLL) at www.enoll.org.

Implementing a living lab can be as simple as defining the boundaries of the lab and using the "try something out and see what happens" method of experimentation. But if you want to get serious about your experimenting, you should take a more sophisticated approach, one that includes (a) establishing the research question or hypothesis, (b) defining the unit of analysis and method of measurement, (c) designing an experiment to answer the question or to prove the hypothesis, (d) implementing the experiment using disciplined research methods, such as the foregoing observation and interview protocols, and (e) interpreting the results.

Whichever research method you use—interviews, observation, surveys, employee idea systems, living labs, or something else—you'll have gained insight into a multitude of customer problems after you've completed it. Which brings us to the next topic—creative problem-solving.

Notes

1 Willie Pietersen. *Strategic Learning: How to be Smarter Than Your Competition and Turn Key Insights Into Competitive Advantage* (New York, NY: John Wiley & Sons, 2010), 51.
2 I don't like focus groups because (a) of the time and expense required to organize them, (b) of the need to simultaneously manage group dynamics (e.g., people who try to dominate the conversation) and get the information I want, (c) the participants tend to anchor on the answers given by others, and (d) participants are sometimes reluctant to say things in front of a group that they would otherwise say in a one- or two-person interview.
3 Janice M. Morse and Lyn Richards, *Readme First for a User's Guide to Qualitative Methods* (Thousand Oaks, CA, 2002). This book is a great introduction to grounded theory and software tools for qualitative data analysis.
4 NVivo is relatively expensive, whereas Dedoose is more affordably priced. You can find information on other qualitative data analysis tools here: http://textanalysis.info/pages/text-analysis-software-classified/content-qualitative-data-analysis.php.
5 Peter Thiel, *Zero to One: Notes on Startups, or How to Build the Future* (London, UK: Virgin Books, 2014), 103.
6 Mark Hurst, *Customers Included: How to Transform Products, Companies, and the World—With a Single Step* 2nd Ed. (New York, NY: Creative Good, 2015), 66.
7 *Ibid*, 56–60.
8 Hy Mariampolski, *Ethnography for Marketers: A Guide to Consumer Immersion* (Thousand Oaks, CA: Sage Publications, 2006).
9 Patricia L. Sunderland and Rita M. Denny, *Doing Anthropology in Consumer Research* (Walnut Creek, CA: Left Coast Press, 2007).
10 Karen Holtzblatt and Hugh Beyer, *Contextual Design: Defining Customer-Centered Systems* 1st Ed. (San Diego, CA: Academic Press, 1998).
11 Karen Holtzblatt, Jessamyn Burns Wendell, and Shelley Wood, *Rapid Contextual Design: A How-to Guide to Key Techniques for User-Centered Design* (San Francisco, CA: Elsevier, 2005).
12 Hurst, *op. cit.*, 105.
13 Clayton M. Christensen and Michael E. Raynor, *The Innovator's Solution: Creating and Sustaining Successful Growth* (Boston, MA: Harvard Business School Press, 2003), 79.
14 Andy Boynton and Bill Fischer, *The Idea Hunter: How to Find The Best Ideas and Make Them Happen* (San Francisco, CA: Jossey-Bass, 2011), 71–73.
15 *Ibid*, 75–76.
16 Hurst, *op. cit.* 94–96.
17 Amy E. Herman, *Visual Intelligence: Sharpen Your Perception, Change Your Life* (Boston, MA: Houghton Mifflin Harcourt, 2016), 25–26.
18 *Ibid*, 26.
19 Shari Tishman, *Slow Looking: The Art and Practice of Learning Through Observation* (New York, NY: Routledge, 2018).
20 D. N. Perkins, *The Mind's Best Work* (Cambridge, MA: Harvard University Press, 1981), 78.
21 Winifred Gallagher, *Rapt: Attention and the Focused Life* (New York, NY: Penguin Books, 2010), 1–2.
22 Gregory Bateson, *Mind and Nature: A Necessary Unity* (New York: Bantam Books, 1979), 32–39

23 Adam Morton, *A Guide Through the Theory of Knowledge* (Malden, MA: Blackwell Publishers, 1997), 33–34.

24 https://quoteinvestigator.com/2015/07/04/seen/. Actually, there is some question as to whether Szent-Gyorgyi was the first to express this idea and whether he said it in exactly this way.

25 BJ Fogg, *Tiny Habits: The Small Habits That Change Everything* (Boston, MA: Houghton Mifflin Harcourt, 2020).

26 Richard K. Lee and Nina E. Goodrich, *Value Innovation Works: Move Mountains…… Drive sustainable, profitable growth! Deliver exceptional value to the most important customers in your value chains. A "How To" guide.* (Richard K. Lee, 2012), 119–120.

27 Louis M. Rea and Richard A. Parker, *Designing Survey Research: A Comprehensive Guide, 4th Ed.* (San Francisco, CA: Jossey-Bass, 2014).

28 Alan G. Robinson and Dean M. Schoeder, *The Idea-Driven Organization: Unlocking the Power of Bottom-up Ideas* (San Francisco, CA: Berrett-Koehler, 2014), 7–11.

29 John Bessant, *High-Involvement Innovation: Building and Sustaining Competitive Advantage Through Continuous Change* (West Sussex, UK: John Wiley & Sons, 2003).

11 Creative Problem-Solving

In simplest terms, a problem exists when there is a gap between an existing state and a goal state and the problem solver doesn't know how to close the gap. The goal, in our case, is to differentiate an offering by providing significantly more of a desired benefit, an additional desired benefit, or both. More specifically, because benefits are provided by attributes, the goal is to create attributes that do a better job of providing the benefits and attributes that provide additional benefits. In this chapter, you're going to learn various methods for solving this type of problem.

Problems

The first job of this chapter is to provide thorough definitions of the terms *problem* and *problem-solving*. We'll start by taking a long look at how others have defined them. Considering that differentiation, and much of the rest of business, requires you to solve problems, it's worth taking the time to develop a deep understanding of what these two terms mean.

The following authors propose problem definitions that center on not knowing how to close the gap between an existing state and a desired state:

- In *The Ideal Problem Solver*, psychology professors John Bransford and Barry Stein write, "A problem exists when there is a discrepancy between an initial state and a goal state, and there is no ready-made solution for the problem solver."[1]
- Operations researchers Colin Eden, Sue Jones, and David Sims, authors of *Messing About in Problems: An Informal Structured Approach to their Identification and Management*, propose this definition of a problem, "We usually refer to ourselves as having a problem if things are not as we would like them to be, and we are not quite sure what to do about it."[2] They also say, "[P]roblems are psychological entities which are often unclear and expressed as anxiety or concern about a situation as well as being expressed as a positive wish for the situation to be different in some way."[3]
- In his book *Techniques of Structured Problem Solving*, communications professor Arthur VanGundy Jr. writes, "A problem can be defined as any situation in which a gap is perceived to exist between what is and what should be."[4]

Consultant John Arnold, author of *The Complete Problem Solver: A Total System for Competitive Problem Solving*, elaborates on the notion of "should be" by advising his readers to ask the following questions when defining a problem:[5]

- "What is not happening that should be happening?" By implication, a problem exists when something is not happening that should be happening. Or, said a bit differently, a problem exists when something is not happening that someone wants to happen.

DOI: 10.4324/9781003271703-12

- "What is happening that should not be happening?" Here, the implication is that a problem exists when something is happening that should not be happening. Or, put differently, a problem exists when something is happening that someone does not want to happen.

In *Swans, Swine, and Swindlers: Coping with the Growing Threat of Mega-Crises and Mega-Messes*, business professors Can Alpaslan and Ian Mitroff go to great lengths to explain what a problem *is not* by distinguishing between an *exercise* and a *problem*:[6]

- To start, Alpaslan and Mitroff give this simple example of an exercise: "If Billy has saved $6 and he needs $11 to buy a game, how much money does he need to save?" In comparison, an example of a problem is figuring out a better way to attract and retain employees. Another example is devising a policy that will minimize the amount of homelessness in a city.
- Exercises are presented to us preformulated in the sense that we do not have to figure out what it is that must be solved. Problems, on the other hand, do not drop out of the sky preformulated. They require that we come to grips with exactly what the problem is.
- An exercise is clearly defined before working on it. Problem definitions become progressively clearer during the problem-solving process.
- Exercises have a single right answer or solution. Problems have more than one possible solution.
- Exercises remain solved because they are static; the nature of the exercise does not change. Problems do not always remain solved because they are dynamic; things change and so too must the solutions.
- Exercises are usually tackled by a single discipline or profession, as would be the case, for example, with an operations research or a chemical engineering exercise. Finding a solution to a problem often requires the efforts of multiple departments, disciplines, or professions.

Consultants Charles Kepner and Benjamin Tregoe, authors of *The New Rational Manager: An Updated Edition for a New World*, describe a problem in the following ways.[7] Note their emphasis on causality and performance:

- "A problem is the visible effect of a cause that resides somewhere in the past."
- A problem exists in "any situation in which an expected level of performance is not being achieved and in which the cause of the unacceptable performance is unknown."
- A problem is "a deviation between expected and actual performance that is of unknown cause."

Business professors Joan Ernst van Aken, Hans Berends, and Hans van der Bij, authors of *Problem Solving in Organizations: A Methodological Handbook for Business Students*, provide a somewhat different take on performance problems:[8]

- "Business problem-solving projects are started to improve the performance of a business system, department, or a company on one or more criteria." The criteria, they note, often have to do with effectiveness or efficiency.
- "A problem can be defined as the result of a certain perception of affairs in the real world with which one or more important stakeholders are dissatisfied."
- The "stakeholders are dissatisfied on the basis of a comparison of their perception of the performance of the business system in question on certain implicit or explicit

performance indicators with some implicit or explicit norms, and they choose the problem to work on because they have the impression that significant performance improvement is feasible within acceptable constraints on time and effort."

The definition of a problem that we're going to use incorporates key concepts from the foregoing definitions. The concepts are italicized in the following piecemeal description of a problem. The piecemeal description is followed by a summary definition.

- A problem involves an *undesired effect*. Loosely defined, an *effect* can be a situation, condition, phenomenon, event, action, behavior, object, capability, characteristic, quality, or property, all of which can be classified as a state of the world. Whatever the case, the effect is the result of one or more *causes*. Thus, problems are about cause and effect.
- Other ways of saying that an effect is *undesired* are to say that it is unsatisfactory, unwanted, or unacceptable. The effect is considered unsatisfactory, unwanted, or unacceptable because it is thought of as being *bad* or because it is thought of as being *less than ideal*, which is to say, not as good as it could be.
- An undesired effect is a problem when a problem solver (person or group) does not possess the *knowledge* required to transform the undesired effect into a *desired effect* because the problem solver doesn't *know what* caused or is causing the effect, or because the problem solver doesn't *know how* to act on the cause(s) to transform the undesired effect into the desired effect, or because of both.
- Desires and knowledge are things that exist in a person's mind (as Eden and his co-authors earlier put it, they are *psychological entities*), which means that the existence and nature of a problem is a matter of *personal belief*. For example, when Competitor A loses market share to Competitor B (the effect), Competitor A will believe it to be an undesired effect and Competitor B will believe it to be a desired effect. Another example is the person who views an undesired effect as a problem because he lacks the knowledge needed to solve it (the know-what and/or the know-how) versus the person who doesn't see it as a problem because she possesses the needed knowledge.

In summary form, our operational definitions are these. A *problem* exists when there is an undesired effect and the problem solver lacks the knowledge required to transform the undesired effect into a desired effect. Unlike exercises, problems do not come preformulated, do not have a single correct solution, do not always remain solved, frequently require a multi-disciplinary team to solve them, and become progressively better defined during the problem-solving process. *Problem-solving* is defined as the process of coming to know the cause(s) of the undesired effect and ways to act on the cause(s) to transform them into the cause(s) of the desired effect.

Figure 11.1 will help you visualize a problem and problem-solving as I've just defined them. The diagram shows that the undesired effect has three causes. Transforming the undesired effect into the desired effect requires that the problem solver determine the causes of the undesired effect and then find ways to act on the causes so as to transform them into things that will cause the desired effect. The question marks in Figure 11.1 indicate where the problem solver may lack the knowledge required to solve the problem. He may not know one or more of the causes of the undesired effect or one or more of the actions that are required to transform the causes.

A simple example of problem-solving is illustrated in Figure 11.2. Imagine that you want to start a fire in your fireplace. The undesired effect is "Fire in the fireplace does not exist" and the desired effect is "Fire in the fireplace does exist." Fire is caused by the existence of

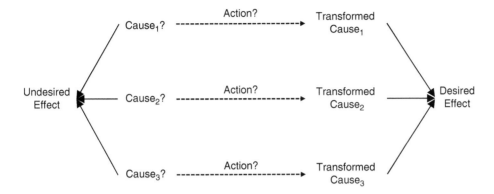

Figure 11.1 Problem-solving is thinking of ways to transform the undesired effect into the desired effect.

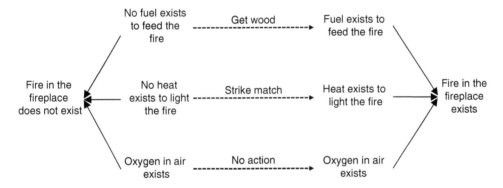

Figure 11.2 An example of transforming an undesired effect into a desired effect.

fuel, heat, and oxygen. In this situation, while oxygen in the air exists, there is no fire in the fireplace because there is no fuel and no heat. So, to act on these two causes of the undesired effect, you get some wood, strike a match, and *voila*, you have a fire.

You might think this qualifies as having solved a "problem," but it actually does not. The reason is that there was no problem in the first place because you *knew* the three causes and you *knew* how to act on them. It would meet our formal definition of a problem, however, if you found yourself lost in the woods without a book of matches or a lighter. Then, like the character played by Tom Hanks in the movie *Cast Away*, you would *not know* how to provide the heat for the fire until it occurred to you to make a hand drill.[9]

Figure 11.3 shows that creating a desired benefit is a form of problem-solving. In this case, the undesired effect is that the desired benefit does not exist (or not enough of the benefit exists). Three states are causing the desired benefit not to exist. Acting on the three states results in bringing the desired benefit into existence.

OXO's Good Grips® handle is a good example of this problem-solving process. As earlier explained, OXO makes large grips for kitchen utensils. OXO's founder had the idea for the product when his wife remarked that her arthritic hands made it difficult for her to grip the thin metal handle of her traditional potato peeler, shown in the left panel of Figure 11.4. He

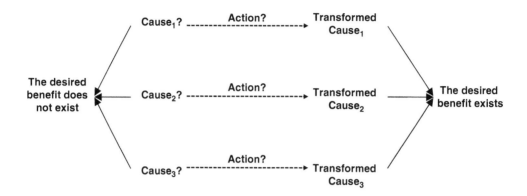

Figure 11.3 Creating desired benefits is a form of problem-solving.

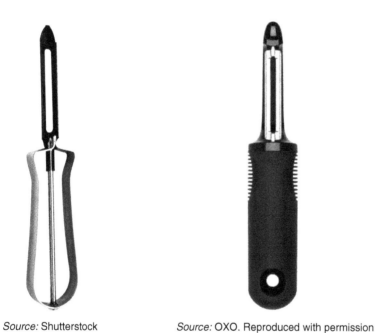

Source: Shutterstock   Source: OXO. Reproduced with permission

Figure 11.4 Traditional vs. OXO Good Grips® potato peeler.
Source: Shutterstock and OXO.

responded by creating a line of large, soft, easy-to-grip handles for potato peelers, shown in the right panel of Figure 11.4, and, later, for all manner of other kitchen utensils. As shown in Figure 11.5, he solved the problem of handles that are hard to hold by acting on each of the causes of the undesired state.

Now that you've considered the foregoing problem-solving diagrams and accompanying descriptions, note the following:

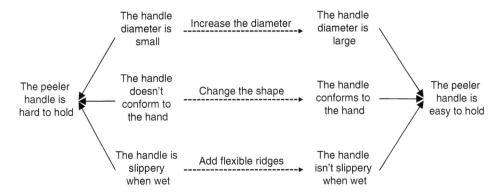

Figure 11.5 Creating the benefit of a potato peeler handle that is easier to hold.

- While not technically correct,[10] I'm using the terms *cause* and *reason* interchangeably, as people often do. Sometimes I speak in terms of the things that are causing a particular state to exist or that will cause a state to exist, i.e., the causes of a state. Other times I talk about the reasons why a state exists or the reasons why a state can be made to exist.
- The undesired effect, desired effect, causes, and transformed causes are all *states of the world* or simply *states*. Again, a *state* can be a situation, condition, phenomenon, event, action, behavior, object, capability, characteristic, quality, or property. In Figures 11.4 and 11.5, for example, the potato peeler handle is initially in the state of being hard to hold be*cause* the handle is in the state of being thin, in the state of not conforming to the hand, and in the state of being slippery when wet. To transform the peeler handle from the state of being hard to hold to the state of being easy to hold, the three causes are transformed into alternate states—the handle is transformed into the state of being wide, the state of fitting the hand, and the state of not being slippery, all of which cause the state "the handle is easy to hold."
- The things that transform each of the initial causes (initial states) into the transformed causes (transformed states) are *actions* or *processes*. (A process consists of a series of actions.) Thus, to *act on a cause* means to perform some action or process that transforms one state into another. In Figure 11.4, the actions are described by using the verbs *increase*, *change*, and *add*. Determining what action or process will achieve the transformation is where creative thinking is required, as will be discussed later in this chapter.
- Most states of the world are the result of multiple causes. In certain circumstances, any one of the causes is *sufficient* to produce the state. In Figure 11.4, for example, any one of the transformed causes is sufficient to make the peeler handle easier to hold. Adding them together makes the handle even easier to hold. If we were to express this as an equation it would be $Cause_1 + Cause_2 + Cause_3 = Desired\ Effect$.[11] In other cases, however, it is *necessary* for all the causes to exist. In these cases, the causes are together described as *necessary and sufficient*, meaning that all the causes are necessary but no one of the causes alone is sufficient. In Figure 11.2, fuel, heat, and oxygen are all necessary to start a fire, but no one of them alone is sufficient to do it. In this case, the equation would be $Cause_1 \times Cause_2 \times Cause_3 = Desired\ Effect$, which means that if any one of the causes is zero (doesn't exist), the desired effect is zero (doesn't exist).

MECE

Sometimes interview and observational research will reveal the undesired effect and its cause(s). For example, between the OXO founder-interviewer and the interviewee (his wife) they were able to discern that a traditional potato peeler handle is hard to hold because the handle is thin, doesn't conform to the hand, and is slippery when wet. However, with complex matters, interviewees are usually only able to say the undesired effect, leaving it to the interviewer to identify the cause(s) of the effect. For example, when a person goes to the doctor and complains of chest pains, it's up to the doctor to diagnose the cause(s) of the pains. Similarly, when a customer tells a computer repair service that his computer boots up too slow, it's the repair service that must diagnose the cause(s) of the boots-up-too-slow effect.

McKinsey & Company, the renowned management consulting firm, is often called on to diagnose the cause(s) of a complex undesired effect, such as a decrease in sales or an increase in employee turnover. To do so, they religiously rely on the MECE (pronounced "me-see") method. I say "religiously" because, as the former McKinsey consultant Ethan Rasiel explains in his book *The McKinsey Way: Using Techniques of the World's Top Strategic Consultants to Help You and Your Business*, "[The MECE method] is the sin qua non of problem-solving at McKinsey. MECE gets pounded into every new associate's head from the moment of entering the Firm. Every document (including internal memos), every presentation, every e-mail and voice mail produced by a McKinsey-ite is supposed to be MECE."[12]

MECE is an acronym that stands for *mutually exclusive, collectively exhaustive*. In the MECE method, an issue tree is used to divide the main issue into a set of sub-issues that contains every aspect of the main issue (the sub-issues are *collectively exhaustive*) and in which none of the sub-issues overlaps another (the sub-issues are *mutually exclusive*). As examples, let's first use the potato peeler handle and then move on to a more complex issue. Imagine you want to use an issue tree to identify all the reasons why the peeler handle is hard to hold. To start, you draw the rectangle on the left side of Figure 11.6 and assume that it contains all the reasons why the peeler handle is hard to hold. Then, as shown in the squares located to the immediate right of the rectangle, you divide the rectangle into the specific reasons why the peeler handle is hard to hold. Your objective should be to identify all the reasons (the list is collectively exhaustive) and to make sure that none of the reasons overlap (the list is mutually exclusive). Notice that, on the right half of the diagram, the transformed causes and desired effect also constitute a MECE issue tree. In this case, the tree consists of a mutually exclusive, collectively exhaustive list of the reasons why the peeler handle is easy to hold.

The next example illustrates a more complex issue tree. In this example, imagine that the undesired effect is that the company's potato peeler sales have decreased and that you're a consultant who has been called in to diagnose the cause(s) of the decrease. To do so, you

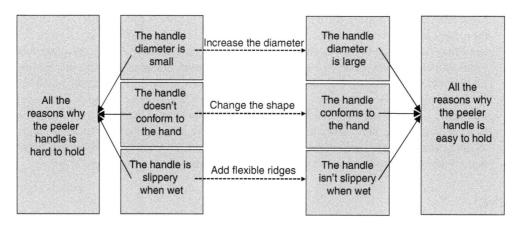

Figure 11.6 Mutually exclusive, collectively exhaustive sets of reasons/causes.

create the issue tree shown in Figure 11.7. Each of the sub-issues is a possible reason why the peeler sales have decreased. In order to create more space, I've eliminated the boxes used in Figure 11.6. And to keep the diagram simple, let's assume that the price of the peeler and its design have been eliminated as possible reasons for the sales decrease. As another way to keep things simple, I haven't extended the issue tree beyond the third level, other than to show the arrows that connect to the fourth level issues.

It's unlikely that all the causes listed for the decrease in peeler sales (the undesired effect) are actual causes, so the next step in the MECE method is to determine which of the causes is responsible for the decrease. To do so, you should use what you know about the situation to develop a hypothesis about the actual cause, then use some form of research (interviews, observation, etc.) to prove or disprove the hypothesis.[13,14] If your hypothesis turns out to be wrong, and/or you think there is more than one cause of the undesired effect, you should repeat the process.

The foregoing two examples are intended to show that the MECE method can be used to diagnose the causes of (or reasons for) any sort of undesirable effect, be it the state of a product attribute like a peeler handle or the state of a company's product sales. The examples are also intended to show that the steps for using a MECE issue tree to create a differentiated offering are to (a) identify the desired benefits of the offering that do not exist, (b) determine the reasons why each desired benefit does not exist, and (c) identify actions that will transform the reasons into reasons why the desired benefit does exist. Devising ways to effect the transformation requires creative thinking, which is the next topic of this chapter. But before we get into that, it will be useful to take a brief look back to see how we got to this point in the book.

A Brief Look Back

So far, you've learned that differentiation is about making your offering different in a way that causes customers to prefer it. Customers prefer an offering when it provides them with significantly more of a desired benefit, additional desired benefits, or both. Benefits and wants/needs are two sides of the same coin; customers want or need benefits that are provided by offerings. By my count, there are six kinds of benefits—physical, mental, emotional, social, economic, and cost/risk reduction. Offerings exist at the level of individual products and services, at the level of bundles and complements, and at the level of entire companies. Offerings have attributes at each of these levels. The attributes perform functions that generate benefits. Customers use the attributes to judge whether the offering will provide them the benefits they desire.

There are three mega-methods you can use to identify the attributes and benefits customers desire. The *segmentation* methods identify segments of customers that desire the same attributes and benefit(s). The *attribute* methods identify the attributes customers use to decide from whom to buy and the reasons why the attributes are important, i.e., the benefits they expect to derive from the attributes. The *action* methods identify the steps customers take before, during, and after they use an offering, the tasks/jobs they perform at each step, the outcomes (benefits) they desire when performing each task/job, and the constraints that stand in the way of obtaining a desired benefit or more of a desired benefit. All the mega-methods employ interview and observation research.

As illustrated on the left half of Figure 11.8, the ultimate purpose of the mega-methods and the research is to identify the benefits that customers desire to gain from an offering, or that they would desire if the offering made the benefits available to them. In other words, the left half is about problem finding. The right half of Figure 11.8 is the problem-solving diagram as it applies to benefits. The problem-solving process starts with the state "the desired benefit

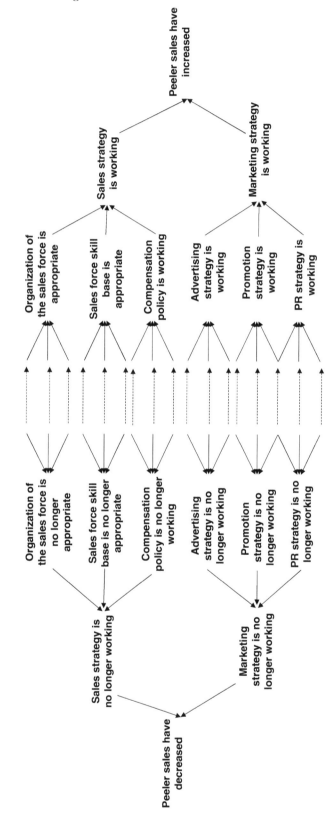

Figure 11.7 Mutually exclusive, collectively exhaustive set of possible reasons peeler sales have decreased.

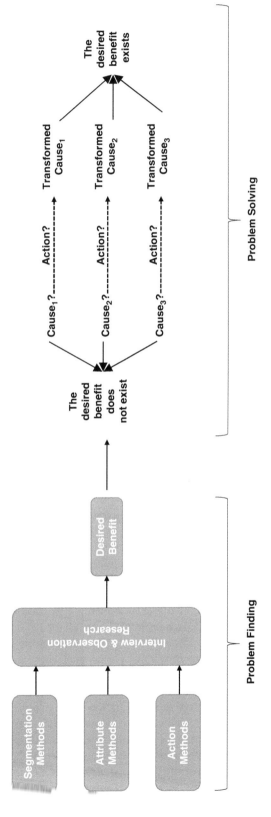

Figure 11.8 It all boils down to desired benefits.

does not exist." It then applies the MECE method to identify the causes of that state. The final step is to identify the actions that will transform the causes of the state "the desired benefit does not exist" into causes of the state "the desired benefit exists." As is next explained, creative thinking is required to identify the actions that will transform the causes.

Creative Thinking

Robert Weisberg is a psychology professor at Temple University who specializes in the study of creative thinking. In a chapter he authored in the book *Tools for Innovation: The Science Behind the Practical Methods That Drive New Ideas*, he explains, "Creativity entails the production of goal-directed novelty…. Creativity results in the intentional production of new things, either ideas or physical objects; the *creative process* or *creative thinking* is the psychological means whereby such novelty is brought about."[15] Where Weisberg defines the output of creative thinking as a *goal-directed novelty*, the philosopher Margaret Boden defines creative output as that which is *novel, non-obvious,* and *valuable*.[16] Paul Thagard, a Canadian philosopher who specializes in cognitive science, uses the following synonyms to elaborate the three concepts—novel (new, original), non-obvious (surprising, unexpected), and valuable (important, useful, appropriate, correct, accurate).[17] It should come as no surprise that these concepts track with the idea of differentiation. Michael Porter focuses on *novelty* when he talks about doing activities differently and doing different activities.[18] Youngme Moon notes that differentiated offerings surprise people by violating their expectations, which is the same as saying that differentiated offerings are *non-obvious*.[19] And my entire treatment of differentiation, including Figure 11.8, centers on benefits, which you now know is equivalent to centering on *value*. In short, a differentiated offering is one that is novel (new, original), non-obvious (surprising, unexpected), and valuable (provides desired benefits).

Weisberg proposes that creative thinking is nothing more than ordinary thinking processes that produce goal-directed novelty. Or, putting it in Boden's terms, creative thinking is nothing more than ordinary thinking that produces something that is novel, non-obvious, and valuable. Among these ordinary thinking processes, Weisberg explains, are *expertise* (the retrieval and use of material from memory), *logic* (both deductive and inductive), and *analogical thinking* (understanding one thing in terms of another).[20] He details the way these thinking processes were used to generate creative output in science (Watson and Crick's discovery of DNA), invention (the Wright Brothers invention of the airplane and Edison's invention of the kinetoscope), art (Picasso's creation of his painting *Guernica*), and of special interest to us, IDEO's design of the differentiated shopping cart pictured on IDEO's website at this link www.ideo.com/post/reimagining-the-shopping-cart.[21] We're going to take a brief look at the way IDEO used expertise, logic, and analogy to redesign the traditional shopping cart before taking a more extensive look at the three types of thinking in the rest of this chapter. (Note that Weisberg explains the IDEO example in substantially more detail than I do, as does Tom Kelley, an IDEO partner, in his book *The Art of Innovation: Lessons in Creativity From IDEO, America's Leading Design Firm*.[22]) We're also going to look at the way the three types of thinking are applied to the OXO potato peeler.

IDEO is a global design firm, perhaps best known for designing Apple's first mouse. In order to demonstrate their design skills, they agreed to a challenge put to them in a 1999 episode of ABC's late-night news show *Nightline*. IDEO was given one week to create a new design for the clumsy shopping cart we've all come to know and hate (or, at least, tolerate). The firm responded by first interviewing and observing supermarket shoppers and managers in order to identify the problematic aspects (undesired states) of shopping carts. Then they used expertise, logic, and analogy to solve the problems. A sampling of the problems IDEO identified and the three types of thinking they used to solve them is provided below:

- Slow Checkout and Embarrassment: IDEO used a combination of *logic* and *expertise* to solve the problems (undesired states) of slow checkout and embarrassment caused by people who, at checkout, discover they don't have enough money to pay for all the items in their shopping cart. They solved the problem by adding the scanner pictured at this link: www.ideo.com/post/reimagining-the-shopping-cart. The scanner automatically tracks the total amount owed for the items that have been scanned, enabling customers to know, before paying for their goods, if they will be short the money needed to pay for them. The logic went something like this: IF checkout is slowed by customers that don't know their total, THEN identify a way for them to know their total before checkout. IDEO's designers then used expertise (their knowledge of electronic gadgets) to think of the scanner as a way for customers to tabulate their total before checkout.
- Unable to Find Items: IDEO used a combination of *logic* and *analogy* to solve the problem (undesired state) of having to track down an employee to ask for help with finding a food item. Their logic ran along the following lines: IF it is necessary to walk around to find an employee to ask, THEN find a way to ask without having to walk around. IDEO used cell phone and walkie-talkie analogies (i.e., concepts pulled from different domains) to come up with the idea of adding a microphone to the scanner so that shoppers could use it to radio an employee to ask for help remotely.
- Child Seat Safety & Utility: IDEO relied on the *analogy* of a roller coaster safety bar to design a pull-over safety bar for the shopping cart's child seat, and the analogy of a child's highchair to add a play surface to the child's seat.
- Pilferage: The homeless steal shopping carts to use the large metal baskets as barbecue grills. IDEO used *logic* to solve the problem: IF the metal shopping cart baskets are being used as barbecue grills, THEN make the baskets out of plastic.

The now-familiar OXO potato peeler serves as a second example of using the three types of thinking to generate a novel, non-obvious, and valuable offering.[23] It will help to refer to Figure 11.5 as you read the following:

- Handle Diameter is Small: Simple logic dictates that IF the handle diameter is too small to hold comfortably, THEN increase the diameter. This takes us to the point of knowing *what* to do, but we still don't know *how* to do it, i.e., we don't know how large the diameter should be. We could figure that out by experimenting with different diameter handles.
- Handle Doesn't Conform to Hand: Here, again, simple logic dictates that IF the shape of the handle doesn't conform to the hand, THEN change the shape to make it conform. This, again, tells us *what* to do without telling us *how* to do it. Analogical thinking is often a good way to figure out the how. To find the analogies we can ask, "What are all the places (domains) in which you find handle grips?" Answers include paintbrush handles, bicycle grips, hand tool grips, knife handles, and so on. Enter the search term "handle grips" on the Google Images page; you'll be amazed at the number and variety of grips that are available to serve as analogs. Most of the time you'll need to adapt the analogs to your particular application.
- Handle is Slippery When Wet: In this instance, applying logic to the stated cause doesn't get us very far. Saying "IF the handle is slippery when wet, THEN make it not slippery when wet" doesn't really tell us *what* to do. It's better to rephrase the cause to make it more specific by saying, "IF the handle is slippery when wet because there is nothing preventing the hand from slipping, THEN add something that prevents the hand from slipping." This says more about *what* to do. If the problem solver has some expertise in

this area, she might be able to pull the *how* from memory. For most people, however, it's more likely that analogical thinking would lead to an answer. Asking where else we find slippery handles might lead us to think of toothbrush handles, where manufacturers have solved the problem by adding ridges that prevent the thumb and fingers from slipping. It may be that OXO adapted this solution to create the flexible ridges on their handles. Looking even further afield to things that prevent slipping when wet, takes us to rubber bathmats and floormats, non-slip flooring tiles, anti-slip tape, the soles of shoes, and (you read it here first) toenail grips for dogs. Enter "things that prevent slipping when wet" into Google Images to see for yourself.

This OXO example is the second place we've run into the distinction between *what* and *how*. Recall that in Chapter 3, I explained that a helpful way to understand the distinction between *what* and *how* is to remember that an offering (the *how*) is a physically manifest thing, whereas the function of the offering is an abstract idea that is assigned to the offering that states *what* it does. In other words, the offering is the physically manifest *how* of the abstract *what*. Creative solutions usually start off as abstract ideas (the *whats*) that require detailing and specification to turn them into physically manifest offerings (the *hows*). Or, putting it more elaborately, creative solutions usually start out in the abstract world of ideas; they are nursed into the physical world of offerings by making the ideas progressively more specific, to the point where the ideas are specific enough to be physically manifested. As is next explained, the abstract and progressively more specific ideas are the product of *logic*, *expertise*, and *analogy* plus the practice of *experimentation*.

Logic

We use logical thinking to reach a conclusion about some fact or truth in the world, which is to say, about what was, is, or will be the case. We also use logical thinking to reach a conclusion about what we (and others) should and shouldn't do. Conclusions about what we should and shouldn't do are often based on conclusions about facts and truth. Both types of conclusions are generated by If-Then thinking. For example, If I hear a roar, Then it's *true* there is a lion, and If there is a lion, Then we *should* run. Or, more compactly put: If roar, Then lion, and If lion, Then run. While our conclusions are the result of If-Then thinking, we rarely phrase them this way. Were you and a friend strolling the Serengeti, it's more likely you would say something like, "I just heard a roar. I think it's a lion. I think we should run," or, even more likely, "Lion! Run!"

The mathematician Eugenia Cheng, author of *The Art of Logic in an Illogical World*, explains that a more concise way of saying If-Then is "implies."[24] So instead of saying If A, Then B, we can say A implies B. In logic and mathematics, she elaborates, "This implication means that whenever A is true, B absolutely has to be true. When A is false the implication doesn't tell us anything."[25] Cheng goes on to explain that a *proof* is a series of implications strung together. For example, A implies B, B implies C, Therefore, A implies C. Outside of mathematics, a proof is usually called an *argument*. It is an argument in the sense that someone is arguing for a conclusion. In the lion example, you argued for the conclusion that you and your friend should run. Your friend might have argued for the conclusion you should hide.

The lion argument is an example of a deductive argument. A syllogism is a deductive argument in which there are two premises (two Ifs) and a conclusion (one Then) that is inferred from the premises. In a syllogism, the "If-Then" and "implies" language is usually jettisoned in favor of a single "Therefore" at the start of the conclusion. The classic example is: All men are mortal. Socrates is a man. Therefore, Socrates is mortal. In her book *The Pyramid Principle: Logic in Writing and Thinking*, Barbara Minto, a former McKinsey &

Company consultant, explains that she finds the usual ways of describing deductive arguments to be confusing. Instead, a deductive argument is better described as doing the following three things:

- "Make a statement about a situation that exists in the world.
- Make another statement about a related situation that exists in the world at the same time. The second statement relates to the first if it comments on either its subject or its predicate.
- State the implication of these two situations existing in the world at the same time."[26]

One way of complying with these three requirements, Minto elaborates, is to say the following.[27] Note how, in the brackets, I've adapted her format to the problem-solving framework illustrated in Figure 11.3:

- "Here's what is going wrong. [The undesired effect.]
- Here's what is causing it. [The cause of the undesired effect.]
- Therefore, here's what we should do about it. [The action that transforms the cause.]"

Remember that Weisberg proposes that creative thinking is nothing more than ordinary thinking processes that produce goal-directed novelty and that logic is one of these ordinary thinking processes. In our case, we want to use logic to identify creative ways (actions) to transform the causes of the undesired effect into causes of the desired effect. The following two examples show how Minto's logical deduction framework can be used to identify creative ways to act on a cause:
IDEO shopping cart example:

- Homeless people steal shopping carts. [The undesired effect.]
- They steal the shopping carts be*cause* they use the metal grills to barbecue food. [The cause of the undesired effect.]
- Therefore, we should make the grills out of something other than metal. [The action that transforms the cause.]

OXO handle example:

- Wet hands slide along potato peeler handles. [The undesired effect.]
- The wet hands slide be*cause* there is no opposing force to stop their sliding. [The cause of the undesired effect.]
- Therefore, we should add something that will provide an opposing force. [The action that transforms the cause.]

Note, again, that both the shopping cart conclusion and the OXO handle conclusion say *what* transformation should be done, but they do not say specifically *how* the transformation should be done, which means that another round of logical deduction is called for. In the shopping cart example, the second round of logical deduction might look like this:
IDEO shopping cart example-second round of logical deduction:

- Homeless people use the metal grills to barbeque. [The undesired effect.]
- They use metal grills to barbeque be*cause* metal doesn't melt when exposed to high heat. [The cause of the undesired effect.]

- Therefore, make the grills out of something that melts or disintegrates when exposed to high heat. [The action that transforms the cause.]

This conclusion gets us closer to an implementable action, but it doesn't get us all the way there. "Make the grills out of something that melts or disintegrates when exposed to high heat" still doesn't tell us precisely *how* to physically manifest something that melts when exposed to high heat. When logic doesn't take us all the way to an implementable answer, one of the other two types of thinking—expertise or analogy—usually does the trick. We can use them by asking the "How can we _____?" question, or its more effective sibling, "What are all the ways we can _____?" question. In the case of the shopping cart, the question is: "What are all the ways we can make the grills out of something that melts or disintegrate when exposed to high heat?" There are two places to search for the answers to this sort of question. The first place is in an expert's head, where an expert is someone who knows something about the subject. The second is out in the world in an analogous domain, where man or nature has already devised a solution. This takes us to the next two sections of this chapter. But before we get to them, we need to look at two ways that deductive arguments can go awry.[28]

The first way a deductive argument can go wrong is the inclusion of *ambiguous terms*. An ambiguous term or phrase is one that can be interpreted to mean more than one thing. Mario Bunge, a philosopher and physicist, explains that ambiguity "can always be removed, in part or entirely, by the adjunction of further signs," including the adjunction of additional words.[29] By way of example, he notes that "political freedom" is less ambiguous than "freedom." In the shopping cart example, consider how the phrase "metal barbeque grill" is less ambiguous than "metal grill," which is itself less ambiguous than "grill." And in the peeler example, consider how the term "handles" is made less ambiguous by adding "thin," "metal," and "potato peeler" to make it clear that we are talking about "thin metal potato peeler handles." Also consider how the phrase "wet and greasy hands" is less ambiguous than the phrase "wet hands." A good way to prevent ambiguity is to look at the key terms in the argument and ask, "What *exactly* do we mean by this term?" or "What *kind* of thing do we mean?" You should keep asking until you reach the point where you can visualize what you are talking about in the context you are talking about it.

A second way logical arguments go wrong is untrue *assumptions*. In *Asking the Right Questions: A Guide to Critical Thinking*, the authors Neil Browne and Stuart Keeley explain, "An assumption is an unstated belief that supports the explicit reasoning."[30] A factual assumption is a belief about what was, is, or will be the case. If the assumption is untrue, the part of the deductive argument it supports is invalid. Factual assumptions usually have to do with the "Here's what is going wrong" statement and the "Here's what is causing it" statement. For example, in the foregoing argument, the statement "Homeless people steal shopping carts" rests on the unstated belief that stealing the shopping carts is, in fact, an undesired effect. What if they only steal the broken shopping carts in the back of the store that are going to be hauled off for recycling? Is it still an undesired effect? A good way to identify assumptions is to repeatedly ask, "What else must be true for this statement to be true?"

Now that we've looked at two ways an argument can go off the tracks, we can get back on the track of looking at the two places to search for answers to the "How can we _____?" question, or in better form, the "What are all the ways we can _____?" question. Remember, the first place to search is in an expert's head. The second is out in the world in an analogous domain, where man or nature has already devised a solution. Also remember, expertise and analogy are often used when logic gets us close, but not close enough, to an action we can implement.

Expertise

Expertise, as described by Weisberg, involves the retrieval and use of material from memory. For our purposes, an expert is anyone who has a whole solution to the problem stored in their memory or all the parts of the solution and the ability to piece them together to form the whole solution. Or an expert is someone who has a part of the solution, which can be pieced together with the parts in other experts' minds to form a whole solution. With both kinds of experts, the challenge is to retrieve the material from memory and piece it together.

One way of retrieving the material from memory is the previously-explained MECE method.[31] Just as the method can be used to identify all the possible causes of an undesired state or effect, it can be used to identify all the possible ways to act on a cause. The process begins by asking the "What are all the ways we can _____?" question. As illustrated in Figure 11.9, the MECE method starts off with a "box" that contains all the possible answers to the question, i.e., a box that is collectively exhaustive. Then the box is subdivided into progressively more specific answers, all of which are mutually exclusive. To keep things mentally manageable, Ethan Rasiel suggests that the number of answers at each level should never be more than five or less than two; three is best.[32] If you have more than five answers, you should state four of them and use an "Other" box for the remainder, then detail the remaining answers at the next-lower level.

The IDEO shopping cart serves as a simple example of using the MECE method to generate ways to act on a cause. Figure 11.10 shows three ways and additional sub-ways of making the shopping cart basket out of something that melts or disintegrates when exposed to high heat. As is usually the case, some answers are better than others, so it will be necessary to select one of the answers as the best based on selection criteria like efficacy, cost, feasibility, and so forth.

Before you settle on a solution, you want to first make sure you're asking the right question. Albert Einstein is supposed to have said, "If I had an hour to solve a problem, I'd spend fifty-five minutes thinking about the problem and five minutes thinking about solutions."[33] A problem hierarchy is a useful tool for thinking about a problem, which is to say, it's a useful way to identify the question you should be answering. As illustrated in Figure 11.11, the way to build a problem hierarchy is to ask "Why?" to move to the left in

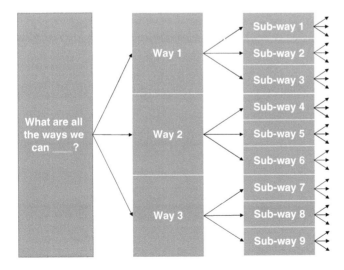

Figure 11.9 Using MECE to answer the "What are all the ways we can _____?" question.

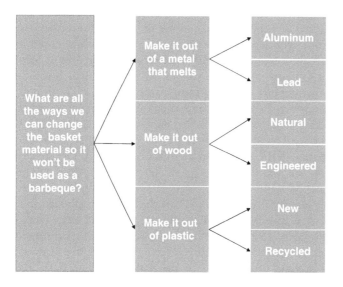

Figure 11.10 An example of using MECE to answer the "What are all the ways we can _____?" question.

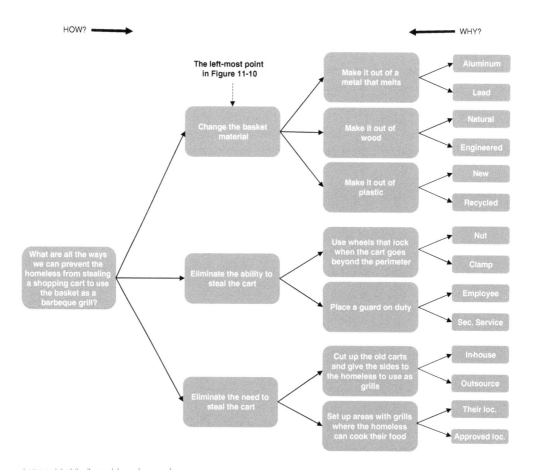

Figure 11.11 A problem hierarchy.

the diagram to the higher-order issues and to ask "How?" to move to the right to the lower-order issues. So, starting at the point of changing the basket material (i.e., the left-most point in Figure 11.10), asking why we want to change the basket material yields the answer "Because we want to prevent the homeless from stealing the shopping cart to use the basket as a barbeque grill," which is transformed into the question, "What are all the ways we can prevent the homeless from stealing a shopping cart to use it as a barbeque grill?" Repeatedly asking "How?" then takes us down two additional branching paths as we move to the right in the diagram.

I started this section by saying that expertise, as described by Weisberg, is about the retrieval and use of material from memory. Ralph Keeney, an emeritus business professor at Duke University, elaborates on this idea in his book *Value-Focused Thinking: A Path to Creative Decisionmaking*:

> The mind is the sole source of alternatives. Either the alternatives are somewhere in the mind waiting to be found, or they can be created from what is in the mind. But in this regard a person's mind is like a vast unexplored space. With such a vast area to search for alternatives, intuitive and informal search strategies are often inadequate. Natural cognitive processes tend to guide our thoughts away from the areas of the mind that hold keys to creative alternatives .... What is needed are *systematic and efficient ways to search* [italics mine] through the mind that negate the natural tendency to think as we have thought before.[34]

MECE diagrams like the ones illustrated in Figures 11.10 and 11.11 are ways of systematically and efficiently searching through the "vast unexplored space" of the mind. Keeney suggests several other ways of doing so, all of which are designed to overcome the cognitive bias known as *anchoring*. People tend to anchor on their first alternative (e.g., the "Change the basket material" alternative in Figure 11.11), or the first alternative they hear, in the sense that the subsequent alternatives they generate all relate to the first (e.g., they all pertain to the alternatives to the right of the "Change the basket material" idea in Figure 11.11). This limits the range, or diversity, of the alternatives they develop in answer to the "What are all the ways we can _____?" question. One of Keeney's methods for exploring the mind centers on objectives and measures of achievement.[35]

An objectives hierarchy (Figure 11.12) consists of an overall objective and one or more levels of sub-objectives. Keeney distinguishes between *fundamental objectives* (aka *end objectives*), which are the fundamental reasons for interest in a situation, and *means objectives*, which are objectives that must be achieved in order to achieve the end objectives. In Figure 11.12, the end objectives are contained in the rectangles and the means objectives are in the ovals. The dotted lines indicate which means objective(s) contribute to accomplishing an end objective. Each end objective is assigned a measure that is used to determine the degree to which the objective is achieved. Keeney calls the measures *attributes*, but to avoid confusion with our use of the term, I refer to them as *measures of achievement* (MOAs). The MOAs are shown at the base of each end objective in the figure.

Keeney explains that thinking about how to better achieve each end objective in the hierarchy, regardless of its level in the hierarchy, can suggest novel alternatives. The objectives should first be considered one at a time, then two at a time, and so on. Because the MOAs for the end objectives define them more clearly, he recommends that the MOAs also be used to stimulate alternatives. Consider in Figure 11.12, for example, how the end objective of making it possible for users to temporarily park their heavy shopping cart and bring multiple small items back to it, and the end objective of making the basket too small to grill on, and the means objectives of using a modular design and making the basket out of plastic,

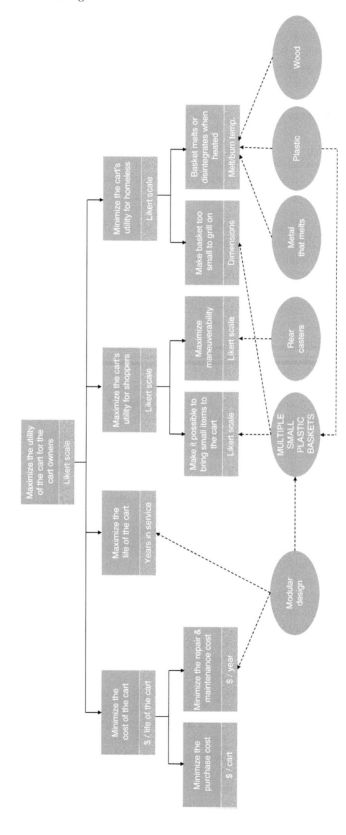

Figure 11.12 An end objectives hierarchy (the rectangles) and the means objectives (the ovals) that achieve the end objectives.

all stimulate the idea of employing multiple small plastic baskets rather than a single large metal basket that the homeless can grill on (see the multiple small plastic baskets shown in the picture at this link: www.ideo.com/post/reimagining-the-shopping-cart).

Consider again what Keeney had to say about alternatives, "Either the alternatives are somewhere in the mind waiting to be found, or they can be created from what is in the mind." The latter option requires people to retrieve the parts of the alternative from various places in their mind and then piece them together into a whole alternative. Or, in the case of a problem-solving group, the parts of the alternative are retrieved from several minds and pieced together by the group or one of its members. Both cases underline the idea that *nothing comes from nothing*, that is, the idea that novel alternatives consist of novel combinations of existing parts. Steven Johnson, the author of *Where Good Ideas Come From: The Natural History of Innovation*, elaborates on the idea by explaining, "Good ideas are not conjured out of thin air; they are built out of a collection of existing parts[.] ... Some of those parts are conceptual: ways of solving problems, or new definitions of what constitutes a problem in the first place. Some of them are, literally, mechanical parts."[36] In other words, creative ideas are novel combinations of existing ideas, and creative artifacts are novel combinations of existing components.

Min Ding, who holds a Ph.D. in marketing and a Ph.D. in molecular, cellular, and developmental biology, is a business professor at Pennsylvania State University. He is the author of *Logical Creative Thinking Methods*.[37] In his book, which contains a wealth of examples of product-, service-, bundle-, complement- and company-level innovations, he details a comprehensive set of methods for piecing together novel combinations of existing ideas and components. Ding explains that logical creative thinking (LCT) is all about search, "LCT posits innovation as a search process and innovators as explorers and consists of a system of logical search methods to identify novel, non-obvious, and valuable concepts,"[38] which is to say, he provides a book-length response to Keeney's proposal that, "What is needed are systematic and efficient ways to search through the mind that negate the natural tendency to think as we have thought before." Considering that differentiation is about creating novel, non-obvious, and valuable offerings, Ding's book gives us a method for differentiating an offering.

The starting point of the LCT process is an actual or hypothetical solution that is relevant to the task at hand (say, a job-to-be-done). For our purposes, the starting point can be a product, a service, a bundle or set of complements, or a company-level component. Ding emphasizes that practitioners should always choose multiple starting points so as to initiate the search from different places. LCT innovation, he goes on to explain, typically occurs at the component level, although it sometimes occurs at the whole solution level. Here, you should remember that the components of products and services are, respectively, objects and events. The components of bundles and complements are products, services, programs, and systems. And the components of companies include their sales & marketing, distribution channel, and customer relationship activities.

The second step of the process, shown in Figure 11.13, is to deconstruct the starting point so as to identify its components. Here, the MECE method is again a useful tool. The starting point can be deconstructed into its physical parts, functions (see again the function analysis methods described at the end of Chapter 4), needs (desired benefits), or in some other way. A useful rule-of-thumb, Ding says, is to deconstruct the starting point into three to six core components. The final deconstruction step is to choose the component(s) that appears to be the most promising.

The third, and main, part of the LCT process involves applying one or more methods to search for a creative solution. Ding classifies the methods at three levels. At the first level, there are the three primary search methods—*reconfiguration*, *replacement*, and *recombination*,

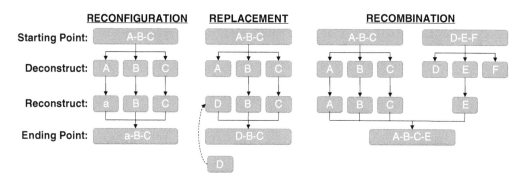

Figure 11.13 The three primary Logical Creative Thinking methods.

each of which is described below and illustrated in Figure 11.13. At the second level, the three methods divide into 12 subcategories of search methods, all of which are listed below. And at the third level, the subcategories divide into 95 sub-subcategories. Ding describes the categories in a way that helps you to choose the method that is most appropriate for a particular search objective:

• Reconfiguration: The reconfiguration method involves deconstructing the starting point into components, modifying one or more of the components, and then reconstructing the components to arrive at the creative solution (ending point). IKEA, for example, took a traditional furniture store (the starting point, or "A–B–C" in the diagram) and modified the salesperson component of the store by locating salespersons at interspersed kiosks ("a" in the diagram), rather than having salespeople approach customers and trail behind them ("A" in the diagram), as is done in a traditional furniture store. Note that the reconfiguration diagram in Figure 11.13 ignores the modifications IKEA made to the other components of a traditional furniture store. Following are the six subcategories of the reconfiguration method:
  1. Duration: Change the lifespan of the component (8 sub-subcategories)
  2. Reduction: Reduce one or more of the components (12 sub-subcategories)
  3. Augmentation: Augment one or more of the components (10 sub-subcategories)
  4. Timelining: Change a relationship over the timeline (12 sub-subcategories)
  5. Spatialization: Change a spatial relationship (7 sub-subcategories)
  6. Causation: Change a functional causal relationship (7 sub-subcategories)

• Replacement: The replacement method involves deconstructing the starting point into components, replacing one or more of the components with a component obtained from elsewhere, and then reconstructing the components to arrive at the ending point (creative solution). Peter Bidstrup, the founder of Doubletree Hotels, used the replacement technique to create (Compri) Hotels,[39] a hotel concept in which he replaced the restaurant and lounge component ("A" in the diagram) of a traditional hotel ("A–B–C" in the diagram) with an airline-style club room ("D" in the diagram). Another example is Southwest Airlines which, early in its life, replaced a price cut needed to match one of its competitor's price cuts with a free bottle of whiskey. Following are the two subcategories of the replacement method:

7. Abstraction: Find a similar component (7 sub-subcategories)
8. <u>Contrarian</u>: Find an opposite component (7 sub-subcategories)

- <u>Recombination</u>: The recombination method involves deconstructing two or more starting points into their components, then combining components from each of them to construct the creative solution. An example is the printer–copier–scanner machines that combine components of printers, copiers, and scanners. Following are the four subcategories of the recombination method:

  9. <u>Sharing</u>: Combine different solutions (9 sub-subcategories)
  10. <u>Cancellation</u>: Use better solutions to remedy weakness (4 sub-subcategories)
  11. <u>Amplification</u>: Combine mutually enhancing solutions (7 sub-subcategories)
  12. <u>Arbitrage</u>: Learn from successful solutions in different contexts (5 sub-subcategories)

In 1945, the French mathematician Jacques S. Hadamard conducted a survey in which he asked scientists to explain the mental processes they used to create their theories. In part of Albert Einstein's response he explained, "Combinatory play seems to be the essential feature in productive thought."[40] He later referred to the combinatory play as "associative play." Whatever you care to call it, Min Ding's LCT method gives you 95 ways to play.

The linguist Derek Bickerton said, "It is only because we can imagine things being different from the way that they are that we are able to change them."[41] Imagining things as being different from the way that they are (or were) is elsewhere referred to as *counterfactual thinking*.[42] The MECE, problem hierarchy, objectives hierarchy, and LCT methods are ways of imagining offerings as being different from the way they are. One problem with managers, however, is that they are often unable to see beyond the way things presently are. That's because they hold rigid beliefs (If-Then rules) about what the offerings in their industry should be, do, or have. For example, after experiencing some number of traditional potato peeler handles, the rule "If potato peeler, Then thin metal handle" gets burned into our brains and the brains of the managers who make them. Every time the managers experience a potato peeler, the association between the If and the Then halves of the rule becomes stronger and more automatic, to the point where they believe the *rule* that potato peelers *should* have thin metal handles. The same goes for the rules "If shopping cart, Then metal basket," "If furniture store aisle, Then straight," "If restaurant, Then wait to be seated," and the countless other subconscious If-Then rules we learn in life without being aware we are learning them.

In *Elastic: Unlocking Your Brain's Ability to Embrace Change*, the physicist Leonard Mlodinow tells the story of how Mr. X made his fortune in the grocery business by surfacing and violating a subconscious rule.[43] (For the full story and the name of the founder and the grocery store chain he founded, you'll have to read Mlodinow's book.) In 1916, Mr. X observed that grocery stores still sold their food in the same way as the general stores we see pictured in western movies, where customers ask the store clerk to pull the items they want off the shelves located behind the counter. In other words, at the start of the century, grocery store owners adhered to the rule "If grocery store goods, Then clerk pulls the goods from behind the counter." This system worked fine when there were only one or two customers in the store, but it was maddeningly slow during busy times. Mr. X prospered by first becoming aware of this subconscious rule (aka *tacit assumption*) and then violating it by creating a grocery store in which the customers themselves pulled the items they wanted off shelves located behind the checkout counters. And so was the modern grocery store born. You can imagine how surprised and delighted customers were when they first encountered this new and faster way of shopping. In fact, they were so delighted that within six years Mr. X was able to build a chain of 1,200 grocery stores in 29 states.

Mlodinow explains how Mr. X's thought process was just another version of the thought process used to solve the nine-dot problem illustrated in Figure 11.14. This 100-year-old problem is a staple of many creativity books, and it is still cited in several academic papers each month, he elaborates. Take some time to try to solve the problem before reading on. Seriously. You'll gain much more from what I next have to say if you make a genuine effort to solve the problem.

Any luck? Probably not. In most experiments, Mlodinow notes, the number of people who are able to solve the problem is fewer than one in ten, and many times it's zero. The reason? Just as, prior to Mr. X, no one surfaced and challenged the subconscious rule that clerks *should* pull the grocery items from shelves rather than customers doing it themselves, you probably failed to surface and challenge your subconscious rule that the lines *should* stay within the nine-dot array rather than extending beyond it, as they do in Figure 11.15. Now think back to some of the other business examples we've examined. Prior to IKEA, how many furniture stores challenged the rule that furniture *should* be sold fully assembled rather than flat-packed? And prior to Sherwin-Williams, how many paint stores challenged the rule that they *should* limit their offering to paint and materials rather than help paint contractors run their business? And prior to Southwest Airlines, how many airlines questioned the rule that they *should* offer food service and interline baggage transfers rather than not offering these services? And prior to Gary Hamel, how many university presidents questioned the rule that universities *should* operate as they do instead of the alternative ways of operating identified in Table 8.1? And on it goes. All of which points to the idea that a useful strategy for identifying ways to differentiate your offering is to make a conscious effort to list and challenge all your subconscious rules about what your offering *should* be, do, or have.

The mental rules that dictate what things *should* be, do, or have are sometimes referred to as *generative rules*, and the entire collection of rules is termed a *generative system*. The rules are considered generative because they generate a particular mental outcome. The generative system that exists in the heads of industry executives determines what is, and is not, possible in the industry—at least to their way of thinking. Prior to IKEA, for example, the generative rules in the furniture industry dictated that a furniture store is one with assembled furniture, straight aisles, no restaurants, no childcare, and so on. While it's possible to use the traditional system of rules to generate *novel* and *valuable* furniture stores (and other offerings), none of them would strike you as *non-obvious* (surprising, unexpected) because they all conform to the traditional system of rules. Margaret Boden explains that the surprise we feel

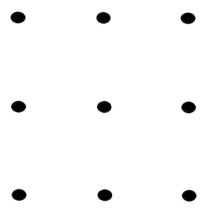

Figure 11.14 The nine-dot problem: connect the dots with four continuous lines without retracing or lifting your pencil from the paper

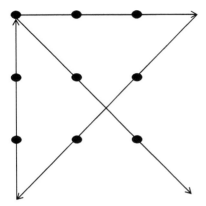

Figure 11.15 The solution to the nine-dot problem; start at the upper-left-most dot.

when we first encounter a creative idea, "often springs from our recognition that it simply *could not* have arisen from the generative rules (implicit or explicit) which we have in mind. With respect to the usual mental processing in the relevant domain (chemistry, poetry, music …), it is not just improbable, but *impossible*."[44] Consider how the surprise you felt when you first encountered an IKEA store, a smartphone, a Swatch Watch, or some other non-obvious offering sprang from the realization that it did not conform to the traditional rules governing what it should be, do, or have.

Mlodinow describes the fundamental method used to search for solutions in the subconscious. This same method can be used to search for solutions in Keeney's "vast unexplored space" of the mind. In fact, the subconscious *is* the vast unexplored space of the mind. The fundamental method consists of the first three stages of the oft-described five-step creative process—preparation, incubation, illumination, evaluation, and verification. There are dozens of stories in science, art, and business in which people vainly work for a period of time to solve a problem (preparation), then give the problem a rest (incubation), only to have the solution suddenly pop into their mind while they're in the shower or otherwise in a relaxed state of mind (illumination). Mlodinow describes how recent research explains the neurological underpinnings of this phenomenon.

The brain contains two fundamental networks. The *executive network* is the network we use when we consciously work to solve a problem, as is the case when employing the MECE, problem hierarchy, objectives hierarchy, and LCT methods and the tactic of surfacing and challenging the rules about what your industry's offering should be, do, or have. In other words, it's the part of the brain we use during the preparation stage of problem-solving. Recent research has revealed the existence of a second network, known as the *default network* or *default mode network*. When our conscious mind is relaxed and not working hard to focus on something, the default network continues to work on the problem subconsciously. The default network is where the incubation occurs. The advantage of the default network is that it can parallel process a gargantuan amount of information, way more than the limited, linear processing that occurs in the executive network. Once the default network has solved the problem, the solution pops into our conscious mind, which is the illumination phase. You have no doubt experienced this many times yourself, such as when you tried to remember someone's name, then gave up, and later had the name pop into your head seemingly out of nowhere.

My reason for explaining all this is to have you appreciate several things. First is the significant and under-appreciated role that the subconscious default network plays in creative thinking. Second is the importance of first putting your executive network to work by using the MECE, problem hierarchy, objectives hierarchy, LCT, and/or rule-listing methods to consciously search your memory for an action that will act on the cause(s) of the undesired state. And not just use the methods, but use them to the point of frustration, because frustration is what kicks your default network into gear and gives it direction and momentum. Third is the value of taking time to relax and give the problem (and other problems) a rest so your executive network doesn't re-engage and override your default network. The final thing to appreciate is that you'll probably need to go through several iterations of the preparation and incubation steps before your mind is lit bright by a solution that is novel, non-obvious, and valuable.

Elkhonon Goldberg, a professor of neurology in the New York University School of Medicine, uses the term "directed wandering" to describe the back-and-forth movement between the sustained, goal-directed effort that occurs during preparation and the subconscious mental wandering that happens during incubation.[45] *Un*directed wandering is what occurs when the default network is wandering the pathways of thought without a particular destination in mind. In contrast, the conscious, goal-directed effort we make during preparation sets the subconscious wandering off in the direction of the goal—hence the term "directed wandering." Goldberg stresses that iterating between the two processes—the sustained, goal-directed effort and the subconscious, directed wandering—is what ultimately makes the creative process successful.

Analogy

While Keeney correctly holds that peoples' minds are the sole source of alternatives, many of those alternatives have migrated out of their minds and into the world. So in addition to searching for solutions in your mind and the minds of others, you should also search for solutions in the world. Analogs are where you want to look.

The first thing to understand about analogy is the difference between a *metaphor* and an *analogy*. A metaphor is a statement that says one thing *is* another. For example, "Life *is* a roller coaster." An analogy, in contrast, is a statement that says one thing *is like* another or, more formally, as illustrated in Figure 11.16, the target domain *is like* the source domain. When the movie character Forest Gump said, "Life *is like* a box of chocolates," for instance, the box of chocolates was the source domain and life was the target domain. To say that one thing is like another thing is to say that they are in some way similar or, to put it another way, that they

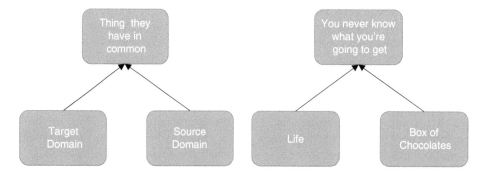

Figure 11.16 To say that the target domain is like the source domain is to say they have something in common.

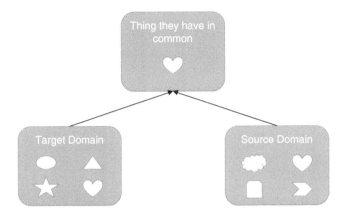

Figure 11.17 The two domains are analogous because they have a characteristic in common.

have something in common—just as life and a box of chocolates have in common that "You never know what you're going to get."

Figure 11.16 illustrates the general idea of analogy, but it doesn't capture all of it. That's because it doesn't do a good job of showing the "thing they have in common," or equivalently, the "in some way they are similar." Figure 11.17 corrects this deficiency. It shows that the source domain has different characteristics (represented by the different shapes), just as a box of chocolates has different characteristics. And it shows that the target domain has different characteristics (also represented by the different shapes), just as life has different characteristics. But the target and source domains do have one characteristic in common (the heart shape), just as life and boxes of chocolate share the one characteristic "You never know what you're going to get." Two (or more) domains are considered *analogous* when they have a characteristic in common.

While Figure 11.17 does a better job of illustrating the nature of analogy, it still doesn't capture one of its key elements, which is that the characteristic the two (or more) things have in common is an abstract idea. Recall that as soon as you start thinking about a general concept (say, the concept of a *chair*) instead of some particular instance of it (*your chair*), you start to climb the ladder of abstraction pictured in Figure 6.3 and Figure 6.4. With every step up the ladder—from *your living room chair* with the coffee stain and the scratch on the leg, to the more general concept of a *living room chair,* to *chair,* to *furniture,* to *décor,* to *asset*—the concepts become progressively more general (abstract), which is to say, they describe fewer and fewer characteristics of *your living room chair.* For example, when *your living room chair* is thought of as a *chair,* more of its characteristics are left out than when it is thought of as a *living room chair.*

With respect to analogies, as illustrated in Figure 11.18, the more abstractly you think about something, such as *your living room chair,* the further the conceptual distance between it and the concept you're using to think about it. As Eugenia Cheng explains, using a much-simplified diagram, an illustration like the one shown in Figure 11.18 "gives us a way of expressing the possibly surprising fact that although thinking about something more abstractly appears to take us *further away* from concrete ideas (vertically in the picture), it enables us to pivot further away from where we started (horizontally), and thus encompass *more ideas,* including concrete ones."[46] To understand what she means, consider the following:

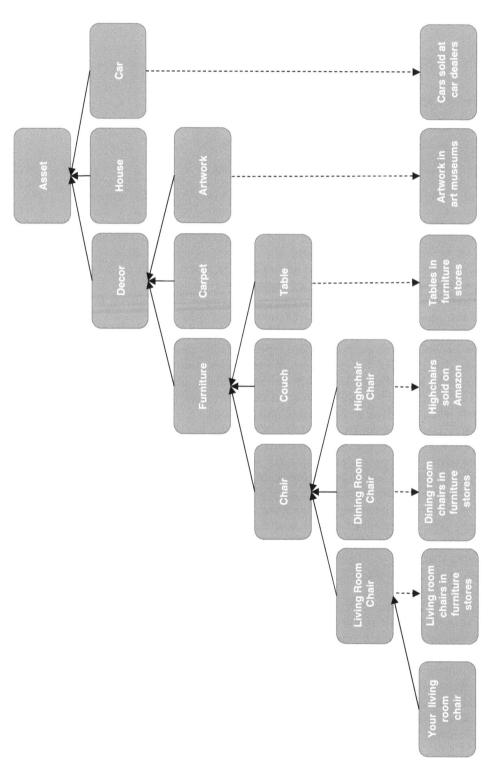

Figure 11.18 Moving up in abstract space increases the vertical and horizontal conceptual distance from the starting point (your living room chair).

- As you proceed up and to the right from *your living room chair*, the concepts become more abstract (i.e., more general), and the vertical conceptual distance between *your living room chair* and the concepts becomes greater. So does the horizontal conceptual distance.
- Also notice that you can specify a place (at the end of the dotted lines) to look for concrete instances of each concept in the diagram, as I have done for some of them, such as looking for concrete instances of artwork in art museums. Then notice that the higher you go in abstract space, the further the horizontal conceptual distance between *your living room chair* and the concrete instances of each concept.
- Finally, consider the large number of concepts in the diagram and the fact that each of them has the potential to serve as an analog. As I said at the start of this section, analogs are where you want to search for creative alternatives. Each of the boxes in Figure 11.18 is a potential source of creative solutions. Imagine, for example, that you are a living room chair manufacturer looking for creative ways to design your chairs. The general concepts and concrete instances shown in the illustration provide you with lots of places to search for characteristics (the equivalent of the heart in Figure 11.17) you can adapt to your living room chairs. Consider, for example, how the play space and eating area of a highchair might be adapted to a living room chair.

Now that you have a better handle on the nature of analogy, let's walk through the method for applying it. As illustrated in Figure 11.19, the first step is to select the characteristic in the target domain that you want to focus on. The second step is to define your objective for the characteristic. For example, the objective may pertain to one of the desired outcomes you identified as part of the jobs-to-be-done method, such as minimizing the time it takes to find a lost item. The third step is to ask and answer some form of the question, "Where else do people try to accomplish this objective?" As shown in Figure 11.18, your answers will reveal various source domains; the more abstract (general) you make the question, the further will be the conceptual distance between your focal characteristic and the source domains. The fourth step is to mine the source domains for ways to achieve your objective, i.e., for solutions you can adapt to your problem.

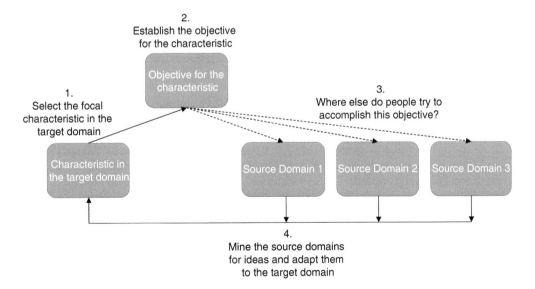

Figure 11.19 Steps for using analogy to find creative solutions

Figure 11.20 illustrates the way IDEO might have used analogy to find ways to arrive at the design of the child seat pictured at this link: www.ideo.com/post/reimagining-the-shopping-cart (though I doubt they went through the thinking process precisely as it is described):

- Starting in the lower left of the figure, IDEO focused on the *child seat* characteristic in the domain of a *traditional shopping cart* (the target domain).
- Moving up one level and to the right, they established the objective *minimize the chance of a young child falling out of the traditional shopping cart seat*. Then they asked themselves where else people try to accomplish this objective. This led IDEO to look at other kinds of traditional shopping carts to see how they try to accomplish this objective, with the goal of adapting the solutions they found to redesigning their shopping cart child seat. For examples, insert "shopping cart child seats" in the search box of Google Images.
- Next, moving another level up and to the right, they made the objective more abstract by phrasing it as *minimize the chance of a young child falling out of a seat* (not a *shopping cart* seat), and they again asked themselves where else people try to accomplish this objective. This led them to look at different kinds of highchair seats, child car seats, stroller seats, and other kinds of seats in which young children are restrained. (Use Google Images to find examples of each kind of seat). And, again, they were looking to find solutions that could be adapted to the redesign of the child seat in their shopping cart.
- Their next step was to go up yet another level and to the right, where they made the objective even more abstract by rephrasing it as *minimize the chance of a person* (not a *young child*) *falling out of a seat*. They then asked themselves where else people try to accomplish this objective, which led them to consider seats in different kinds of amusement park rides, wheelchairs, racecars, and other kinds of seats where people are somehow restrained. (Search for examples of each using Google Images.) Here, again, they mined each of these source domains for ideas that could be adapted to the redesign of the child seat in their shopping cart.

In the end, IDEO adapted the pullover lap bar of an amusement park ride, the play space of a highchair, and the cup holder of a car seat to create the redesigned shopping cart child seat pictured at this link: www.ideo.com/post/reimagining-the-shopping-cart.

Once again, as shown in Figure 11.19, the simpler way of applying analogy is to focus on a problem (undesired effect) or objective in the target domain and ask, "Where else do you find this problem?" or "Where else do people have this objective?" Then search for corresponding source domains, mine the source domains for solutions, and adapt the solutions to the target domain. An interesting example is provided by Australia's *Designing Out Crime* partnership.[47] The partnership was faced with the problem of alcohol-fueled fights in Sydney's Kings Cross district, where the pubs and clubs empty as many as 30,000 young adults onto the main strip at closing time. The partnership's designers asked, "Where else are people faced with the problem of tens of thousands of young adults, many of whom are prone to alcohol-driven violence?" They identified music festivals as a source domain, mined it, and discovered numerous solutions that could be adapted to their problem.

Another way to apply analogical thinking, whether you use the simpler method or the more elaborate abstraction hierarchy, is to start with a desired physical, mental, emotional, social, economic, or cost/risk reduction benefit. Let's say, for example, you want customers to enjoy the emotional benefit of feeling curious. To apply the simpler method, you would ask something like, "Where else are people made to feel curious in a way that they enjoy?" One place is in novels, where writers hook readers by keeping them curious about what will happen next. A bit of web research (a great way to find and mine source domains) reveals that

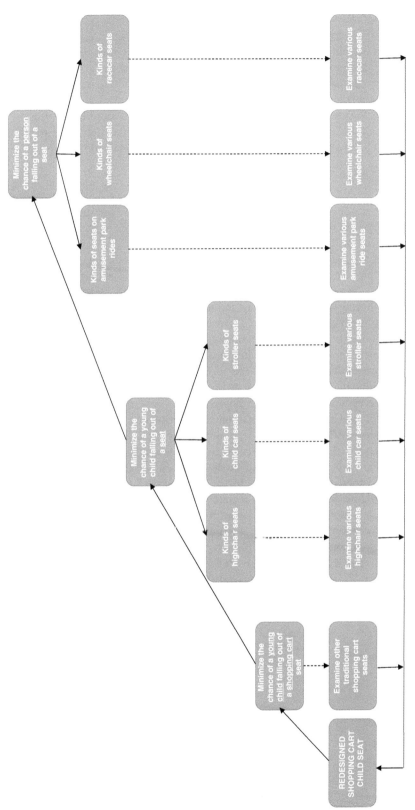

Figure 11.20 Using analogy to search for ways to improve a shopping cart child seat.

writers use three methods to stimulate curiosity—questions, surprise, and a gap in knowledge created by foreshadowing or drip-feeding important information.[48] You could dig deeper by asking, "Where else do people use a gap in knowledge to stimulate curiosity?" This might lead you to think of amusement park rides, like the Pirates of the Caribbean ride at Disneyland, where they stimulate curiosity by using a winding path to create a gap in knowledge that keeps people wondering what's around the next bend. And, again, you could dig deeper by asking, "Where else do people use winding paths to stimulate curiosity?" Which might lead you to IKEA, where, as you previously learned, the stores use winding aisles to stimulate customers' curiosity about what lies around the next bend.

Experimentation

Most of the initial ideas that are generated using the foregoing methods are just the seed of a fully grown solution. That's because the problem isn't understood fully enough to make the solution requirements complete. In his book *Design Thinking: Understanding How Designers Think and Work*, the emeritus design professor and prolific author Nigel Cross comments on the "tricky relationship" between a problem and a solution when he says, "In the process of designing, the problem and the solution develop together."[49] Elsewhere he and Kees Dorst, also a design professor and prolific author, speak of the problem and solution as "co-evolving."[50] One way to flesh out the solution requirements, known as *rapid prototyping*, is to develop a "quick and dirty" prototype solution, show it to customers[51] or otherwise analyze it to determine where it's deficient, translate the deficiencies into new solution requirements, and use the new requirements to develop a more evolved prototype.[52] As shown in Figure 11.21, the process is repeated, each time by making incremental improvements to the prototype, or the operationalized offering itself, until an acceptable solution is developed.

The iconic red Netflix envelope is a great example of experimentation.[53] It took hundreds of iterations for Netflix to perfect the size, shape, padding, and materials that would optimize the envelope for delivery by the US postal service and to meet other design requirements. Initially, in 1999, the envelope was white and made of heavy cardboard. In 2000, Netflix switched to yellow, and then to red in 2001. In the same year, the company also experimented with a lighter plastic envelope before realizing that paper was the better option for the environment. In 2003, Netflix added bar codes to make it easier to sort and return the envelopes. Subsequent versions of the envelopes incorporated works of art, which were inspired by customers' doodles and graffiti on the return envelopes. In 2016, for Halloween, they held their first customer art contest. With each iteration of the envelope, Netflix learned more about the envelope "problem" and improved upon its solution.

We've spent a lot of time in this chapter learning creative ways to produce desired benefits. Now it's time to convert the benefits into a value proposition.

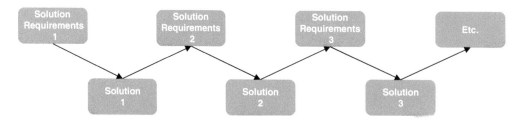

Figure 11.21 Each solution exposes additional ways in which the solution requirements are deficient.

Notes

1 John D. Bransford and Barry S. Stein, *The Ideal Problem Solver: A Guide for Improving Thinking, Learning, and Creativity*, 2nd Edition (New York, NY: W.H. Freeman and Company, 1993), 7.

2 Colin Eden and David Sims, *Messing About in Problems: An Informal Structured Approach to Their Identification and Management* (Oxford, UK: Pergamon Press, 1983), 12.

3 *Ibid*, 14.

4 Arthur B. VanGundy Jr., *Techniques of Structured Problem Solving*, 2nd Ed. (New York, NY: Van Nostrand Reinhold, 1988), 3.

5 John D. Arnold, *The Complete Problem Solver: A Total System For Competitive Decision Making* (New York, NY: John Wiley & Sons, 1992), 12.

6 Can M. Alpaslan and Ian I. Mitroff, *Swans, Swine, and Swindlers: Coping with the Growing Threat of Mega-Crises and Mega-Messes* (Stanford, CA: Stanford University Press, 2011), 17–20.

7 Charles H. Kepner and Benjamin B. Tregoe, *The New Rational Manager: An Updated Edition for a New World* (Princeton, NJ: Princeton Research Press, 1997), 22–24.

8 Joan Ernst van Aken, Hans Berends and Hans van der Bij, *Problem Solving in Organizations: A Methodological Handbook for Business Students* (Cambridge, UK: Cambridge University Press, 2007), 7–9.

9 A hand drill is a wooden spindle that is pressed against a fireboard and rapidly rolled between the hands to generate enough heat to light a tinder nest of dry grass.

10 A *cause* produces an effect, whereas a *reason* supports a decision or opinion. Despite the difference, the two terms are often treated as synonyms.

11 David A. Levy, *Tools of Critical Thinking: Metathoughts for Psychology* (Boston, MA: Allyn and Bacon, 1997), 72.

12 Ethan M. Rasiel, *The McKinsey Way: Using the Techniques of the World's Top Strategic Consultants to Help You and Your Business* (New York, NY: McGraw-Hill, 1999), 6.

13 Ken Watanabe, *Problem Solving 101: A Simple Book for Smart People* (New York, NY: Penguin Group, 2009). This international bestseller by a former McKinsey & Company consultant provides a simple, easy-to-understand explanation of the MECE method, including a method for hypothesis testing.

14 Arnaud Chevallier, *Strategic Thinking in Complex Problem Solving* (New York, NY: Oxford University Press, 2016). Written by an associate vice provost at Rice University, this book provides a detailed explanation of the MECE method, including the way to go about hypothesis testing.

15 Robert W. Weisberg, "On 'Out-Of-The-Box' Thinking in Creativity," in *Tools for Innovation: The Science Behind the Practical Methods That Drive New Ideas*, ed. Arthur B. Markman and Kristin L. Wood (New York, NY: Oxford University Press, 2009), 24.

16 Margaret A. Boden, *The Creative Mind: Myths & Mechanisms* (New York, NY: Basic Books, 1990), 30.

17 Paul Thagard, *How Scientific Creativity Results From Three Brain Mechanisms*, http://obf.edu.pl/docs/knew2014-slides/thagard.eureka.6.poland.pdf.

18 Michael Porter, "What is Strategy?" *Harvard Business Review*, November-December, 1996, 64.

19 Youngme Moon, *Different: Escaping the Competitive Herd* (New York, NY: Crown Business, 2010), 220.

20 Robert W. Weisberg, *Creativity: Understanding Innovation in Problem Solving, Science, Invention, and the Arts* (Hoboken, NJ: John Wiley & Sons, 2006). Weisberg elaborates on these types of thinking, and others, in this book-length treatment of creativity.

21 Weisberg, "On 'Out-Of-The-Box' Thinking," 28–41.

22 Tom Kelley, *The Art of Innovation: Lessons in Creativity From IDEO, America's Leading Design Firm* (London, UK: Profile Books Ltd., 2016), 8–14, 70–71.

23 If you think the OXO potato peeler handle is obvious, consider that the traditional potato peeler was invented in 1947 and the OXO handle was introduced in 1990, which means it took 43 years for someone to see the "obvious." This is another example of things hidden in plain view.

24 Eugenia Cheng, *The Art of Logic in an Illogical World* (New York, NY: Basic Books, 2018), 32.

25 *Ibid*.

26 Barbara Minto, *The Pyramid Principle: Logic in Writing and Thinking* (Harlow, Essex, UK: Prentice Hall, 2009), 64–66.

27 *Ibid*, 66:

28 There are other ways logical arguments go wrong, but we won't get into them. Eugenia Cheng's book and most critical thinking books describe the other ways.

29 Mario Bunge, *Philosophy of Science, Volume I: From Problem to Theory* Revised Ed. (New Brunswick, NJ: Transaction Publishers, 1998), 110.

30 M. Neil Browne and Stuart M. Keeley, *Asking the Right Questions: A Guild to Critical Thinking* 5th Ed. (Upper Saddle River, NJ: Prentice Hall, 1998), 52.

31 Kevin P. Coyne and Shawn T. Coyne, *Brainsteering: A Better Approach to Breakthrough Ideas* (New York, NY: Harper Business, 2011). The Coyne brothers, both former McKinsey & Company consultants, provide a book-length exposition of the idea of using the MECE method to search for ideas.

32 Rasiel, *op. cit.*, 8.

33 https://quoteinvestigator.com/2014/05/22/solve/.

34 Ralph L. Keeney, *Value-Focused Thinking: A Path to Creative Decisionmaking* (Cambridge, MA: Harvard University Press, 1992), 198.

35 *Ibid*, 201–211.

36 Steven Johnson, *Where Good Ideas Come From: The Natural History of Innovation* (New York, NY: Riverhead Books, 2010), 35.

37 Min Ding, *Logical Creative Thinking Methods* (New York, NY: Routledge, 2020). This is one of the best books on creative thinking I've encountered. You can find more on Ding's Logical Creative Thinking method by entering "lct.institute" into your search bar.

38 *Ibid*, 5.

39 (Compri) Hotels were later renamed Doubletree Club hotels by the company that acquired Doubletree Hotels.

40 Albert Einstein, as quoted by Maria Popova, "How Einstein Thought: Why 'Combinatory Play' Is the Secret of Genius," *Brain Pickings* website, https://www.brainpickings.org/2013/08/14/how-einstein-thought-combinatorial-creativity/. The website contains Einstein's complete response to Hadamard's inquiry.

41 Derek Bickerton, *Language & Species* (Chicago, IL: The University of Chicago Press, 1990), 117.

42 Judea Pearl and Dana Mackenzie, *The Book of Why: The New Science of Cause and Effect* (New York, NY: Hatchette Book Group, 2018), 28.

43 Leonard Mlodinow, *Elastic: Unlocking Your Brain's Ability to Embrace Change* (New York, NY: Vintage Books, 2018), 174–182.

44 Boden, *op. cit.*, 41.

45 Elkhonon Goldberg, *Creativity: The Human Brain in the Age of Innovation* (New York, NY: Oxford University Press, 2018), 132–140.

46 Cheng, *op. cit.*, 213.

47 Kees Dorst, *Frame Innovation: Create New Thinking by Design* (Cambridge, MA: The MIT Press, 2015), 31–34.

48 Angela Ackerman and Becca Puglisi, "Three Powerful Techniques to Harness A Reader's Curiosity," *Writers Helping Writers* website, https://writershelpingwriters.net/2018/01/three-powerful-techniques-harness-readers-curiosity/.

49 Nigel Cross, *Design Thinking: Understanding How Designers Think and Work* (London, UK: Bloomsbury, 2011), 11.

50 Kees Dorst and Nigel Cross, "Creativity in the design process: co-evolution of problem-solution," *Design Studies*, 22(5), 425–437.

51 Living labs, which were explained in the last chapter, are a great place to obtain feedback on prototypes.

52 Todd Zaki Warfel, *Prototyping: A Practitioner's Guide* (Brooklyn, NY: Rosenfeld Media, 2009).

53 "The Iconic Red Envelope: The Best Mail in America," *DVD.com*, http://blog.dvd.netflix.com/new-dvd-releases/the-evolution-of-the-mailer.

12　The Value Proposition

Why should I buy from you instead of your competitors? What makes you different? As I said at the start of this book, whether they say it or think it, customers are forever hitting you with this two-punch combination. They may not ask the question in exactly this way. They may ask: *Why should I buy from you instead of somebody else?* Or they may ask about another next-best alternative, like: *Why should I buy from you instead of doing it myself?* Or: *Why should I buy from you instead of not buying from anyone?* Or: *Why should I buy your new version when your last version works fine?* However they phrase it, it's the most important question customers will ever ask you. So you better have a good answer. A *compelling* answer. An answer that *sells*. That's where the value proposition comes in.

Benefit Proposition

The *value proposition* states the *value* you *propose* (promise) to provide your customers. In Chapter 2, you learned that *Value = Benefits – Price*, which means the value proposition is the *benefits – price proposition*. More casual is to say that value is *benefits for price*, which makes the value proposition the *benefits for price proposition*. Even more casual, and easier to think about, is to put price in the back of your mind and think of the value proposition as simply the *benefits proposition*. In Chapter 3, you learned that, by my count, there are six kinds of benefits—physical, mental, emotional, social, economic, and cost/risk reduction. And you learned that customers sometimes ladder the benefits one on top of the other (see Table 10.1). Ultimately, it's the benefits customers perceive they will receive from an of-fering that differentiate it. While it's correct to say that benefits, plural, are what differentiate your offering, that seems to fly in the face of what I next have to say, which is that the value proposition is better thought of as the *benefit proposition*.

In Chapter 6, I quoted Niraj Dawar, who said, "In any product category, customers find it easier to mentally associate each criterion with a single brand and to associate each brand with a single criterion."[1] As examples, I noted that most people associate Volvo with safety, Toyota with reliability, and BMW with drivability. Why? Because that's the benefit these brands always emphasize, the one thing they most want customers to remember about them.

Just as the car brands emphasize one key benefit, so should you. All your marketing materials and sales pitches should highlight the one benefit you most want customers to associate with your offering. Why? Because in a world where customers are inundated with information, they're not going to remember much of what you say. If you list all your benefits, they'll remember none of them. It's going to be in one ear and out the other. A helpful way to think about this is to imagine yourself lying on the bed of nails in the left panel of Figure 12.1. Which one of the nails do you think you'll remember? Now imagine lying on the single nail in the right panel. Do you think you'll remember that nail? Substitute benefits for nails, and you get the point. (Pun intended.)

DOI: 10.4324/9781003271703-13

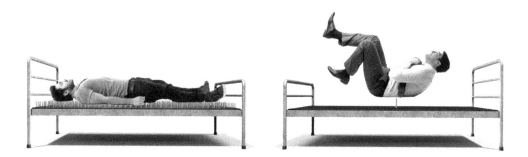

Figure 12.1 Emphasizing a single benefit makes it more memorable.
Source: David Holt Design, Adobe.

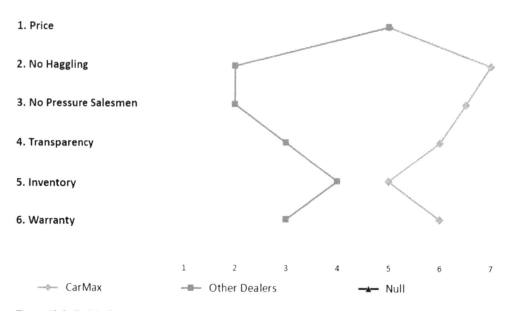

CARMAX STRATEGY CANVAS

1. Price

2. No Haggling

3. No Pressure Salesmen

4. Transparency

5. Inventory

6. Warranty

—◆— CarMax   —■— Other Dealers   —▲— Null

Figure 12.2 CarMax's strategy canvas.

So how do you decide which benefit to emphasize? The short answer is that the benefit should be slightly abstract, should be desired by the target of your differentiation strategy, and should be provided by your offering's key differentiating attributes. For the long answer, consider again the idea of a strategy canvas. Figure 12.2 contains the strategy canvas for CarMax, a chain of used car dealerships. Remember that the strategy canvas lists the purchase criteria, in order of importance, and it shows how well a company's offering performs on the criteria relative to its competitors. CarMax differentiates itself by outperforming other used car dealers on no-haggle pricing, no-pressure salesmen, transparent operations, a large inventory of cars, and a strong warranty.

For CarMax, the challenge is to convert their superior performance on the purchase criteria into the single benefit they will always emphasize. A good way to do the conversion is to first identify the principal physical, mental, emotional, social, economic, or cost/risk reduction benefit of the superior performance on each of the purchase criteria. With CarMax, the principal benefit of the no-haggle pricing, no-pressure salesmen, transparent operations, and strong warranty is the emotional benefit of reduced stress, and the principal benefit of the large inventory of cars is the physical benefit of not having to run around town to find the desired car, which ladders up to the benefit of reduced stress. The next step is to synthesize the principal benefits, or some number of them, into a single, comprehensive benefit. For CarMax, the benefit is a *stress-free car-buying experience*.

OnStar, GM's in-vehicle safety and security system, serves as another good example. The purchase criteria, shown in Figure 12.3, are the ability to call for crash assistance, roadside assistance, navigation assistance, remote unlocking, and stolen car assistance. One could say that the principal benefit of OnStar's superior performance on the purchase criteria is the mental benefit of knowing that help is only a phone call away, which can be laddered up to the key emotional benefit of *peace of mind while driving*.

As I said, the key benefit should be *slightly* abstract, meaning that it should be abstract enough to synthesize all, or several, of the individual benefits, but not so abstract as to render it meaningless. For CarMax customers, a *stress-free car-buying experience* is more meaningful than the more general benefit of a *good car-buying experience* or a *better car-buying experience*. Where the first option is specific enough to understand its meaning, the latter two are so general that it's difficult to know what they mean. The same goes for OnStar's key benefit, *peace of mind while driving*. It's general enough to encapsulate the benefits of OnStar's individual attributes, but not so general as to be meaningless, as would be the case if the key benefit was *a great driving experience* or *a superior driving experience*. If you suspect your key

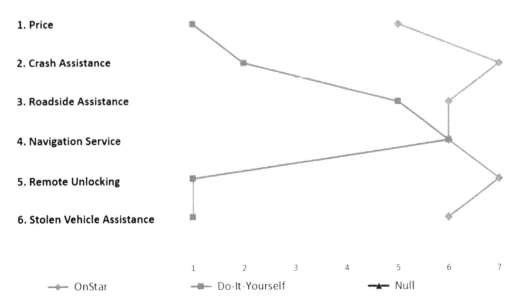

Figure 12.3 OnStar's strategy canvas.

benefit is too abstract, ask why it delivers the overly abstract benefit. For example, by asking themselves why their car-buying experience is a *good car-buying experience*, CarMax's managers might have answered that the car-buying experience is good because it's stress free.

The CarMax and OnStar examples make it look easy to identify the key benefit. But looks can be deceiving. Consider that CarMax might have settled on *peace of mind while buying* and OnStar on *a stress-free driving experience*. Both are reasonably accurate descriptions of their key benefit, but neither captures the benefit as well as the original description. The fact is that it's hard to know when you've arrived at the "right" answer, so it's worth taking the time to explore subtle differences in wording until you intuit that you're expressing your key benefit in just the right way. As Mark Twain said, "The difference between the almost right word and the right word is really a large matter—'tis the difference between the lightning-bug and the lightning." And here, for the third time, it's worth considering what OnStar's former CEO, Chet Huber, had to say about the *real job*—that it's "… crazy powerful, if you get it right."[2] The same applies to the key benefit--it's crazy powerful if you get it right.

Comparing the CarMax and OnStar examples with the example of IKEA conveys another lesson. Putting the subtlety of the process aside for a moment, creating the key benefit for CarMax and OnStar looks relatively easy because, in each case, all their offering attributes generate the same kind of benefit—stress reduction in the first case and peace of mind in the second. But that's not always the case. In some cases, you have to cobble together a more disparate set of benefits into a single idea. Sometimes that's possible and sometimes it's not. IKEA is an example of the latter. As shown in Figure 12.4, IKEA outperforms other contemporary furniture stores by providing lower prices, immediate delivery, and a comprehensive offering of furniture and houseware. The corresponding benefits are, respectively, *affordability* (economic benefit), *instant gratification* (emotional benefit), and the *time-savings* of one-stop-shopping (cost/risk reduction benefit). Unless IKEA is able to identify a slightly

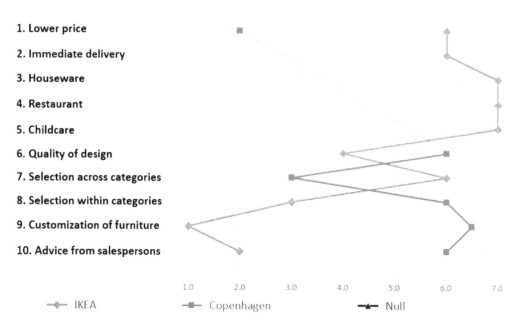

Figure 12.4 IKEA's strategy canvas.

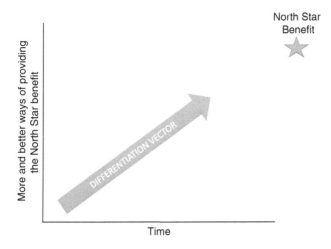

Figure 12.5 The North Star benefit sets the direction of the differentiation vector.

abstract benefit that incorporates these three disparate benefits, they're faced with the difficult decision of selecting one of them in order to comply with the one-key-benefit rule. But rules are made to be broken, and the one-key-benefit rule is one of them. Sometimes the best option is to find a concise, memorable way of combining two or three (never more than three) differentiating benefits—say, in IKEA's case, something like, "Save money. Save time. Enjoy it today."

An important aside is that your key benefit should serve as the *North Star benefit* for your product development and operational improvement efforts. Consider OnStar again, whose key benefit is *peace of mind while driving.* As earlier explained in the context of the jobs-to-be-done method, this North Star benefit has driven product improvements like crash assistance, roadside assistance, navigation assistance, stolen car assistance, remote unlocking, and remote diagnosis when the check engine light comes on. OnStar's North Star benefit has also driven the way its operational processes are performed, including the way its call center agents are trained and the way OnStar helps GM salespeople explain the offering to prospective customers. Related to the concept of a North Star benefit is the concept of a *differentiation vector.*[3] As illustrated in Figure 12.5, the North Star benefit establishes the direction of the differentiation vector, and the vector is extended by finding more and better ways of providing the benefit.

Reasons-to-Believe

Again, the value proposition answers the questions: *Why should I buy from you instead of your competitors? What makes you different?* The answer runs along the following lines: *Because we promise to provide benefit X, which our competitors do not* and/or *we promise to provide significantly more of benefit Y than is provided by our competitors.* But "talk is cheap," as the saying goes, so telling the benefit you promise to provide isn't enough. Customers also want what business consultant Doug Hall calls *reasons-to-believe* you'll deliver the promised benefit.[4] As detailed below, the seven most common reasons-to-believe are a compelling explanation, case studies and statistics, thought leadership, warranties and guarantees, testimonials, prior experience with your offering, and what Michael Porter terms *signals of value.*[5]

A compelling explanation is one that clearly and convincingly explains how the benefit will be created and delivered. Compelling explanations are usually key to B2B value propositions, where the customer wants to know exactly how the seller will deliver the promised economic benefit. A good example is the real estate investment trust AmREIT. As explained by Cynthia Montgomery, in an industry where the three most important attributes are location, location, and location, AmREIT's strategy was to buy shopping centers located on what they termed, and later trademarked, the Irreplaceable Corner™.[6] The six criteria they used to define an irreplaceable corner were a corner location, high barriers to entry, a high traffic count, a dense daytime population, a dense nighttime population, and high household income in the surrounding neighborhood. To convince big-money investors to invest with them instead of their competitors, AmREIT created a graph in which the Y-axis was average household Income in a one-mile radius and the X-axis was the number of households in a three-mile radius. The graph showed that AmREIT's shopping center portfolio was much further up and to the right than its competitors' portfolios, thereby providing a simple, compelling visual explanation of why the location of AmREIT's portfolio was superior to their competitors' portfolios.

Anderson and his co-authors describe another sort of explanation, called a *value word equation*, that is especially suited to B2B customers.[7] A value word equation uses words and simple mathematical operators (e.g., $+$, $-$, x, and $\div$) to precisely calculate the monetary worth of the promised financial benefit, such as cost savings or incremental revenue. As compared to explanations that rely on complicated, hard-to-follow spreadsheets, value word equations clearly explain why the monetary worth of an offering is greater than that of the next-best alternative.

Demonstrations are another way to explain how you will deliver a promised benefit. The infomercials you see on late-night television provide lots of examples—demonstrations of wipes that soak up more liquid, gadgets that do a better job of slicing and dicing, and gizmos that enable you to call for help when you've fallen and can't get up. Cutaway models (e.g., shoes that are sawed in half longitudinally), scale models, and simulations are other ways to create convincing demonstrations.

Law, consulting, and other professional service firms employ another kind of explanation. They use the biographies of their professionals to explain why they provide superior advice. For example, the firms may point out that all their professionals graduated from a top-tier law school or business school or that they all have ten or more years of specialized experience.

The second kind of reason-to-believe is *case studies and statistics*. Case studies are a favorite of consultants and service providers, both of whom use them to describe the great things they were able to do for similarly situated clients. A well-written case study employs the fundamental elements of storytelling—*setting* (the type of company and its situation), *characters* (the roles played by the people involved, e.g., the CEO), *plot* (with a beginning, middle, and end), the *conflict* (the client's problem), and the *resolution* (the way the problem was solved and the real-number results that were achieved).[8] It's always a good practice to use the principles of graphic design, such as headers, bullet points, and images, to make the case study easy to scan and read. You might also want to try presenting the case study in different formats, including the traditional written format, an infographic, a webinar, a video, or a podcast. Always remember that case studies are more believable when customers have a way to confirm the claims made in them and when the claims state actual dollars rather than terms like "a lot" or "twice as much."

Standalone statistics are another reason-to-believe. Like case studies, they are more effective when they can be verified or when they are independently prepared or verified. Consumer Reports, which is in the business of testing and reporting various product claims and statistics, is an example of independent verification. Another example is the Environmental Protection Agency (EPA), which verifies the miles-per gallon statistics reported by car manufacturers. A third example is the consumer ratings and comments on social media sites like Amazon.com, Travelocity, and Yelp.

Thought leadership is the third type of reason-to-believe. This is another favorite of consulting, legal, and other professional service firms, though it can be applied by many kinds of companies. Thought leadership is about being a leader in the creation and dissemination of ideas in a particular field or practice. The ideas are disseminated in white papers, research studies, blogs, industry and professional publications, company-sponsored journals, emails, seminars, workshops, and even entire books. Thought leadership can also include the creation of think tanks and institutes dedicated to advancing the thinking in a field. In his book *Thought Leadership: Prompting Businesses to Think and Learn*, the writer Laurie Young explains that leading-edge ideas are frequently derived from the intersection of two or more disciplines, by research, and by analysis, new perspectives, creative stimulation, and intuition.[9]

The fourth kind of reason-to-believe is *warranties and guarantees*. The difference between the two is largely a matter of word choice. Any promise about the quality, condition, or reliability of a product that a seller makes and that customers rely on can create a warranty or guarantee. If the product fails to fulfill the promise, it can usually be returned, repaired, or replaced. An example is CarMax's 7-day money-back guarantee and their 90-day/4,000-mile limited warranty. Another example is the earlier-described division of ICI that sells explosives to quarries. It uses the blast data it collects to guarantee that a certain percentage of rocks will fall within a specified size range.

Testimonials are the fifth kind of reason-to-believe. The person making the testimonial can be a satisfied customer or an authority figure that customers are inclined to trust, like a celebrity or an expert in the field. Quotes are the most popular form of testimonials. The most direct way to obtain them is to ask customers to provide a testimonial quote. Another way to obtain quotes is to pull screenshots from Facebook posts and Twitter updates, with the customer's permission, of course. Live and videotaped interviews are an alternative to written testimonials. And press reviews, like movie or restaurant reviews, are persuasive because they come from sources that are qualified to speak on the topic.

The sixth kind of reason-to-believe is *prior experience* with your offering. There are a variety of ways to provide the experience. One way is to sit on a board or committee with prospective customers, which gives them a chance to experience your abilities. Another is to do seminars, webinars, and speeches where you're able to demonstrate your, or your company's, expertise. Sampling is an additional way to let customers experience your product before they buy it. If you've ever "dined" at Costco, you know that letting people sample foods and beverages is a popular way to promote them. Another example of sampling is software firms that promote their products by letting users sample a limited version of their software.

A final kind of reason to believe is a signal of value. Michael Porter defines *signals of value* as "the means used by the customer to infer or judge what a supplier's actual value is."[10] *Signaling criteria* are signals of value that serve as purchase criteria. Among the signaling criteria described by Porter are reputation, cumulative advertising, the outward appearance of the product, the appearance and size of facilities, time in business, and the list of customers that are served. Other signals of value include awards, prestigious positions on boards and committees, company size, a high rate of client retention, a large percentage of new business from referrals, a high success rate, and a high growth rate. In fact, just about everything you do—from the way you dress, to the way you speak, to your table manners—can serve as a signal of value. Or not, as the comedian Rita Rudner humorously made clear when she quipped, "I was going to have cosmetic surgery until I noticed that the doctor's office was full of portraits by Picasso."[11] A worthwhile exercise is to create a journey map that identifies all the points of contact with your customers, then inventory the signals of value at each point, and finally decide whether they are conveying what you want them to convey.

Another thing to say about reasons-to-believe is this. In most cases, a company's value proposition centers on the key benefit generated by one or more of its attributes. In some cases, however, the company doesn't have any additional or better benefits to offer—or at least not yet—so it must rely on doing a superior job of providing reasons-to-believe. While it's best to provide one or more unique benefits, having one or more superior reasons-to-believe can be a way of differentiating your offering.

And one last thing to say about key benefits and reasons to believe. They should be true! Customers aren't stupid. If you lie about your offering, they'll figure it out. Then they'll broadcast it far and wide on social media. Plus, as the actor Wilford Brimley used to say in the Quaker Oats commercials, "It's the right thing to do." Which brings us to the topic of micro-scripts.

Micro-scripts

The final part of creating your value proposition is to distill the differentiating aspects of your offering down to a memorable tagline or statement. In his book *The Micro-Script Rules: It's not what people hear. It's what they repeat …,*" the branding consultant Bill Schley explains an effective way of doing so.[12] He refers to the distilled statement as a *micro-script*. A micro-script is a short, memorable claim—anywhere from one word to a sentence or two—that people can't help but remember and want to repeat to others. It's made memorable and repeatable by using *a metaphor, vivid imagery,* or *rhythmic sounds.* Classic examples are M&M's "Melts in your mouth, not in your hands," Maxwell House coffee's "Good to the last drop," LifeAlert's "I've fallen, and I can't get up," and, of course, Wilford Brimley's "It's the right thing to do." Contemporary examples are "1,000 songs in your pocket," which Steve Jobs used to introduce the iPod, Geico's "15 minutes saves you 15%," and Nike's extraordinarily successful "Just do it" tagline.

Putting it All Together

As I see it, a value proposition, which is better thought of as a benefit proposition, consists of the four elements illustrated in Figure 12.6. The first element is your differentiators—the attributes you offer that your competitors don't, or the attributes that outperform your

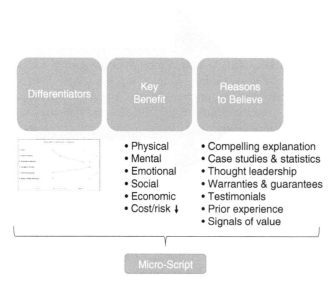

Figure 12.6 Elements of the value proposition.

competitor's attributes, or both. The second element is the key benefit (or 2–3 benefits, if you must) you choose to emphasize in all your sales and marketing efforts. The reasons-to-believe you will deliver the promised benefit(s) make up the third element of the value proposition. And the fourth element is the micro-script that captures the first three elements in a way that customers will remember and want to repeat to others.

Your value proposition should comply with the three criteria of an effective value proposition. The first criterion is that the key benefit corresponds with an important want or need. That will be the case if the benefit is produced by superior performance on one or more of the high-ranking purchase criteria on the strategy canvas. The second criterion rests on the elemental idea that differentiation is about being different, which means you want to make sure your differentiating benefit isn't already claimed by a competitor. As earlier explained, it's nearly impossible to displace a benefit that is already positioned in the minds of customers because customers view the first company to claim the benefit as the real thing and everyone else as impersonators. The third criterion of an effective value proposition is that it be produced by activities that you are able to perform and your competitors are not or by activities that you are able to perform significantly (an order-of-magnitude) better than your competitors. It makes no sense to base your value proposition on a benefit that can be easily reproduced by your rivals, which brings us to the topic of the next chapter—the activity system.

Notes

1 Niraj Dawar, *Tilt: Shifting Your Strategy from Products to Customers* (Boston, MA: Harvard Business Review Press, 2013), 133.
2 Clayton M. Christensen, Taddy Hall, Karen Dillon, and David S. Duncan, *Competing Against Luck: The Story of Innovation and Customer Choice* (New York, NY: HarperCollins Publishers, 2016), 204.
3 Michael E. McGrath, *Product Strategy For High Technology Companies: Accelerating Your Business to Web Speed* (New York, NY: McGraw-Hill, 2001), 164–168.
4 Doug Hall, *Jump Start Your Business Brain: Win More, Lose Less, and Make More Money With Your New Products, Services, Sales and Advertising* (Cincinnati, OH: Brain Brew Books, 2001), 91–130.
5 Michael Porter. *Competitive Advantage: Creating and Sustaining Superior Performance* (New York, NY: The Free Press, 1985), 138 & 144–150.
6 Cynthia Montgomery, *The Strategist: Be The Leader Your Business Needs* (New York, NY: Harper Business, 2012), 85–88.
7 James C. Anderson, Nirmalya Kumar, and James A. Narus, *Value Merchants: Demonstrating and Documenting Superior Value in Business Markets* (Boston, MA: Harvard Business School Press, 2007), 51–57.
8 James Scott Bell, *Plot and Structure: Techniques and Exercises for Crafting a Plot That Grips Readers From Start to Finish* (Cincinnati, OH: Writer's Digest Books, 2004).
9 Laurie Young, *Thought Leadership: Prompting Businesses to Think and Learn* (Philadelphia, PA: Kogan Page, Ltd., 2013), 77–85.
10 Porter, *op. cit.,* 142.
11 https://www.just-one-liners.com/i-was-going-to-have-cosmetic-surgery-until-i-noticed-that-the-doctors-office-was-full-of-portraits-by-picasso/.
12 Bill Schley, *The Micro-Script Rules: It's not what people hear. It's what they repeat…"* (New York, NY: N.W. Widener, 2010).

13 The Activity System

Throughout this book, I have highlighted Michael Porter's assertion that "[T]he essence of strategy is in the activities—choosing to perform activities differently or to perform different activities than rivals."[1] As earlier explained, he used IKEA as an example. Two activities that IKEA performs differently are grouping furniture by room type and the immediate delivery that is enabled by making it possible for customers to take their furniture home with them. And three activities that IKEA performs that conventional furniture stores do not are providing a restaurant, a childcare service, and houseware. All these are activities that are performed "onstage" in the sense that they are things customers can see or otherwise experience. But a company's activity system also includes the "backstage" activities that produce the onstage activities. In this chapter, we're going to look at several ways of identifying the backstage activities. We'll stick with the example of IKEA and focus on their *immediate delivery* attribute.

The Value Chain/Network/Shop

Porter notes that "Every firm is a collection of activities that are performed to design, produce, market, deliver, and support its product."[2] As explained in Chapter 9 and illustrated again in Figure 13.1, he uses the *value chain* framework to describe a company's activity system.[3] Alternate frameworks are the *value network* and the *value shop*, which were also explained in Chapter 9. The value chain shows the general kinds of activities that a business engages in during the process of transforming inputs into the outputs that comprise its offering. The *primary activities* are listed in sequence along the bottom of the value chain, and the *support activities* rest on top of the primary activities. Except for portions of the Marketing & Sales activities and Service activities, all the activities shown in the value chain are generic backstage activities, which makes the value chain framework a useful tool for identifying the backstage activities that contribute to performing an onstage activity. In this example, we're interested in the backstage activities that produce IKEA's *offer immediate delivery* attribute.

The Strategy Wheel

Another framework you can use to inventory the backstage activities that produce an onstage activity is the strategy wheel. An example is shown in Figure 13.2. The strategy wheel is usually started by placing your company's purpose in the center of the wheel. In our case, we're going to place a differentiating attribute in the center, which in the IKEA example is the *offer immediate delivery* attribute. The next step is to identify the design, procurement, manufacturing, and other activities that enable IKEA to offer immediate delivery.

DOI: 10.4324/9781003271703-14

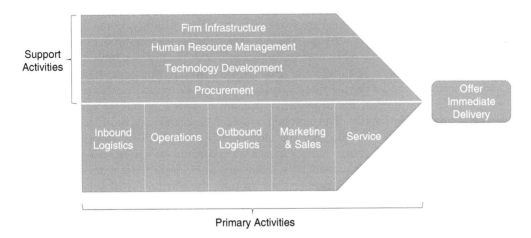

Figure 13.1 Use the value chain to identify the backstage activities that enable IKEA to offer immediate delivery.

Source: Adapted from *Competitive Advantage: Creating and Sustaining Superior Performance*, Figure 2.2, page 37.

Figure 13.2 Use the strategy wheel to identify the backstage activities that enable IKEA to offer immediate delivery.

Source: David Holt Design.

The Dependency Diagram

The value chain and strategy wheel are two useful tools for inventorying the activities required to offer a differentiating attribute. The *dependency diagram* is a third tool, one that I find particularly helpful, especially when used in conjunction with the first two tools. Here, again, we'll use IKEA's *offer immediate delivery* attribute as the example. This time, however, we'll extend the example to identify the specific activities that make immediate delivery possible.

As shown in Figure 13.3, the dependency diagram is started by placing *offer immediate delivery* at the top of the diagram. The next step is to ask: What activity(s) must we perform to offer immediate delivery? In this case, the answer is *enable self-delivery by customers*. The question is then repeated: What activity(s) must we perform to enable self-delivery by customers? The answers are that enabling self-delivery depends on the activities *enable self-assembly by customers* and *offer flat-packed furniture*. In turn, the *offer flat-packed furniture* activity depends on the activity *provide in-store warehouse*. The question is then asked of each of these activities. The activity *provide in-store warehouse* depends on the activity *build large stores*, which depends on the activity *locate in suburbs,* where the land is more plentiful and affordable. The *offer flat-packed furniture* activity also depends on the activities *perform design in-house* and *create modular designs*. In turn, the activity *perform design in-house* depends on the activity *accumulate design skills*, and the activity *create modular designs* depends on the activities *develop supply chain* and *accumulate design skills*. To keep things simple, I've stopped here. But a quick scan of the value chain and the strategy wheel—which should always be used in conjunction with the dependency diagram—will make you realize that there are more activities to consider. For example, building large stores depends on financing activities and accumulating design skills depends on hiring and training activities.

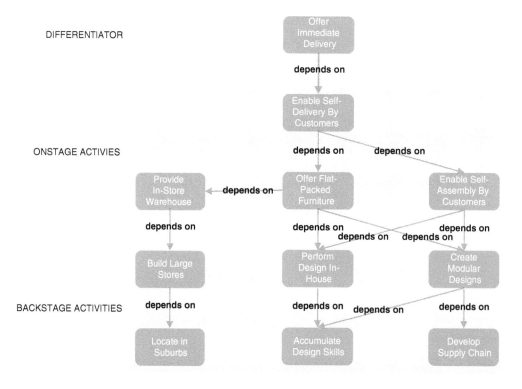

Figure 13.3 Using a dependency diagram to identify the activities required to offer immediate delivery.

There are several things to note about the foregoing dependency diagram. The first thing is that it can be converted into an *enablement diagram* or a *driver diagram* by reversing the direction of the arrows. Each activity then enables or drives the activity at the end of the arrow. But it's easier to start at the top with the differentiating attribute and work down through the dependency relationships rather than start at the bottom and work up to the differentiator. Sometimes, however, important activities are revealed by first working from the top down to complete the dependency diagram and then working from the bottom up by asking of each activity: What else does this activity enable? It's always a good idea to place the enablement diagrams for each differentiator next to one another in order to identify activities that enable more than one activity. For example, in the foregoing IKEA activity diagram, the *build large stores* activity also enables IKEA to *offer a wider range of goods*, which is another differentiator identified in Figure 12.4.

The second thing to note is that the differentiator depends on a cascade of activities, including other onstage activities and the backstage activities they depend on. With some activities (e.g., *build large stores*), it's hard to say whether the activity is an onstage activity or a backstage activity. But that's not worth worrying about. The main idea is to capture the cascade of dependencies. Also note that all the activities are phrased as a verb followed by a short noun phrase, which is an effective way of describing an activity or action and is consistent with the nomenclature used for functions, as described in Chapter 4. It's okay to think in terms of *actions* rather than *activities* if you find that easier to do, so long as you don't confuse the term with the way it's used in Chapter 9.

The third thing to note, once again, is the importance of doing the activities differently or doing different activities—the higher in the diagram, the better. Imagine, for example, what would have become of IKEA had it focused on trying to be faster at the *same* old method of delivering fully assembled furniture instead of taking the *different* path of enabling self-delivery by customers. Here, again, it's helpful to remember Youngme Moon's observation, "What we consider to be different depends on what we consider to be the norm .... In fact, trying to define what is different is like trying to define what is opposite[.]"[4] To implement her observation, first consider how everyone else is performing the activities. Then imagine ways to perform them differently or ways to perform different activities altogether. Imagining how to do things differently involves the same creative thinking you learned earlier—expertise, logic, and analogy. You can also imagine ways to be different by using the attribute line (aka Hotelling line) method described in Chapter 8.

It takes time to first identify the cascade of activities in the dependency diagram and then find ways to do them differently, which surfaces another thing that is worthy of note—the importance of taking the time to thoroughly think through the dependency diagrams for each of your differentiators. The activity system is where the rubber meets the road. At this point in the strategy-making process, you've gone to great lengths to decide *what* attributes you're going to use to differentiate your offering. Now you need to determine *how* you're going to make those attributes a reality. You and your management team should take whatever time is required to do the job right.

Determining what will be required to realize your strategy is one reason for spending sufficient time on the dependency diagram. The second reason is to verify that the activities are coherent, which is to say, that each activity works to enable the one(s) above it rather than working at cross purposes with it. Cynthia Montgomery provides some illuminating examples of CEOs and management teams who took the time to map their activity system, only to discover that the system, or parts of it, didn't support their strategy or, worse, that their strategy wasn't feasible.[5] The third reason for thinking long and hard about your activity system is to make it more difficult for your competitors to copy your strategy. Taking the time to design a coherent system of differentiated activities, especially the backstage activities that your competitors are unable to see, is an effective way of devising a sustainable differentiation strategy.

Digging Deeper

You can make your strategy even more difficult to copy by digging deeper into each activity. Some of the digging should occur as part of the initial strategy-making process. The rest of it should happen over time as part of a continuous improvement process. One way to dig into each activity is to use a modified version of the journalist's questions—*what, where, when, who, why, which, how,* and *how much* (6WH^2). With regard to IKEA's *locate in the suburbs* activity, for example, you might ask: *Why* else should we locate in the suburbs? (You already know the principal reason—the land is more plentiful and affordable.) In *which* cities would it be best for us to locate in the suburbs? In *what* sequence should we open stores in these cities? *What* kind of suburbs are best? *Where* in the suburbs should we locate? *Who* would be willing to drive to a store in the suburbs? *How* will we identify potential sites? *How much* land will we require? *How much* money can we afford to spend on the land? And so on.

Another way to dig deeper into the activities is to understand that an activity involves inputs that are transformed into an output. The output is the completed activity, just as *our stores are located in suburbs* is the output of the activity *locate in the suburbs*. The inputs are the *resources* that are required to complete the activity, such as capital, people, time, equipment, land, material, and information. In IKEA's case, the fundamental question is: What are all the things we must have to locate our stores in the suburbs? The answer will include things like debt and equity capital, information regarding available sites, people to evaluate and purchase the sites, people to design the buildings and oversee their construction, people to stock the stores, people to hire and train employees, office space and equipment for the people, and a transportation system to move the initial inventory to the stores and periodically replenish it. Underlying all these issues are the key differentiation questions: How can we do these activities differently? What different activities can we do?

Once your strategy is in place, you can improve it by implementing a continuous improvement method. In *Improving Performance: How to Manage the White Space on the Organization Chart*, the performance improvement consultants Geary Rummler and Alan Brache explain a method for digging down through a company to identify ways to improve its performance at the organization level, at the process (inter-functional) level, and at the job/performer (individual employee and equipment) level.[6] As explained in Chapter 6, employee idea systems are another way of improving performance. The implementation of hundreds, even thousands, of employee ideas makes a company's differentiation strategy extremely difficult to copy. Consider again the Toyota Production System and the Danaher Business System described in Chapter 6, which combine high-performance employee idea systems and the Japanese continuous improvement process called *Kaizen*.[7]

This description of the activity system brings us to the end of the practice part of this book. The last thing to learn is how to put the practices together.

Notes

1 Michael Porter, "What is Strategy?" *Harvard Business Review*, November-December, 1996, 64.
2 Michael Porter. *Competitive Strategy: Techniques for Analyzing Industries and Competitors* (New York, NY: The Free Press, 1980), 36.
3 *Ibid*, 33–61.
4 Youngme Moon, *Different: Escaping the Competitive Herd* (New York, NY: Crown Business, 2010), 194.

5 Cynthia Montgomery, *The Strategist: Be The Leader Your Business Needs* (New York, NY: Harper Business, 2012), Montgomery, 91–95.

6 Geary A. Rummler and Alan P. Brache, *Improving Performance: How to Manage the White Space on the Organization Chart* 3rd Ed. (Hoboken, NJ: Jossey-Bass, 2013).

7 Masaaki Imai, *Gemba Kaizen: A Commonsense Approach to a Continuous Improvement Strategy* (New York, NY: McGraw-Hill, 2012).

14 The Strategy Process

Thus far, you've learned about the pieces of the strategy-making process. Now it's time to piece them together. The explanation won't take long because you've already learned most of what you need to know. As shown in Figure 14.1, a differentiation strategy consists of a coherent combination of answers to five questions.

Target

Who are we targeting? Because differentiation strategies are segment specific, you must first decide what segment to target. First decide on the supply chain segment, then on a market segment within the supply chain segment, and finally decide on one or more of the roles (decision-maker, support team, and end-user) played by the people within the market segment. The various ways of segmenting a supply chain and a market were explained in Chapter 7.

You can usually start by devising a differentiation strategy for an entire supply chain segment (say, all the end-users) and later iterate to create more specific strategies for one or more of the market segments within the supply chain segment. For example, a hotel company might start by creating a differentiation strategy for all the end-users of its hotels and later create more refined differentiation strategies that account for the unique purchase criteria of people who are traveling for the purpose of business, for the purpose of attending a meeting at the hotel, and for the purpose of leisure. In another, later iteration of the strategy-making process, the hotel company might create an even more refined differentiation strategy that accounts for the unique needs of the decision-maker, support team, and end-users. With business travelers, for example, the decision-maker might be a corporate travel department, the support team might consist of the people back in the office with whom the traveler works, and the end-user is the business traveler him- or herself.

Benefits

What benefits do they desire? The attributes of offerings perform functions that deliver benefits. Ultimately, differentiation is about providing customers with more of a desired benefit, additional desired benefits, or both. As you now know, to my way of thinking, there are six kinds of benefits—physical, mental, emotional, social, economic, and cost/risk reduction. The six kinds of benefits were explained at length in Chapter 3. Ways of looking for opportunities to provide the benefits that are desired (i.e., ways of looking for differentiation opportunities) are the function analysis, segmentation, attribute, and action methods explained in Chapters 4, 7, 8, and 9, respectively. Kansei engineering, explained in Chapter 3, is specifically designed to identify mental-emotional benefits. In all cases, customer research, explained in Chapter 10, is used to discover and understand the desired benefits.

DOI: 10.4324/9781003271703-14

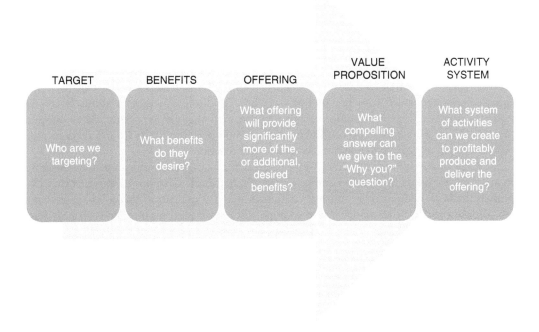

Figure 14.1 A differentiation strategy is a coherent combination of answers to five questions.

Offering

What offering will provide significantly more of the, or additional, desired benefits? As summarized in Table 14.1 and explained in Chapter 5, offerings exist at the level of individual products and services, where the components are objects and events, at the level of bundles and complements, where the components are products, services, programs, and systems, and at the level of the company, where the components are the company's sales & marketing activities, distribution channels, and customer relationship activities. At all three levels, the components are characterized by multiple attributes (property values). Chapter 11 explains that innovative offerings consist of combinations of components that are novel (different), non-obvious (because they break a "should" rule), and valuable (because they provide more and better benefits).

Table 14.1 Offering levels and the components at each level

Level	Components
Products	Objects
Services	Events
Bundles	Products, Services, Programs & Systems
Complements	Products, Services, Programs & Systems
Company	Sales & Marketing Activities
	Channels of Distribution
	Customer Relationship Activities

Chapter 11 also explains that creating the attributes that produce a desired benefit is fundamentally about creative problem-solving. The creative problem-solving process entails using the MECE method to identify the states that cause the desired benefit not to exist, then using creative thinking to identify ways to act on the states to transform them into states that cause the desired benefit to exist (Figure 11.1). Creative thinking includes logic, expertise, and analogy. Logical thinking employs deduction. Expertise is about using various methods—MECE, an objectives hierarchy, the LCT method, and listing and challenging the "should" rules—to search memory (yours and others) for whole solutions or parts of solutions that can be pieced together to form a whole solution. Analogy is about searching analogous domains for whole solutions and solution parts that can be combined to create a whole solution. With each type of thinking, you should periodically pause and relax to give your subconscious default network time to devise a solution.

Physically manifesting the abstract, skeletal ideas that are produced by creative thinking requires that the ideas be detailed and enriched (fleshed out). Chapter 11 explains that experimenting with progressively more specific prototypes (rapid prototyping) is an effective way of doing so. Each more-specific prototype discloses design requirements that its less-specific predecessor did not.

Value Proposition

What compelling answer can we give to the "Why you?" question? In the Introduction, you learned that your company is forever being asked the one-two question: *Why should I buy from you instead of your competitors? What makes you different?* Chapter 12 explained that your answer to the question, your value proposition, should consist of the one key benefit you want to emphasize in all your marketing and sales activities plus some number of the seven kinds of reasons to believe you will deliver the promised benefit. Ultimately, you should distill the value proposition down to a micro-script that people will remember and want to repeat to others.

Activity System

What system of activities can we create to profitably produce and deliver the offering? It has been emphasized throughout this book that the essence of a differentiation strategy is choosing to perform activities differently than your competitors, or to perform different activities altogether, or both. Each activity is part of a system of activities. Some (the customer-facing activities) are performed "onstage." Others are performed "backstage" to produce the onstage activities. Chapter 13 explained three tools for designing the activity system—the value chain/network/shop, the strategy wheel, and the dependency diagram. While you are doing the designing, it's important to remember that each activity costs money and, as explained in Chapter 1, you have a competitive advantage when, and only when, your offering is more profitable than your competitors' offerings.

Comprehensive, Iterative, and Ongoing

As is next explained, the strategy-making process should be comprehensive, iterative, and ongoing:

- Comprehensive: Your strategy-making process should be comprehensive in the sense that you ultimately develop differentiation strategies for all the appropriate supply chain segments, the target market segments within them, and the roles played in each of the target market segments. If you don't have the time or human resources to do a comprehensive analysis during the first year of the strategy-making process, do it in subsequent years. Rome wasn't built in a day.

- <u>Iterative</u>: You should periodically repeat the strategy-making process for each of the target markets to ensure that the strategies remain current and to continuously improve them.

- <u>Ongoing</u>: Considering the importance of your differentiation strategy and the time required to comprehensively iterate through the strategy-making process, the process should be ongoing. Rather than an annual one-and-done (and ignore) strategy session, the strategy-making team should meet routinely (say, monthly) to assess and elaborate the existing strategy and extend it to other segments. The status and efficacy of the strategy should be a standing item on the executive committee's agenda. And each functional department should routinely review the status and efficacy of its contribution to implementing the strategy. In short, you should embed the strategy-making process in your company by making it part of your routine.

Another piece of advice is to conduct the strategy-making workshops in the mornings in three- to four-hour bursts over the course of several days. This ensures that the team members are fresh enough to do their best thinking, and it also gives the team members' subconscious time to mull things over between the workshops.

The bottom line of this book is this. If you compete in an industry in which one or more of your competitors has implemented a successful differentiation strategy, you can *differentiate or die*. If you compete in an industry where no one is successfully differentiating their offering, you can *differentiate and prosper*. Either way you look at it, creating and sustaining an effective differentiation strategy is the single most important thing you can do. So get on with it. And keep on with it.

Index

Page numbers in italics indicate a figure and page numbers in bold indicate a table on the corresponding page.

For Product Safety Concerns and Information please contact our EU
representative GPSR@taylorandfrancis.com
Taylor & Francis Verlag GmbH, Kaufingerstraße 24, 80331 München, Germany

www.ingramcontent.com/pod-product-compliance
Ingram Content Group UK Ltd.
Pitfield, Milton Keynes, MK11 3LW, UK
UKHW050932180425

457613UK00015B/371